On Frost and Eliot

On Frost and Eliot

William H. Pritchard

pdb

PAUL DRY BOOKS

Philadelphia 2025

First Paul Dry Books Edition, 2025

Paul Dry Books, Inc
Philadelphia, Pennsylvania
www.pauldrybooks.com

Designed and typeset by Gopa & Ted2, Inc.

Printed in the United States of America

Library of Congress Control Number: 2025931215
ISBN 978-1-58988-202-7

Table of Contents

Introduction

THERE ARE of course many ways to demonstrate the unlikeness of Robert Frost and T.S. Eliot, and my purpose in juxtaposing them is to establish their differences even as their respective greatness is acknowledged. Perhaps overall the differences can be suggested by recognizing the large divergence in voice through which they approach us. Here is a paragraph from Eliot's book of 1931, *After Strange Gods*, never reprinted by him. He is visiting America officially to deliver the Norton Lectures at Harvard and upon arrival describes his response to his native land revisited:

> My local feelings were stirred very sadly by my first view of New England, on arriving from Montreal, and journeying all day through the beautiful desolate country of Vermont. Those hills, I suppose, had once been covered with primaeval forest; the forest was razed to make sheep pastures for the English settlers; now the sheep are gone, and most of the descendants of the settlers, and a new forest appeared blazing with the melancholy glory of October maple and beech and birch scattered among the evergreens; and after this process of scarlet and gold and purple wilderness you descend to the sordor of the half-dead milltowns of southern New Hampshire and Massachusetts. It is not necessarily those lands which are the most fertile or most favored in climate that seem to me the happiest, but those in which a long struggle of adaptation between man and his environment has brought out the best qualities of both; in which the landscape has been moulded by numerous generations of one race, and in which the landscape in turn has modified the race to its own character. And those New England mountains seemed to me to

> give evidence of a human success so meagre and transitory as to be more desperate than the desert.

This passage from near the beginning of *After Strange Gods* sounds like the end of something, and even as we're familiar with other, similar expressions of Eliotic pessimism, this one about emptiness and desolation and "sordor" stands out for its rhetorical weight. By the end of the paragraph things have gone sufficiently downhill to forestall any readerly optimism, and we're left with hopelessness only. To cheer us up, perhaps a letter of Frost's will do, written about what happened the night later that year when he met Eliot at an occasion in Boston. The subject is a poem Frost had recently written of which Eliot and others were unaware.

> I find it's the sort of poem that can be put to all sorts of uses. You heard me put it to two or three.... To top it off I managed the other night to bring it in on a serious occasion I couldn't take seriously in Boston. T. S. Eliot said he would read a poem if I would. I made him a counter offer. I said I would write mine while he was reading his. I went to work on all the play cards I could gather pretending to make mine up as fast as I could. When my turn came I was not quite finished but said I would do the best I could with the last stanza extempore. I stumbled a little for verisimilitude. Someone exclaimed "Quite a feat" and next day the Atlantic begged the poem for publication. All were so unexpectedly solemn that I hadn't the courage to disabuse them. My lie kept me awake one whole night.

The poem, "A Record Stride," is one of Frost's most clever and elaborate in its performance of what is called "light verse," though Frost didn't use the term. What we would like to hear more about is Eliot's response. What did he say to Frost about the poem, and was he taken in by the trick as others were? When the two passages are considered as representative of their authors, something may be suggested about why Frost and Eliot should be an unlikely pair. At the risk of simplifying each of them, we can place Eliot's lament over the land's disappointment to the American returned from his adopted country next to the utterance of a man who never really left home and whom we may think of as contesting the right to lament by one who had. This seems more than plausible in light of the following outburst of Frost's to his daughter Lesley a couple of years after the above utterance. It comes at the end of a lengthy (for him) and very interesting letter to her about modernist poetry—what Pound and Eliot had wrought. Frost poses the question which of the two—Pound or Eliot— "means the most," and says that Eliot "has written in the throes of getting religion and forswearing a world gone bad with war." Then this surprising conclusion to the question: "That seems deep. But I don't know. Waste Lands—your great grandmother on the grandmother on your mother's side! I doubt if anything was laid waste by war that was not laid by peace before." This is a perplexing statement even for a master of them like Frost: yes, this is a blow at *The Waste Land*, a poem far from one of Frost's favorites. But who could have predicted what we may call the grandmother's entrance? As demonstrated by the earlier trick with the poem, Frost couldn't play fair if he tried, which is exactly what he didn't try to do, handing us the grandmother instead of the poem.

The more personal motive for my interest in juxtaposing these poets may seem less than compelling, perhaps not even sensible. It has been my impulse, at least since college days, to play the game of ranking. It was never enough for me to analyze and praise the achievement of a writer; he or she also had to be put next to another writer for the purpose of establishing the superiority of one to the other. When I wrote *Lives of the Modern Poets* forty years ago, I wasn't content with my valuation of one of them until placed next to another in the competition for poetic honors. The poets who in that book presented themselves as most likely candidates were Yeats, Eliot, Frost, and Stevens. Hardy I judged to be in a slightly distinct historical period, Pound was too much for me to take in, leaving E. A. Robinson, Hart Crane, and William Carlos Williams as distinguished also-rans. When it came to a further narrowing in the contest, I vacillated: both Yeats and Stevens were already supported by eminent critics who put my then youthful efforts in the shade. Stevens especially, with the support of Harold Bloom and Helen Vendler, was a formidable candidate for top ranking. My holding out for Frost as the winner might have been too easy a choice, dictated too much by my familiarity over the years with his work. And what if Auden had snuck into the sacred group? There was a late evening at Harvard in graduate school days when a bunch of us gathered in Richard Poirier's Kirkland House rooms to witness what felt like a mighty battle for supremacy between an eloquent John Hollander touting Auden at the top of things and Poirier's advocacy of Frost. The contest was surely a draw, but perhaps Eliot surpassed them both for variety and intellectual challenge.

That world seems worlds rather than decades away. Just to limit the contest to poets, where now are the superstars? Is there for today's readers of poetry anything comparable to those nine modern poets as subject for contested ascriptions of value? I'm aware of the perils of "valorizing" one writer or period at the expense of another. And yet…and yet? The game of ranking was a way of passionately registering one's literary taste, claiming that such affirmations and negations made all the difference. In my own case, the major difference I see between my preferences then and now was the accession of Eliot, joining Frost as the most significant candidates for greatness. I account for my steadily increasing admiration of Eliot by adducing his criticism as making up for a relatively slim output of poems. His achievement rests upon the combination of poems and criticism we are still—particularly with the criticism—coming to terms with.

The game wasn't confined to the seriousness and pleasure of an amateur for whom questions of ranking and evaluation were predominant. The premier critic of American poetry and poets from those decades, Randall Jarrell, wrote frequently about the age, which he titled "The Age of Criticism." In the essays comprising *Poetry and the Age*, Jarrell chastised that age for its promoting of literary criticism above the works that criticism was presumably written to help us appreciate. Reading his passionate, often very funny aspersions about readers who were, alas, less bold and daring in their taste than he, one protests that SURELY this is an exaggeration. Certainly exaggeration was Jarrell's natural mode as a critic, but he put his finger on something central to the literary scene as it flourished and exhausted itself in the later decades of the twentieth century. It was a scene that Frost and Eliot would have viewed—if at all—with detachment rather than alarm and that today's onlookers must feel is a very long way away. As for Jarrell's strictures about how criticism was overreaching itself, that is something a shade ironic coming from a writer whose critical legacy included essays on Whitman, Yeats, Frost, Stevens, Marianne Moore, William Carlos Williams, plus a number of worthy if less than major figures.

In juxtaposing Frost and Eliot my major effort is to remind readers of the unlikely pair whose operations around the poems they wrote remain of great interest, aspects of which may be unfamiliar even to admirers of their verse. They include relevant prose, commentary, letters and other musings, biographical facts, and selections from what seem to me some of the best criticism of each man, much of this material overseen and commented on by me. I should expect that a reader moving around these territories will make critical accountings of much that I missed in putting them together. My overall purpose is not to institute a contest with designated winner and loser, but to bring out the competitive energies of two men of letters who did not rest in clearly marked-out lines of force. Although there is to be no more ranking, Frost gets the last word in this introduction because it's short and telling and reminds us of how central the notion of play was for each man: "I play Euchre and he plays Eucharist," he wrote in a letter. That is a way of putting it, and more than satisfactory.

Part I: Frost

The Designs of Robert Frost

> You are not going to make the mistake that Pound makes of assuming that my simplicity is that of the untutored child. I am not undesigning.
> (Frost to Thomas B. Mosher, 17 July 1913)

BOTH IN HIS letters and his poetry, the assertions of Robert Frost (1874-1963) have a way of performing what it is they promise, and the above one, written home from England to a Maine publisher and collector, is typical. In it the writer proves that his supposed "simplicity"—Frost's first book of poems, *A Boy's Will,* was being praised at the time by Pound and others for just that quality—is really not so simple. Yet he proves it not by insisting that, in fact, he is full of design (one of his best poems is titled "Design") but rather that he is "not undesigning." The subtle difference between a positive assertion and one made with a double negative is what Frost's poetry, and indeed his writing generally, demands that a good reader hear. One of his most important formulations, made in a letter from about the same period to his American friend and ex-student John Bartlett, puts a case for the centrality of listening to poetry:

> It is so and not otherwise that we get the variety that makes it fun to write and read. *The ear does it.* The ear is the only true writer and the only true reader. I have known people who could read without hearing the sentence sounds and they were the fastest readers. Eye readers we call them. They can get the meaning by glances. But they are bad readers because they miss the best part of what a good writer puts into his work.
> (22 February 1914)

He does not just say, dutifully, that in the activity of reading poetry both eye and ear are important; rather that "The ear is the *only* [my italics] true writer and...reader." There is a priority here that is crucial to Frost's artistic career, as well as to his life outside the poems.

It is also the belief on which he staked his identity as a poet who would speak to a wider audience than could ever be spoken to by his contemporaries—Pound or Eliot or Stevens. Frost had no desire to be what he termed "caviare to the crowd," saying in another letter home that "there is a kind of success called 'of esteem' and it butters no parsnips." From the very beginning of his publishing career in England in 1913-14 he was determined, he said, to "reach out" to "the general reader who buys books in their thousands." By way of accomplishing this, he proceeded not by setting himself up as a purveyor of this or that idea about life (although the rural nature of his material proved attractive to readers) but by writing as if there were people out there ready to hear what he had to say. Or they could be "made" to hear it by their being entertained and delighted with exactly rendered tones of speech, with something they had heard somewhere before—with what he called, most tellingly, the "sound of sense."

He defined this sound of sense, the "living part of a poem" (as he put it in January 1914), as "intonation entangled somehow in the syntax idiom and meaning of a sentence," and as "only there for those who have heard it previously in conversation." By so defining things he placed himself in corrective opposition to the brilliant practices of poets like Tennyson and Swinburne whose great successes, Frost insisted, were a matter of harmonized consonants and vowels, of "effects in assonation":

> But they were on the wrong track or at any rate on a short track. They went the length of it. Anyone else who goes that way must go after them. And that's where most of them are going. I alone of English writers have consciously set myself to make music out of what I may call the sound of sense.
>
> (4 July 1913)

No matter that at the time Frost wrote these sentences, contemporaries of his such as Hardy and Yeats were doing something very much like making "music" out of the "sound of sense" (Hardy's *Satires of Circumstance* and Yeats's *Responsibilities* were both published in 1914). Frost needed to imagine himself as engaged in a heroic enterprise and as doing it on his own, even doing it in another country than his own.

He had come to England with his wife Elinor and their four children after some years on a farm in Derry, New Hampshire. There, while raising chickens without notable success or undue energy, he became interested in the talk of his neighbors, turning round in his head the voices that would fill many of his poems. Most of his first three published books of poetry were written in some form or other during this time at the Derry farm, and in retrospect Frost saw the often lonely, isolated life he lived there as a preparation for a wider, public, and above all a poetic life:

> I kept farm, so to speak, for nearly ten years, but less as a farmer than as a fugitive from the world that seemed to me to "disallow" me. It was all instinctive, but I can see now that I went away to save myself and fix myself before I measured my strength against all creation.
>
> (22 March 1915)

Such measuring began modestly, as he moved back toward the world by accepting jobs as English teacher in private academies in New England, but more grandly when in 1911 he sold the farm and moved to England for purposes of nothing less than seeking his poetic fortune. Although he knew no one in the mother country, through his own enterprise and good luck, and through the interested efforts of contemporaries he met there like F. S. Flint and Ezra Pound, he had—by the time the war forced him to return to America in the winter of 1915—published two volumes *(A Boy's Will,* 1913, and *North of Boston,* 1914) with a third one (*Mountain Interval,* 1916) virtually ready for the press. He had also made a number of interesting and useful alliances, with the Georgian poets and especially with Edward Thomas (whose vocation as a poet Frost first encouraged), and he had accomplished the strong beginnings of a reputation that was only to grow in the years to come.

Thomas proved to be the most perceptive critic of Frost's early work. Reviewers of *A Boy's Will,* while well-disposed toward the American poet ("He is without sham and without affectation," said Pound), were content to praise the poems for their simplicity. Yet the term is inadequate to characterize the artful complication of Frost's style in his first book. Consider the octet from a sonnet, "The Vantage Point":

If tired of trees I seek again mankind,
Well I know where to hie me—in the dawn,
To a slope where the cattle keep the lawn.
There amid lolling juniper reclined,
Myself unseen, I see in white defined
Far off the homes of men, and farther still,
The graves of men on an opposing hill,
Living or dead, whichever are to mind.

The rhyme pattern is "not undesigning," nor is the sound of sense in the accent that must be given to "Well" (it is of course an adverb, not an interjection), nor is the suspended, quite elaborate syntax of the eight-line sentence with its aptly pointed dash in line two or its use of commas in lines five and eight. This is a poem which toys with the idea that the "I" can do anything, turn whicheer way he pleases, contemplate what or whomever he chooses to contemplate, as the spirit moves him. Its tone is mild and unboastful, as if this were merely the way things are, and as if we were being vouchsafed no more than the facts:

And if by noon I have too much of these,
I have but to turn on my arm, and lo,
The sunburned hillside sets my face aglow,
My breathing shakes the bluet like a breeze,
I smell the earth, I smell the bruisèd plant,
I look into the crater of the ant.

The sestet is a different kind of sentence, to be delivered in one breath, as the series of declarative assertions with strong, simple, sometimes repeated verbs ("sets," "shakes," "smell," "look") render the up-close inspection of natural things provided by this new vantage point. "Never if you can do it," Frost wrote to Bartlett, "write a sentence which does not posture specially." The difference between the first and second parts of "The Vantage Point" is registered by the reader as something heard, by the way the rhythm of the sentence plays itself off against the metrical grid: "The possibilities for tune from the dramatic tones of meaning struck across the rigidity of a limited meter are endless," Frost was to write in "The Figure a Poem Makes" (1938).

Looked at historically, particularly with reference to nineteenth-century American poetry, Frost's practice was a refreshing and a revolutionary subverting of what passed for the Grand Style in all too many post-Civil War writers. As may be noted by browsing through Bliss Carman's *Oxford Book of American Verse* (1928), the strutting dignity with which those poems set forth their noble sentiments is matched only by their rhythmic inertness ("I do not know beneath what sky / Nor on what seas shall be thy fate; / I only know it shall be high, / I only know it shall be great"—Richard Hovey). It was Frost's distinction to banish such inertness by writing lines like the following (from another early poem, "Storm Fear"), where a man voices his uncertainties in the face of a winter storm:

> I count our strength,
> Two and a child,
> Those of us not asleep subdued to mark
> How the cold creeps as the fire dies at length—
> How drifts are piled,
> Dooryard and road ungraded,
> Till even the comforting barn grows far away,
> And my heart owns a doubt
> Whether 'tis in us to arise with day
> And save ourselves unaided.

One partly understands why the poem from which these concluding lines are taken was thought of as "simple." There are only three words of more than two syllables. The named circumstances, the feeling of helplessness and fear, are easily available ones, as familiar—even as comforting—as the barn used to be until the snow made it seem far away.

But almost immediately we notice how the disposition of words and line lengths and rhymes is anything but simple. The poem's overall pace is attractive partly through the variations in line-lengths: "Two and a child" *looks* like feeble protection when compared with "How the cold creeps as the fire dies at length," which takes as long to say as it did to feel the creeping cold and dying fire. At the same time the rhymes make for continuity and suppleness of movement by never quite coming when you expect them, by having the last word of "Those of us not asleep subdued to mark" rhyme with the ends of lines much earlier in the poem; by having the key word "doubt" in the third from final line go back to an early line ("Come out! Come out!"); by deferring over the course of five lines the unobvious rhyming pair of "ungraded" and "unaided." And "simplicity" is hardly the name for the effect gained by using the surprising word "subdued," placed as it is quite daringly after "asleep," by way of subtly naming a state of acute yet feeble awareness. Nor are we simply dealing with a bad snowstorm; it is not just that the people may need to be plowed out, but that this situation inspires a tremor of metaphysical worry, no more nor less than that, as real and perhaps as transient as the storm itself, or the poem. Such a movement from the level of sense to that of spirit is unpretentious and unobtrusive, but from the very beginning it lay at the heart of Frost's enterprise as a poet, and there was nothing simple about it.

A Boy's Will also contained a number of poems in which Frost revealed his affiliations with, rather than his divergences from, the Tennysonian-Swinburnian "track," poems in which "effects of assonation" are both noticeable and artful. But the more original work—the poems just mentioned, plus "October," "The Tuft of Flowers," and "Mowing"—was first payment on his witty boast to Bartlett (4 July 1913) that "To be perfectly frank with you I am one of the most notable craftsmen of my time. That will transpire presently." He was also shrewd enough to have ready a second book whose style and subject was quite distinct from that of *A Boy's Will. North of Boston,* originally billed in his publisher David Nutt's catalogue as "Farm Servants and Other People," capitalized on Frost's perception that he was thought of as somebody who did the "farm" thing in poetry. This "book of people," as his dedication to his wife called it, consisted of some fifteen longer poems, and although an "I" occasionally appears (notably in "Mending Wall," "After Apple-Picking," and "The Wood-Pile") the focus is not mainly on the subjective presence that pervaded *A Boy's Will.* Nor is there heard the bittersweet lyric voice from that first volume, with its appealing combination of wistfulness, regret, quiet irony, and gentle protest. In its place we hear voices in conflict with and correction of one another, "characters" who are not to be identified with someone named Robert Frost. So the most dramatic of the poems in *North of Boston* begins this way:

> He saw her from the bottom of the stairs
> Before she saw him. She was starting down,
> Looking back over her shoulder at some fear.
> She took a doubtful step and then undid it
> To raise herself and look again. He spoke
> Advancing toward her: "What is it you see

> From up there always—for I want to know."
> She turned and sank upon her skirts at that,
> And her face changed from terrified to dull.
> He said to gain time: "What is it you see?"
> Mounting until she cowered under him.
> "I will find out now—you must tell me, dear."

As "Home Burial" develops and the woman begins to talk back to her husband, the narrator pretty much disappears, forbears the making of characterizing, explanatory comment about the accusations and resentments his protagonists express to each other. And the poem's excitement comes wholly from their play of voices.

Frost claimed that for a time, in his years of "isolation" on the Derry farm, he preferred "stocks and stones to people," but that before long he was listening to the way they talked:

> I like the actuality of gossip, the intimacy of it. Say what you will effects of actuality and intimacy are the greatest aim an artist can have. The sense of intimacy gives the thrill of sincerity. A story must always release a meaning more readily to those who read than life itself as it ever goes releases meaning.
>
> (22 March 1915)

This "releasing" was to be effected, however, not by a narrator who at a certain moment stopped the music and laid out the correct understanding of what was happening, but through nothing more than whatever the voices in conflict added up to—and the reader had to do the adding up. Concurrently Frost lowered the diction of these poems "to a level even Wordsworth stayed above," as he wittily put it. This was a risky decision insofar as, judged by individual lines of poems, the work did not look much like "poetry," at least as many readers in 1914 expected poetry to look and sound. The effort was toward realism, toward achieving "the thrill of sincerity" which could come from human speech artfully imagined so as to give the impression that no one was running the show, that these people had just begun to talk and that we were privileged to overhear them.

At the same time, poems such as "Home Burial," "The Death of the Hired Man" (which achieved anthology popularity), "The Black Cottage," "A Servant to Servants," and others, were no mere exercises in technical craftsmanship detached from moral and human concerns. In one of his highly perceptive reviews of the volume (he reviewed it no less than three times!) Edward Thomas boldly spoke of *North of Boston* as containing "masterpieces of deep and mysterious tenderness." And a contemporary critic, Margery Sabin, has put saliently the larger motive out of which these poems derived their energies and resonance:

> Frost in 1914 wanted to believe—and wrote poems out of that belief—that human vitality takes on a suprapersonal existence in the established intonations of speech, intonations which the individual may draw on for personal expression and, perhaps even more important, for the reassuring recognition that his single life is connected to other lives. What Frost calls "the abstract vitality of our speech" gives reassurance that the life within us is not eccentric or monstrous. It ceases to be monstrous once it participates in the verbal forms through which other people also enact their lives.
>
> ("The Fate of the Frost Speaker," *Raritan,* Fall 1982)

One of the loveliest demonstrations of such "reassurance" comes at the end of "The Black Cottage" and may serve also to suggest how, even though Frost claimed to be writing in a "low" style, the poems show moments of heightened awareness and imagination in which characters are led, as if by a power outside them, into an eloquence of utterance that is "poetic" even by the traditional standard.

In "The Black Cottage" the narrator and his friend, a minister, stop on their walk to visit an abandoned house where an old woman lived whose husband and sons had died in the Civil War and whom the minister knew as a long-time member of his congregation. In reminiscing, he is led to speculate about the passing of time, the changing and eroding of all things, and in reaction he suddenly begins to imagine through language a "desert land" of which he would be the monarch, this land dedicated to permanence—" to the truths we keep coming back and back to":

> "So desert it would have to be, so walled
> By mountain ranges half in summer snow,
> No one would covet it or think it worth

The pains of conquering to force change on.
Scattered oases where men dwelt, but mostly
Sand dunes held loosely in tamarisk
Blown over and over themselves in idleness.
Sand grains should sugar in the natal dew
The babe born to the desert, the sandstorm
Retard mid-waste my cowering caravans—
"There are bees in this wall." He struck the clapboards,
Fierce heads looked out; small bodies pivoted.
We rose to go. Sunset blazed on the windows.

Edward Thomas observed that most of the poems in *North of Boston* were written in "the good old English idiom of blank verse," but this verse, anything but homely, is of great richness and convolution, marked by a propulsive forward movement and a diction ("Scattered," "idleness," "retard") as "high" as its visionary subject requires. Yet that there are impulses other than the visionary (the minister is really indulging his own version of a boy's will) is acknowledged by the end of the poem, when suddenly the bees make themselves felt and the syntax shortens into terse declaratives, subject and verb and object. Ezra Pound remarked in his review of *North of Boston* that "The Black Cottage" is "very clearly stated." Clarity of statement, however, is not a sufficient term to suggest the dramatic and compositional force of the poem.

It might be argued—and indeed it has been by more than one critic of Frost—that *North of Boston* is his most original book of poems and that he was never to write another one as distinctive. And it is true that, as a narrative poet, he began to rely more on the performing resources of a central speaker-entertainer who sounded much like Frost himself—the Frost, that is, who upon his return to America early in 1915 became increasingly a public figure, a great success as a reader of his poetry in colleges and clubs, a humorous entertainer who could be depended upon to put on a show as spellbinding as Dickens's or Mark Twain's. It is worth insisting also on the increasing importance of Frost's role as a teacher, not just or even mainly in the classroom. Beginning in 1917, when Alexander Meiklejohn hired him at Amherst College, he maintained to the end of his life academic affiliations of various sorts with Amherst, the University of Michigan, Harvard, and Dartmouth. But he liked to refer to himself as a "symbolic teacher," just as—while he continued to be a farmer ("I always have a farm in my backyard," he would say)—it was a symbolic rather than "real" farming in which he engaged. Frost's teaching went on less in the classroom course than from the public lecture podium and in the countless conversations (often of a monologue sort) he conducted with undergraduates, teachers, and ordinary "lay" readers ("I want to reach out to all sorts and kinds") who were convinced they had some special relationship to this extraordinary person.

As he became more successful, more in demand, more of an entertainer, he risked—and did not always avoid—declining into a predictable act, the distinctness of his poetry lost in what Randall Jarrell called "the public figure's relishing consciousness of himself." Yet despite that figure's sometimes blotting out the very private genius of Frost's art, the heartening fact is that, although he never wrote another book like *North of Boston,* he continued to write poems for almost fifty years until his death in 1963, and up through the publication of *Steeple Bush* (in 1947, when he was over seventy) wrote them on a fairly regular basis. Some of his finest efforts may be found in the first fifteen poems of *A Witness Tree,* a volume published in 1942 at the end of a decade in which he endured the death of his favorite daughter, the death of his wife, and the suicide of his son. Earlier, *Mountain Interval* (1916) and *New Hampshire* (1923, which won him the first of his four Pulitzer prizes) not only contained some of the best poems he was ever to write (a short list would include "An Old Man's Winter Night," "Birches," "A Star in a Stone-Boat," "'Out, Out—'," "To Earthward," "Two Look at Two," "Stopping by Woods on a Snowy Evening," and "The Road Not Taken") but showed a fusion in many of the poems between lyric and narrative impulses. While *A Boy's Will* was predominantly a "subjective" book of lyrics, and *North of Boston* an "objective" book of narratives, stories with people in them, it now became more difficult to classify many poems which had elements of both.

For example, "An Old Man's Winter Night" (from *Mountain Interval*) tells the story of how an aged man "keeps" his house and farm as the darkness of the night and his attendant old age press in upon him. In the early lines of the poem, Frost's manner is designedly "awkward" so as to present the man's situation in verse no more elegant or eloquent than its subject—a diminished life:

> What kept his eyes from giving back the gaze
> Was the lamp tilted near them in his hand.

What kept him from remembering what it was
That brought him to that creaking room was age.

Yet as "An Old Man's Winter Night" moves to its conclusion, and as the man prepares to retire for the night, its manner mixes lyric, "poetical" pathos with an ironic, more prose-like understanding and acceptance:

He consigned to the moon—such as she was,
So late-arising—to the broken moon,
As better than the sun in any case
For such a charge, his snow upon the roof,
His icicles along the wall to keep;
And slept. The log that shifted with a jolt
Once in the stove, disturbed him and he shifted,
And eased his heavy breathing, but still slept.
One aged man—one man—can't keep a house,
A farm, a countryside, or if he can,
It's thus he does it of a winter night.

This is poetry which invites us to sympathize with, to feel for the pathetic old man alone, close to insensibility, whose gesture to the moon ("broken" itself) is the rueful one so beautifully presented in the word "consigned." Yet as the situation invites pity, a studied wryness in the narrative treatment makes pity impossible (the moon is "in any case" better than the sun, at least as far as looking after icicles and snow goes). With the words "One aged man—one man—can't keep a house / A farm, a countryside" we seem to be moving out toward some large cosmic statement about human loneliness, of how our circumstances and surroundings always outmatch us, especially as age and isolation come on apace. Yet just before such a statement is attained, and in the middle of the penultimate line, Frost turns back on it: "...or if he can, / It's thus he does it of a winter night." In "Mowing," the mysterious key assertion is that "The fact is the sweetest dream that labor knows." "An Old Man's Winter Night" is a poem, finally, that respects the fact of a life, of man's existence, rather than how that life can be used to illustrate cosmic or moral meanings. Whether he can or can't "keep" a farm, a house, or a countryside, is not as important as to respect the fact of what he is, to see what he has done and is still doing: "It's thus he does it of a winter night."

The playfulness that permeates Frost's poetry is partly a matter of its dependence on such largely unspecified words as "thus" or "keep" or "does." "Something there is that doesn't love a wall," "Mending Wall" begins, and along with the poem's speaker we are brought up against "something" in the poem that organizes our attention in a fresh way. At the end of "Two Look at Two" (from *New Hampshire)* a pair of lovers have been climbing a mountain and, almost at the point of turning back, first see a doe looking at them, then later a buck who eyes them quizzically. These confrontations are presented with delicacy and lightness of touch; but the end of the poem moves into something beyond lightness, as the buck breaks the spell by passing "unscared" along the wall which separates animal from human:

> Two had seen two, whichever side you spoke from.
> "This *must* be all." It was all. Still they stood,
> A great wave from it going over them,
> As if the earth in one unlooked-for favor
> Had made them certain earth returned their love.

Frost's poetry is filled with such "as if" moments, in which what his essay "The Figure a Poem Makes" called "a momentary stay against confusion" is enacted by the poem. The "great wave" which goes over the couple at the end of "Two Look at Two" is testimony that human beings can feel about "the earth," can imagine "as if" moments in ways the earth itself, for all its solidity, cannot. Frost's generosity and boldness toward our human ways of making significance of life have not been remarked on enough.

If, after *North of Boston,* his narratives are as a rule less dramatic, more relaxed, even garrulous in their pace, and usually spoken by Frost-the-bard (who makes his longest and most wisecracking appearance in the long poem "New Hampshire"), his lyric poetry up through the 1942 *Witness Tree* reveals riches only hinted at by the poems in *A Boy's Will.* Randall Jarrell's wonderful essay "To the Laodiceans" is the best introduction to this body of work which calls forth all the lively responsiveness a reader can bring to it. A short list of poems may suggest how variously expressive they are in range of style and tone. In addition to ones previously mentioned, consider "Spring Pools," "Acquainted with the Night," "The Onset," "Nothing Gold Can Stay," "The Need of Being Versed in Country Things," "Neither Out Far Nor In Deep," "Provide, Provide," "Design," "The Silken

Tent," "I Could Give All to Time," "The Most of It," and "Never Again Would Birds' Song Be the Same." This is to choose only twelve titles from a group which, without much lowering the overall quality of writing, could be expanded to double, even triple the size. In these poems Frost writes as a post-Romantic (or post-post-Romantic) poet, both acknowledging the visionary impulses that found expression in Wordsworth and Shelley (and closer to home in Emerson and Thoreau) and subjecting those impulses to ironic, frequently humorous treatment.

Most often the impulse in the poem is toward some permanence, toward something more than a *momentary* stay against confusion, as is represented, say, by the desert paradise of the minister's imaginings in "The Black Cottage." Typically a Frost lyric presents the attractive temptation to stop or to rest in a notion of fixity; or, alternatively, to give in to the flux, "to go with the drift of things" (as in the early "Reluctance"). Then, at a crucial point in the lyric, this impulse is countered by a contrary one, a "backward motion" (in the language of "West-Running Brook", Frost's most metaphysical poem) in which our human will expresses itself. The gesture of refusal—or of self-preservation—may on occasion be a lofty one, as it is in "West-Running Brook": "Not just a swerving, but a throwing back, / As if regret were in it and were sacred." Or it may be accomplished with the lovely and humorous grace of these final lines from "Come In," a little poem in which the speaker is powerfully affected by the music of a thrush singing from within a wood. The man hears the thrush's sound as like "a call to come in / To the dark and lament": yet he politely declines the invitation:

> But no, I was out for stars:
> I would not come in.
> I meant not even if asked,
> And I hadn't been.

The extra bonus of that final line is the sort of payment readers come to expect from a good Frost poem which, like the man himself, is not undesigning.

Like that of his great predecessor Ralph Waldo Emerson, Frost's work has never been sufficiently appreciated in England (though, paradoxically, England gave him his start), perhaps in part by way of a reaction to the rather promiscuous admiration he has inspired from so many sorts of

American readers, many of whom have no time for T. S. Eliot or Wallace Stevens. But Frost's poetry is as difficult and as rewarding as that of his distinguished contemporaries. If, for some American readers, the homely nature of his materials—cows and apples and stone walls—predisposes them to like the poetry because it is made out of them, they are no more simpleminded than "cosmopolitan" readers who feel easy with mythical allusions in Eliot but disdain cows and apple trees as a fit vehicle for serious poetry. We would do well to heed Frost's own dictum to an American friend in 1914, when he told Sidney Cox that the true poet's pleasure lay in making "his own words as he goes" rather than depending upon words whose meanings were fixed:

> We write of things we see and we write in accents we hear. Thus we gather both our material and our technique with the imagination from life; and our technique becomes as much material as material itself.

It was this principle that Pound saluted in Frost when in his review of *North of Boston* he said, conclusively, "I know more of farm life than I did before I had read his poems. That means I know more of 'life'."

—*The New Pelican Guide to English Literature, Volume 9: American Literature* edited by Boris Ford (London: Penguin, 1988).

Frost Departmentalized

ALMOST ANYONE you run into these days, fresh from reading the second volume of Lawrance Thompson's biography, or perhaps someone's review of it, will ask what you think of Frost now, now that he has been painstakingly exposed as the monster some always knew, or hoped, he really was.[1] If the newly-enlightened person is forgiving, he may say that it just goes to show how we're all human, nobody's perfect—as some curious legend had it Frost was. Or he may compliment himself that, though no poet, at least he takes better care of his family than did the bard from New Hampshire or Vermont. The line that best sums up this sense of Frost exposed, either wittingly or unwittingly, through Thompson's book, is found in Helen Vendler's acute and influential review in the *New York Times Book Review*: noting that Thompson's volume is subtitled "The Years of Triumph" Mrs. Vendler remarked "If this be triumph, what is disaster?" And she went on forcefully to argue that Thompson is capable of "criminal blandness" in his attempts to (in his own words) "Offer a balanced delineation that mingles sympathy with critical detachment," that in fact he sides with Frost whenever it suits him, and that through seven hundred pages of what she terms "doughy prose" it becomes abundantly clear Frost was a much worse character than Thompson can possibly admit. I found the prose often as doughy as does Mrs. Vendler, but exactly for that reason I am unwilling to join her in assuming that we can wade through the dough and come upon Frost plain, that is, monstrous.

To begin with, anyone familiar with the *Selected Letters* which Mr. Thompson edited and published six years ago will find little to shock him in the new biographical volume. Many of those letters are quoted at length

1. ROBERT FROST: The Years of Triumph 1915-1938, by *Lawrance Thompson*. Holt, Rinehart and Winston.

in this volume, but now often as illustrative substantiation for the narrative Thompson is weaving; for example, in the *Letters* volume Thompson quoted the following paragraph from a letter to Lincoln MacVeagh (Frost's agent at Henry Holt) about Carl Sandburg's appearance at the University of Michigan, where Frost was spending a year as resident artist:

> We've been having a dose of Carl Sandburg. He's another person I find it hard to do justice to. He was possibly [three] hours in town and he spent one of those washing his white hair and toughening his expression for his public performance. His mandolin pleased some people, his poetry a very few and his infantile talk none. His affectations have almost buried him out of sight. He is probably the most artificial and studied ruffian the world has had. Lesley says his two long poems in The New Republic and The Dial are as ridiculous as his carriage and articulation. He has developed rapidly since I saw him two years ago. I heard someone say he was the kind of writer who had everything to gain and nothing to lose by being translated into another language.

Now, in the narrative describing the visits of various poets Frost brought to Michigan, Thompson tells us that Frost disliked Sandburg, that Sandburg had praised free verse in the lecture, then accompanied himself on the guitar and sung American folksongs including one with the lines "Oh my name it is Sam Hall, and I hate you one and all, damn your eyes." And Thompson introduces Frost's letter by remarking coyly: "Most of the hating was done by Robert Frost that afternoon in Hill Auditorium, and Sandburg had scarcely left town when Frost reacted bitterly in a letter to MacVeagh," after which we get the paragraph quoted above. Now to me the remarks about Sandburg seem brilliantly right: Frost has found exactly the words that do full justice to "the most artificial and studied ruffian the world has had." The picture of Sandburg spending one hour out of his brief stay "washing his white hair and toughening his expression" is true only in the sense that poems are true which can't be gainsaid or dislodged once the right words have been found to write them in. But Thompson, preoccupied with making his narrative move along in a lively manner, decides to raise a few eyebrows by making the play on "hate" and so moves from the Sandburg song to what we then are supposed to accept as Frost's Real Feelings: hate and a "bitter reaction" to Sandburg via MacVeagh.

I suppose if a biographer chooses to see only hate and bitterness in this letter, and to ignore the studied wit with which contempt is molded into a fine comic creation, then at least we could delight in the letter and provide our own reading of it.[2] But not content to leave things at that, Thompson has performed an act of supererogation by providing, as he loves to, a special index with sixty-three topical subheads which will help to "illuminate the complicated and contradictory responses of Frost as man and as artist. To expedite reference and cross-reference, the topical subheads are grouped here with page numbers." How thoroughly departmental! If, in Thompson's word, you "browse" your way through these sixty-three topical subheads you will eventually come to "Vindictiveness," and if undeterred you follow up that subhead you will encounter a list, in alphabetical order, of "RF's vindictive gestures against" people all the way from "Arnold, Matthew" (a poor dead literary figure) through "King, Stanley" (a poor dead president of Amherst College) and on through most contemporary poets and for good measure Frost's wife, son, and sister. The assumption is that at one point or another in his life Frost was vindictive toward Matthew Arnold, Stanley King, his wife, Carl Sandburg, Amy Lowell and the rest. Thompson seems to have no doubts that he has found the perfectly accurate word to label, in each case, what really went on.

Since the reader is invited to use this special index, I complied by compiling a list of the following "topical sub-heads" as an indication of the traits Thompson thinks worth emphasizing in Frost's character. My selected list, in alphabetical order runs: "Anti-intellectual" "Baffler-teaser-deceiver" "Brute" "Charlatan" "Cowardice" "Depression, Moods of" "Enemies" "Fear" "Gossip" "Hate" "Insanity" "Jealousy" "Misunderstanding" "Murderer" "Pretender" "Puritan" "Rage" "Retaliations, Poetic" "Revenge" "Self-Centeredness" "Spoiled Child" and finally "Vindictive." On the other side of the ledger I note "Friendship," but no headings under the following

2. As in the case of the following sentences from a letter to Untermeyer after Amy Lowell's death; Thompson gives us the ins and outs of Frost's "malice" towards her, then quotes without comment this epitaph: "I did go before the assembled college to say in effect that really no one minded her outrageousness because it never thrust home: in life she didn't know where the feelings were to hurt them, any more than in poetry she knew where they were to touch them. I refused to weaken abjectly." Is "malice" the right word for this—or something more complicated?

titles which I have constructed for myself: "Intellectual" "Bravery" "Exhilaration, Moods of" "Hope" "Love" "Sanity" "Understanding" "Loyalty." I conclude that Thompson feels these qualities are not worthy of indexing in Frost; yet Ridgeley Torrence is quoted as saying in 1919 "He is a man, a noble character in addition to being a noble poet," and two years later the reporter from the Boston Traveler remarked upon the "remarkable face of the man...strong features that radiate peace, contentment, and the perfectly balanced solidarity of the inner man." Why not index entries on "nobility" or "strength"? Or were Torrence and the reporter simply deceived?

Yet Thompson has found room to include the eye-catching category of "Murderer," and presuming that by this point in the book we are still naive enough to question the appropriateness of that term as naming an important aspect of Frost's character we could look it up in the index and find under it three entries, the first of which directs us to a statement Frost made in a letter to Witter Bynner begging off writing a preface to Bynner's poetry. Frost asks for forgiveness then adds "even as I hope to be forgiven a murder I did once," which remark Thompson believes refers to guilty feelings over the death of his first child. The second entry refers us to Lesley Frost's grief-stricken accusation, after her mother's death, that Frost was somehow responsible. The third, and it would seem most significant, entry is this: "RF recalls five people he wanted to murder, 439-440." Turning back to page 439 we come upon the poem "A Roadside Stand," whose reference to "greedy good-doers" pretty clearly has the New Deal in mind and which ends with Frost musing about how these poor people who run this pathetic stand might be relieved to be put "at one stroke out of their pain," after which he wonders how *he* would like it if they offered to do that to him. Not very memorable verse, and with its sentiment worn pretty simply on its sleeve. But Thompson moves in with the heavy artillery:

> Murder, and even the desire to murder for justice rather than for mercy, never stayed out of Frost's consciousness too long. He had thought of entitling this poem, sarcastically, "Euthanasia," but part of what bothered him as literary strategy was his recent tendency to let his new poems reflect all too many of his murderous thoughts.

We are then conducted through a series of footnoted memories (introduced with the phrase "He could remember…") of various people whom at one time or other Frost would like to have done away with: "In England, there came a day when he would have taken pleasure in murdering Ezra Pound. Not long after he returned to the United States, he had thought of killing his old enemy, Ellery Sedgwick, editor of the *Atlantic Monthly*." And he had once used "razor words in public to achieve a murderous revenge" on his old Pinkerton school-boss. For Thompson there is no difference between word and thing: if you say you'd like to cut Pound's throat then you are entertaining thoughts of murdering him. If you are filled with rage against Ellery Sedgwick's lordly treatment of you, then you "had thought of killing him," as if Frost was ready to stomp into the Atlantic Monthly office and gun Sedgwick down, frock coat and all. Or that using "razor words" to achieve "murderous revenge" is really about the same thing as cutting someone's jugular.

Thompson's extraordinary literal-mindedness is perhaps most depressingly evident in what was already a full-blown campaign in his edition of the letters and first volume of biography, namely the proving that Frost was a man of "deep religious faith." From the thousands of words in text and notes devoted to this matter I will point briefly to one sequence in order to suggest how, if you are Thompson, you go about such proof. It is really very simple: take the assertion "Some may know what they seek in school or church" (from "A Star in a Stone-boat"), which looks subversive in regard to matters of religion, and handle it this way: "He continued to enjoy casting himself in the role of rebel and skeptic, even though his actual position in matters of belief was far more conservative and orthodox than he permitted his public to guess." At this point a footnote teases you to seek out verification for Thompson's knowledge of Frost's "actual position" in these matters. But, alas, Footnote 21 of Chapter 17 says only "For a discussion of this ambivalent and Uriel-like posture, see note 40 of Chapter 6." Figuring this next one will really provide the goods, and so following along patiently, we eventually come to a discussion of Frost's relation to Emerson's poem "Uriel": a complicated matter, and perhaps more complicated than the text's bold phrase about his "actual position" might lead us to suspect. You can do anything with words, though: just extract a subversive-looking utterance from the poem, call it "apparent skepticism" and move on to the next poem. If the poem is the playful "An Empty Threat," quote the end of it, then add "In spite of all his teasings, aimed at the doubts (or even the beliefs) of those whose opinions differed from his, Frost was essentially concerned with using his poetry for the purpose of affirming his own religious belief." It is of course the biographer's privilege to strike through the mask and move about confidently in the realm of essence where all apparent skepticism is really deep religious faith. But it reminds me of an incident on *Meet the Press* some years ago when the indefatigable Lawrence Spivack was pressing Frost to say that on the whole his life had been a happy one, while Frost kept claiming it all depended on how he felt when he got up in the morning. Time ran out before Spivack got the answer he wanted; time doesn't of course run out on Mr. Thompson.

One poem Thompson fails to mention, in his discussion of Frost's deep religious faith, was the following unpublished verse which I quote from the memory of having heard Frost satisfiedly recite it:

> Mary had a little lamb,
> His name was Jesus Christ;
> God, not Joseph, was the ram
> But Joseph took it nice.

Would one want to say that this poem was *really* a self-defensive mask for Frost's richly deep feelings about Christ and his parents? Or would it be less tendentious, more playful perhaps, to say that the poem was a momentary score for a poet who cared more about the delights of performance than he cared about anything else? On the occasion of one public reading he was asked by a true-hearted soul from the audience whether he, Frost, was ever confused. Do you know a game called *Confusion,* Frost asked? No, the questioner did not. Let's play it, said Frost: first I'll ask you, are you confused? Yes, stoutly answered the sincere questioner. Now you ask me, invited Frost. Are *you* confused, Mr. Frost? *No*—you lose, answered Frost, and with that the game was over. What can you do with that sort of ruthless play? Thompson's response is to understand, to understand, and once more to understand: as a biographer he never admits to confusion of any sort, and this perhaps accounts for the oppressive manner in which he sits on his subject with labels and schemes. And indices.

But can we brush all these matters aside, push through "the facts" as Thompson painstakingly sets them down and penetrate to the Real Frost? One of the seemingly most telling points in Mrs. Vendler's review is made when she quotes as an illustration of Thompson's "criminal blandness" the following sentence about Frost's son Carol: "There had never been any sustained affection between him and his father, and on many occasions each had antagonized the other in ways which had built up lasting enmities." Mrs. Vendler says:

> Surely this is to apportion blame equally: Thompson forgets that Carol was a baby and Frost a man when it all started. What is a father who has no "sustained affection" for his son but a monster? A terrifying lack in Frost is made to sound like a peccadillo.

But Mrs. Vendler too easily ignores the fact that "sustained affection" is Thompson's phrase, and she wrongly makes use of what she has already characterized as "doughy prose" to leap to a rhetorical question about Frost as monster. What does she know that enables her to be clear about this "terrifying lack" in Frost? How many fathers, if put on the spot, could be trusted to judge whether they really did or did not truly have "sustained affection" for their sons? Does the fact that Carol eventually killed himself constitute unfailing proof that his father was derelict in affection? From the biography it looks to me that Frost was a man who paid enormous attention to his children, no doubt both marvelous and crippling as such attention often turns out to be. My own inclination is to judge not lest I be judged.

Furthermore I would insist, contra Mrs. Vendler, that the life recounted in these pages is not "a sad life," at least no more so than any poet's whose experience is all our experience intensified: "We poets in our youth begin in gladness; / But thereof come in the end despondency and madness." And that all the spite or pettiness or malice of character which this biographer details with such solemn and judgmental care fall away not only when we read the poems from those "Years of Triumph" (triumphs like "An Old Man's Winter Night" or "Putting in the Seed" or "The Hill Wife" or "To Earthward" or "West-Running Brook") but when we read a letter such as this one, written after Frost's daughter Marjorie had died tragically:

> Well, the blow has fallen. The noblest of us all is dead and has taken our hearts out of the world with her. It was a terrible seven weeks' fight—too indelibly terrible on the imagination. No death in war could more than match it for suffering and heroic

> endurance. Why all this talk in favor of peace? Peace has her victories over poor mortals no less merciless than war. Marge always said she would rather die in a gutter than in a hospital. But it was in a hospital she was caught to die after more than a hundred serum injections and blood transfusions. We were torn afresh every day between the temptations of letting her go untortured or cruelly trying to save her. The only consolation we have is the memory of her greatness through all. Never out of delirium for the last four weeks her responses were of course incorrect. She got little or nothing of what we said to her. The only way I could reach her was by putting my hand backward and forward between us as in counting out and saying with over-emphasis *You*—and—*Me*. The last time I did that, the day before she died, she smiled faintly and answered "All the same," frowned slightly and made it "Always the same."...The classical theory was not born out in her case that a fine and innocent nature released by madness from the inhibitions of society will give way to all the indecencies. Everything she said, however quaint and awry, was of an almost straining loftiness. It was as if her ruling passion must have been to be wise and good, or it could not have been so strong in death. But curse all doctors who for a moment let down and neglect in childbirth the scientific precautions they have been taught in school. We thought to move heaven and earth—heaven with prayers and earth with money. We moved nothing. And here we are Cadmus and Harmonia not yet placed safely in changed forms.

One of the ways you felt in Frost's presence was elevated: he had the power momentarily to turn all our sad lives into something else. His own life becomes "sad," the "Years of Triumph" a hollow phrase, only when a biographer's single-minded explanations of that life are allowed to outweigh the voice which speaks out through poem or letter and leads us by a renewal of words to a renewal of our own possibilities for life. The Play's the thing, Play's the thing, Frost said in his preface to Robinson's last poem. Though the following sonnet from Robert Lowell's *Notebook* is about Frost at a point in his career beyond which the present book leaves off, it leaves things open in a way more biographers should aspire to:

Robert Frost at midnight, the audience gone
to vapor, the great act laid on the shelf in mothballs,
his voice musical, raw and raw—he writes in the flyleaf:
"Robert Lowell from Robert Frost, his friend in the art."
"Sometimes I feel too full of myself," I say.
And he, misunderstanding, "When I am low,
I stray away. My son wasn't your kind. The night
we told him Merrill Moore would come to treat him
he said, 'I'll kill him first.' One of my daughters thought things,
knew every male she met was out to make her;
the way she dresses, she couldn't make a whorehouse."
And I, "Sometimes I'm so happy I can't stand myself."
And he, "When I am too full of joy, I think
how little good my health did anyone near me."

—*Hudson Review*, Winter 1970-71.

Frost Revised

IF YOU'VE dropped in at the local bookstore lately you may have noticed that the familiar green *Complete Poems of Robert Frost, 1949* has been replaced by a new collected edition called *The Poetry of Robert Frost,* followed by, in smaller letters, "Edited by Edward Connery Lathem." Running through the titles of other collections of famous modern poets—*The Collected Poems of W. B. Yeats,* or *T. S. Eliot: Collected Poems,* or *The Collected Poems of Wallace Stevens*—you may recall that none of those collections (one of them made posthumously) was edited by anyone, and you may wonder, therefore, why it is that Frost's poetry was judged to stand in need of editing. A publisher's note at the beginning of this volume tells us that, although the time has not yet come for a variorum or a definitive edition, "the current need is for a convenient volume both for general readers and scholars, scrupulously edited for textual accuracy"; and that because of Holt's long association with Frost, the book is thus published with special pride.

How convenient is the volume, and should Holt, Rinehart and Winston be proud of it? Its major addition to the 1949 *Complete Poems* is Frost's last book of poems, *In the Clearing* (1962), hitherto available only separately. The new volume has 607 pages, where its predecessor had 666; it is priced at $10.95, a few dollars more than the collections of the poets mentioned above. It is sturdily double-bound, as was the 1949 edition, and the poems are line-numbered as they were not previously—an advantage to critics and teachers, especially when dealing with longer poems. But since almost 100 pages of the volume are taken up by an editor's statement and the textual apparatus which follows it, let us scan those pages for what they tell us about the spirit and principles brought to the presentation of Frost's poems.

As one would expect, the bibliographical and textual notes are occupied mainly with documenting divergent readings, citing variants from the different editions, providing place and date of first publication. The typographical character and organization of the individual volumes—some of which were retained at least in part in *Complete Poems, 1949*—are now relegated to, and described in, the notes. In some cases this means that material absent from *Complete Poems, 1949,* but present in the individual volumes as they appeared, has now reappeared in the textual notes; in this connection it is particularly pleasant to have handy once more the original glosses to the poems from *A Boy's Will*—"The youth is persuaded that he will be rather more than less himself for having forsworn the world" etc. But a good deal is lost too: no longer are we permitted the luxury of no more than one poem to a page (as in the *Complete Poems* edition), so that if we open to pages 12-13 we come upon the last two lines of "To the Thawing Wind," immediately followed on the page by "A Prayer in Spring," which in turn is followed by the first five lines of the first stanza of "Flower-Gathering"; then on to page 13 and the remaining three lines and second stanza of that poem, which is then followed by "Rose Pogonias." In other words, the pages are crowded, the poems often broken up unattractively. And much of the pleasure of those very short poems (originally introduced as *Quantula* in *A Witness Tree,* and preserved within the text of *Complete Poems, 1949*) is now lost. Most of the fun of "The Secret Sits"—"We dance round in a ring and suppose, / But the Secret sits in the middle and knows"—was to come upon the poem sitting there on a big white page in gnomic isolation; the same goes for "An Answer"—"But Islands of the Blessèd, bless you, son, / I never came upon a blessèd one." In the new edition these poems share two pages along with seven other poems, and quarters are cramped.

These inconveniences, losses of fine old ways of presenting Frost's poems, would probably be forgivable: one could sigh about publishing costs, though that sigh might be tempered by the guess that Holt, Rinehart and Winston has made a fair amount of money from their Frost sales. But the editing of the poems goes beyond a listing of variants or dates of publication: Mr. Lathem is also responsible for "changes introduced by the present editor that constitute departures from copy-texts." The main copy-text is *Complete Poems, 1949,* but departures from it have been made "both for the correction of errors and for achieving greater textual clarity." I'm not quite sure what "greater textual clarity" means in principle; but in fact it seems to mean that the editor has seen fit to correct or improve Frost's punctuation of his own poems when that punctuation for one reason or another is deemed inadequate or misleading or awkward or whatever.

Though he does not elucidate specifically, it is clear that the editor thinks one of the best ways to correct error or achieve textual clarity is to declare war on the hyphen; so "witch-hazel" or "sleigh-bells" or "window-pane" or "star-like" now become "witch hazel," "sleigh bells," "window pane," and "starlike." Aside from what seems to me the needless and presumptuous fiddling involved in such emendations, what happens when the amusing line from "Fireflies in the Garden" about how though the fireflies aren't stars they "Achieve at times a very star-like start" now becomes "starlike"? Or when the humorous command in "Clear and Colder"—"Then take some left-over winter" becomes "leftover"? Or even more annoying in "Birches," where "As ice-storms do" now becomes "As ice storms do," a somewhat duller deed; or "snow-crust" becomes "snow crust"; or where Truth used to break in "With all her matter-of-fact about the ice-storm" she now breaks in without the fine emphasis those hyphens provide? What has happened to all the hyphens? A friend of mine suggested that perhaps the editor was bequeathed some large basket in which to store hyphens, and that after picking them out of the poems, he has so stored them.

But he must own an equally large basket of commas—seasoned with more emphatic dashes—eager to find their way into some poem or other, because Mr. Lathem has been as lavish in his providing of them as he has been saving of hyphens. Here are three instances of small changes made in some of Frost's best and most familiar poems; the reader may judge how small the changes are. In "An Old Man's Winter Night" the lines describing the old man's preparation for sleep used to read this way:

> He consigned to the moon, such as she was,
> So late-arising, to the broken moon
> As better than the sun in any case
> For such a charge, his snow upon the roof,
> His icicles along the wall to keep;
> And slept....

The editor emends the first two lines to read:

> He consigned to the moon—such as she was,
> So late-arising—to the broken moon

Evidently Frost's steady unbroken trail of commas was not emphatic enough for Mr. Lathem's taste, which judged that "such as she was, / So late-arising" needed the more special treatment provided by surrounding dashes. A second example: the Oven Bird's message used to be delivered this way:

> He says the early petal-fall is past
> When pear and cherry bloom went down in showers
> On sunny days a moment overcast;

Now a comma has been placed after "past," supposedly to warn us against the strong enjambment that sustains our voice from one line to the next. Did Frost not know what he was doing when he "omitted" the comma? Finally the famous lines from "Stopping by Woods on a Snowy Evening":

> Whose woods these are I think I know.
> His house is in the village though;

now read

> Whose woods these are I think I know.
> His house is in the village, though;

while "The woods are lovely, dark and deep," now has an added comma after "dark." It is as if a prim schoolmaster were at work, showing his concern for Robert's getting the correct punctuation into the business or friendly letter so that his English will be Good and Understood By All, rather than "Under a spell so the wrong ones can't find it, / So can't get saved." Perhaps the absence of a comma can be a very positive presence in the spell cast by a poem. In the case of "Stopping by Woods," the substantive change in tone introduced by the editor's emendation of a comma before "though"—"His house is in the village, though"—turns the speaker into a coyly twinkling fellow with all too much of a clever tongue lodged in his cheek. Robert Frost was more impersonal than that, and his jokes were harder to catch.

One of his poems ended (and still ends) with the following lines: "For I am There, / And what I would not part with I have kept." On the evidence of this edition I'd have to say, alas not all kept, but regrettably parted with and not, so far as I can see from the evidence, by the poet's own wish. I think some sort of explanation is due from Holt and the editor: until one is convincingly forthcoming I would advise you to save, as I have, the $10.95. If you don't already own a *Complete Poems, 1949* look up, by dint of hard labor, a secondhand bookstore where they will very likely have a copy someone recently and mistakenly has replaced by the new edition.

—*Atlantic,* October 1970.

Robert Frost Collected Poems, Prose, and Plays

IT IS ENTIRELY fitting that the first twentieth-century American poet to be published in the Library of America series is Robert Frost. These one thousand pages of his poetry and prose (there are three plays as well, but they don't matter) constitute the most varied, humanly satisfying, and technically interesting body of verse by any modern American poet, not excepting Wallace Stevens or T. S. Eliot. They also contain an invaluable body of theoretical and critical writing *about* the art of poetry. To have such riches available for the first time in a single, compact, affordable volume, is a testimony to how, in a world where reading and criticizing poetry counts less and less, intelligent editorial tribute has been paid to the poet who counts more and more.

Frost has been well served by the two critics who collaborated on making the selection. Richard Poirier, one of the founders of the Library of America, has written what is still the most ambitious and rewarding critical discussion of Frost's poetry (*Robert Frost: The Work of Knowing,* 1978); Mark Richardson, whose doctoral dissertation was an edition of Frost's prose, has uncovered many interesting out-of-the-way items and has, I suspect, been instrumental in writing the very useful series of notes to both prose and verse. But what these editors have done that most deserves our gratitude is their restoration of Frost's *Complete Poems* (1949) as the proper text for the volumes of verse he brought out from *A Boy's Will* (1913) through *Steeple Bush* (1947).

That such a seemingly conservative editorial decision nevertheless deserves remarking is the result of a bad mistake made twenty-five years ago by Frost's publisher, Holt, Rinehart and Winston, when they decided to bring out a "comprehensive and authoritative" edition of the poetry. Claiming to be "scrupulously edited for textual accuracy," the book that resulted was nothing of the sort, since its editor, Edward Connery Lathem, went about "improving" the poems by repunctuating them when he thought they demanded it. So hyphens and commas were added or subtracted as Lathem saw fit, and Frost's usually lightly punctuated verse was tampered with to make it fit what the editor saw as more correct grammatical practice. To take one simple though egregious example of such tampering: "Stopping by Woods on a Snowy Evening," a poem nobody in the world ever thought stood in need of editorial attention, was unwisely granted it when Lathem added two commas to its four stanzas. The first comma changed line two, "His house is in the village though" to "His house is in the village, though"; the second turned "The woods are lovely, dark and deep" into "The woods are lovely, dark, and deep." (Poirier has pointed out that in Frost's original line the woods were not just "lovely, dark, and deep" but "lovely, [i.e.] dark and deep." In both cases an easy, unemphatic presentation was made to sound prim and "correct," while rhythmic and tonal implications were disregarded, even reversed, by editorial fussing. So to get rid of Lathem's corrections and additions was in itself a first-rate decision.

Frost's last book of poetry, *In the Clearing,* published the year before he died and with a pretty high percentage of forgettable poems, is likewise restored to its pre-Lathemized state. But of more interest to students of the poet are eighty or so poems, most of them hitherto uncollected, many written when Frost was a young man, some of them published in magazines. They include "La Noche Triste," composed when he was sixteen, about Cortes's retreat from Tenochtitlan ("The Montezumas are no more, / Gone is their regal throne"), and the class hymn he wrote for his high school graduation. There is "Twilight," the title poem of a little booklet he had hand-printed to woo his classmate sweetheart and future wife, Elinor White; there is a morbid, even suicidal piece, called "Despair," written sometime in the 1890s ("I am like a dead diver after all's / Done, still held fast in the weeds' snare below"); and there is the touching poem he wrote after he sold his Derry farm and prepared to depart for England. "On the Sale of My Farm" ends with this delicate gesture of regret:

> Only be it understood,
> It shall be no trespassing
> If I come again some spring
> In the grey disguise of years,
> Seeking ache of memory here.

There are also a number of satirical poems, friendly verse letters to friends, and an unfriendly one written but not sent to Ezra Pound. Frost's occasional penchant for the bawdy is strongly revealed here in "Pride of Ancestry," which begins on this promising note:

> The Deacon's wife was a bit desirish
> And liked her sex relations wild
> So she lay with one of the shanty Irish
> And he begot the Deacon's child.

I am sorry however to see no sign of the little poem he used to say in hopes of shocking pious believers: "Mary had a little lamb, / Its name was Jesus Christ. / God, not Joseph, was the ram, / But Joseph took it nice."

In the prose collected here we encounter repeatedly striking formulations about reading and writing; many of them—the more notable for being hot off the griddle—came when Frost, living in England, wrote home to American friends, using them as sounding boards for his poetic "theory." Selections of his letters edited by his biographer Lawrance Thompson and by his friend Louis Untermeyer have been unavailable for years: a pity, since Frost was a wonderfully humorous, if occasionally exasperating, letter writer. The new collection picks out central ones about the importance of sentence sounds and of imagining the speaking voice. Decades later, in a series of apothegms written for the *Atlantic Monthly* under the title "Poetry and School," Frost took a last crack at the notion of reading poetry without listening to it: "The eye reader is a barbarian. So also is the writer for the eye reader, who needn't care how badly he writes since he doesn't care how badly he is read." The "best reader" will be "one who will read, can read, no faster than he can hear the lines and sentences in his mind's eye as if read aloud. Frequenting poetry has slowed him down by its metric and measured pace." These apothegms conclude with the one everybody knows about how, for pleasure, he would as soon write free verse as play tennis with the net down.

Frost was of course, among other things, a teacher, even though his courses at Pinkerton Academy, the University of Michigan, and Amherst College were to say the least unconventional. "We go to college to be given one more chance to learn to read in case we haven't learned in High School"; once we have learned that, he believed, the rest would follow. (He once defined college as a place to hang around until you catch on, after which you might be well advised—as he did—to light out for some other territory.) Frost delighted in not saying the obvious things about how "English" was the department where you went to improve your "writing skills," as the current depressing parlance has it. No, he says, "We write in school chiefly because to try our hand at writing should make us better readers." (I tell students that when their parents nag them about their writing they should ask Mom and Dad about how parental reading of Shakespeare or Milton has been going recently.) "The chief reason for going to school is to get the impression fixed for life that there is a book side to everything," he writes; that impression, not at all easy to come by for most students, even at elite colleges and universities, is something rather different from improving writing skills so as to be effective in business or law later on.

But after all is said and done, it's the poems that matter, and the Library of America's volume gives us the opportunity of reading through a life of poetry, from "Into My Own," the first poem in *A Boy's Will,* to "In winter in the woods alone...," the final, untitled one from *In the Clearing.* It's a poetic world large and difficult enough to get lost in; also one you can't exhaust, since there are always new poems that did not quite register before, or old ones that sound slightly different this time around. No one has ever spoken more convincingly and truly about Frost's world than Randall Jarrell did in his great essay "To the Laodiceans," when he insisted that Frost's poetry is like the world we know:

> the world with its animals and plants and, most of all, its people: people working, thinking about things, falling in love, taking naps; in these poems men are not only the glory and jest and riddle of the world, but also the habit of the world, its strange ordinariness, its ordinary strangeness, and they too trudge down the ruts along which the planets move in their courses. Frost is that rare thing, a complete or representative poet.... When you know Frost's poems you know surprisingly well how the world seemed to one man, and what it was to seem that way.

—Originally published in the *Boston Globe,*
October 22, 1995 as "First Frost."

The Notebooks of Robert Frost

The Notebooks of Robert Frost,
edited by Robert Faggen

THIS IS THE FIRST in a projected series of works by Robert Frost that will include editions of his poems, essays, and letters, published by the Belknap Press of Harvard University under the general editorship of Robert Faggen. Mr. Faggen, author of a book about Frost and science (*Robert Frost and the Challenge of Darwin*), has undertaken the truly heroic task of presenting Frost's notebooks, which, forty-three years after the poet's death in 1963, have been used only sparingly by scholars. Spanning six decades, from the 1890s to the early 1960s, they consist physically of the homeliest of materials: dime-store spiral pads and school theme books that Frost, so Faggen tells us in a useful introduction, kept with him in his movings from place to place and his busy life of reading engagements for diverse audiences. The editorial challenge they present is due in part to their helter-skelter character. There is no clear chronological ordering: a single notebook may contain entries from widely different times in Frost's life, while the layout of individual pages seems almost willfully capricious, with sentences going in various directions. Deciphering many of them is also a problem—the word illegible appears frequently in the editor's interpolations.[1]

But the deepest challenge they present, even to a reader familiar with Frost's poetry, lies in the way they simultaneously invite us to colloquy

1. Since this was written, doubt has been cast on Faggen's editorial practice by two critics, James Sitar and William Logan, who accuse him of inaccurately transcribing many items in the notebooks. Since Faggen has spent years editing them, my sense is that he should be trusted, despite whatever mistakes there turn out to be.

while fending us off. A 1917 letter of Frost's suggests a principle behind these notebook entries: "You get more credit for thinking if you restate formulas or cite cases which fall easily under formulae. But all the fun is outside, saying things that suggest formulae but won't formulate—that almost but don't quite formulate." In another letter quoted by Faggen, Frost informs his correspondent, "I have written to keep the curious out of the secret places of my mind both in my verse and in my letters to such as you." The notebooks might be thought to reveal those secret places more than did his poems and letters; yet, in their combination of what the editor calls "candor and cryptic evasion," they offer no easy and direct road to what Frost the human being "really" believed about central matters.

One of the most charming and pertinent of the entries is this four-line ditty:

> Nothing ever so sincere
> That unless it's out of sheer
> Mischief and a little queer
> It won't prove a bore to hear.

A "sincere," mischief-lacking poem is a bore to hear because absent from it are the twists and turns, the changes of tone, the "special posture" of individual sentence sounds that Frost, in his insistence on "ear" rather than "eye" reading, makes central to the reading and writing of poetry. He is also committed to humor: "I am never more serious than when joking," was one of his repeated avowals.

The poem just quoted is an example of a Frostian "joke" that is serious as well. But in one of the many entries that address themselves to what a poem is, or is like, or should be like, we get the following:

> The poem must have as good a point as an anecdote or a joke. It is the more effective if it has something analogous to the practical joke—an action—a "put up job" such as being carried out as a serenade or valentine or requiem or memorial address.

Notable here is the insistence on poetry as an action, something carried out with purpose in mind (elsewhere he refers to a poem as a "deed"), a practical joke, "sheer / Mischief and a little queer." The reader is engaged in an analogous activity, as when, in one of the many entries directed at teaching, students are advised, "Don't tell the poem in other and worse English of your own to show you understand it. But say something of your own based on the poem (*not* an opinion of it though)." To respond adequately to the "put up job" of a poem, it is not enough to call it beautiful or say you don't like it; you need rather to do something to keep the ball in play.

Another word for this recommended activity, within the poem or in response to it, is one of Frost's favorite words—performance. He addresses the matter directly with this admonition: "Performance in poetry and in life is recognition and admission of the fact that things are not to be too well understood." "Are not to be," rather than "are not," underscoring the insistence that nothing be closed down too confidently, too quickly. Faggen reminds us in his introduction of the poet's respect for, indeed fascination with, uncertainty and chaos. This is the "confusion" that in his crucial essay, "The Figure a Poem Makes," he said the poem provided a "momentary stay against." Only a momentary one, mind you.

Lest one get the impression that the notebooks are wall-to-wall nuggets of detachable Frostian wisdoms, it should be said that much of the material is relatively, sometimes wholly impenetrable, even with the editor's best efforts at annotation. For example, the following entry:

> Story of the Gaget Gimlet no Longer Manufactured.
> " " Hiring the One-armed Teacher
> " " The Woodpecker's Daughter.
> Nothing Fatal but Death Stigma
> Of an [?Albenes] Tatoo
> Brat Buster
> Do you read [?Serviss]

The items that precede and follow this one shed no light on it, nor does Faggen venture to comment. It is one of the occasions in which an attempted look into the composer's mind reveals nothing—which is to say that any reader is going to skim a lot, looking for a moment when something shines through. Some items are repeated so often as to testify to how fond Frost was of them, such as "All men are created free and equally funny"; or "I hate the poor don't you Yes and I hate the rich. I hate them both as such." In one item he questions and answers this condition of hatred: "Why do I hate them. Because they bother me so. I have to think of them when there are so many other things I want to think of."

At moments we get memorable glimpses into Frost the bad boy who prided himself on "running away" from colleges (Dartmouth, Harvard) and like an earlier Frank Sinatra did things his way. He never missed the chance to bait Archibald MacLeish, especially after MacLeish's verse play *J.B.* was published. He takes MacLeish's much-anthologized poem "Ars Poetica," whose final lines reverently intone "A poem should not mean / But be," and corrects it, by moving the words around, to: "It should be mean." "You have to be attractive enough to get people within striking distance," he noted, and the strike could be lethal. At other times the operative word is sly, as in this piece of timeless advice: "Keep on writing to her after marriage with a view to marrying her later in life when her husband dies or fails her." Then there are purely humorous entries that make us think of Mark Twain, as when Frost defines a "regionalist" as "one who picked out a region (such as the abdomen fundament or elbow) and has a pain in it."

The editor rightly points out the predominance of epigrammatic meditations in the notebooks—Frost says in one of them that students "must be taught that the fun of being epigrammatic is the legitimate fun of literature." Although I haven't seen the comparison made, there are compelling similarities of temperament and serious wit between Frost and the great Renaissance poet Ben Jonson, whose first collection of poems was titled *Epigrams.* Jonson later published *Timber, Or, Discoveries* "made upon men and matter, as they have flowed out of his daily readings." Perhaps the finest moments in Frost's notebooks are ones, always coming out of the blue, in which his discovery is such as to strike us as truly never said before. Sometimes they are about matters one wouldn't have expected him especially to reflect on, like the following two on alcoholic intake. In one of them he shrewdly imagines his way into the kind of person who is prey to drink: "Drink is a medicine for the too strict by nature. No one needs it who has ever lost himself without it." We are not allowed merely to feel superior to these overstrict people, nor are we invited to dismiss the following expansion of it: "Getting drunk is the glorification of waste—pouring libation {to the God of Waste} not onto the fire but into yourself. It is squandering with complete submissiveness to the nature of things your time your wealth your faculties." Faggen comments on Frost's frequent preoccupation with "waste," including a resonant line from his poem "Pod of the Milkweed":

"But waste was of the essence of the scheme." Perhaps there is something to be said even for squandering central human qualities—time, wealth, faculties—in the interests of a gesture as large-scaled as "complete submission to the nature of things." In such formulations as these, the clever epigrammatist moves into realms rather deeper and less to be taken in "fun." "Life is a punishment. All we can contribute to it is gracefulness in taking the punishment." Nothing to ponder there; it has to be swallowed straight.

The editor cautions us to be wary of the "seductive finality" of some of the entries, and this is best done by trying to see the aphorisms and epigrams in the light of others that qualify or even contradict the one in question. Frost notes that "The tone of plain statement is one tone and not to be despised. All the same it has been my great object in poetry to avoid the use of it." These notebooks testify to how hard he worked at not being easily understood: "I should like to be so subtle at this game," he wrote in a letter, "as to seem to the casual person altogether obvious." For the game, which he played over sixty years, the following entry may stand as a motto: "I have made a life study out of what I can say."

—*Weekly Standard*, September 10, 2006.

The Flip Side of Frost

The Collected Prose of Robert Frost
Edited by Mark Richardson
Belknap/Harvard University, 378 pp., $39.95

A YEAR AGO *The Notebooks of Robert Frost* appeared, the first of a number of works by Frost to be published by Harvard University's Belknap Press. Now, following on its heels, comes this welcome edition of Frost's prose, seventy-six items ranging from a paragraph to a few pages, edited by Mark Richardson in exemplary fashion; that is, in addition to adhering to the most scrupulous editorial practice, Richardson has provided 120 pages of notes. The notes don't merely identify people and allusions—allusions often, as is Frost's wont, that are cryptic or teasing—but provide valuable documentation of "Frost's habits of composition" so as to make up a "loosely consequential narrative of Frost's total career as a writer of prose."

As Richardson states in his introduction, Frost was reluctant to publish his prose, even to write it with publication in mind. His Norton lectures at Harvard in 1936 were supposed to be collected into a book; he neglected to do this, and if there ever was a manuscript it has been conveniently lost. "Something in me still fights off the written prose," he wrote a correspondent about the book he had just fought off. Richardson doesn't say as much, but I suspect this impulse had to do with Frost's fear that in writing prose about poetry—about his own poetry—he might be providing readers with what he didn't want to provide: a systematic theory of how writing poetry was or should be done. His letters, especially the ones written home from England in 1912-13, are full of declarations about matters such as the sound of sense, the play of voice rhythm against metrical pattern, and the need for each line of verse to have its special vocal posture. But he was wary of putting the vivid life of something tossed off in a letter or a lecture into book form. Although he promised to give his publisher, Henry Holt, a collection of his prose in 1941, no such collection was forthcoming. After his death, a slim volume of his prose was published; now Richardson has sought out and included all the prose Frost was known to have prepared, with whatever mixed feelings, for print.

About a third of these items are early ones, some of them columns and editorials Frost wrote for his high-school newspaper in Lawrence. There are also a few stories he wrote for his children, and others he published in a poultry magazine when he was an unsuccessful chicken farmer. Richardson describes the prevailing tone of many of these early pieces as "both coy and cocky." It was a manner he never really lost, inasmuch as even his later, most serious reflections about poetry and life were seldom put forth without an aggressive air of keeping always one step ahead of the reader. "I am never more serious than when joking," he said more than once. In his "serious" essay "The Figure a Poem Makes," he speaks trenchantly of poetry as beginning in delight and ending in wisdom and as "a momentary stay against confusion." But the essay begins abruptly and confusingly by declaring: "Abstraction is an old story with the philosophers, but it has been like a new toy in the hands of the artists of our day." Who is speaking, and about what? He continues: "Why can't we have any one quality of poetry we choose by itself? We can have in thought. Then it will go hard if we can't in practice. Our lives for it." Even a reader tuned to Frost's playful mode will have trouble locating himself in relation to those sentences that are hardly even sentences. The disorienting of readerly expectations is always part of the game.

"The Figure a Poem Makes," for many years placed as an introduction to Frost's "Collected Poems," is one of a number of valuable, original essays in which, without overtly theorizing, Frost gave us his theory of poetry. Richardson thinks "The Constant Symbol" is his greatest essay in poetics; I would give the award to "Education by Poetry" and single out for special note his introduction to E. A. Robinson's "King Jasper," in which among other things Frost distinguished between griefs and grievances, poetry's subject being the former. Also wonderful, although not exactly an essay, are the twenty-eight pithy brevities he titled "Poetry and School." Any teacher of first-year college students would do well to share some of these brevities, such as "We go to college to be given one more chance to learn to read in case we hadn't learned in High School. Once we have learned to read the rest can be trusted to add itself unto us."

Frost's ambiguous, even disdainful relation to higher education is well known, and he was convinced of the baleful effect studying poetry can have on its appreciation. Education by poetry—true education—proceeded in a more wayward and disinterested manner. As early as 1910 he described his English curriculum at the academy in Derry, N.H., where he was teaching, as follows: "Expression in oral reading rather than intelligent comment is made the test of appreciation." Poetry, he always insisted, was a deed, and the student does a true deed when he can read aloud with expressively correct feeling the lines of a poem, instead of writing a paper about its theme or meaning. One hundred years later we have not taken the measure of many of the radical thoughts that fill these meditative monologues.

—*Boston Globe*, March 2, 2008.

Frost In His Letters

FROST IN HIS LETTERS: we might ask about the title, its appropriateness as a subject of study, of literary commentary. How many English or American writers can plausibly be approached as if their "letters" were a genre worth taking seriously for the special pleasures and rewards to be found in them? Academic libraries fill up with multi-volumed collections of letters by the great writers—Wordsworth, Dickens, Charlotte Brontë, Tennyson, Hardy, Bernard Shaw, Henry James—but who reads them, much less owns them? (James, maybe, in a one-volume selection from the four volumes.) As a young student of literature I had it implanted in my mind by no less an authority than Lionel Trilling, that there were two great writers of letters in English—Keats and D.H. Lawrence. There's certainly a case to be made for each, though who wants to work through the nine volumes of Lawrence's letters that have now been published? Unless they're subsidized, university-sponsored collections of letters surely have no appeal for publishers: fifteen years ago Houghton Mifflin published Randall Jarrell's letters, wonderfully engaging pages I found them, which sold poorly. (Robie Macauley, then an editor at Houghton Mifflin, told me that only Flannery O'Connor's letters had made it into paperback.)

Surely Frost's letters have not been clamored for by readers who presumably love his poetry, at least not to the extent that Frost's publisher was willing to keep them in print. Lawrance Thompson's *Selected Letters* and Louis Untermeyer's collection of Frost's letters to him, both published by Holt in the year after Frost's death, have been out of print for decades, along with the valuable *Family Letters of Robert Frost*, edited by Arnold Grade. The *Library of America* Frost has usefully printed some pages of letters dealing especially with matters of poetic form and Frost's "theory" of verse. Other publishers of his poetic contemporaries have done better by them, keeping Pound's and Stevens's letters in print, as well as the first and only volume published so far of T. S. Eliot's. I want to direct these remarks not—if I may draw a dangerous distinction—at the "content" of Frost's letters, at what he "had to say" about poetry or love or heroism—but at the distinct and memorable way he said those things. The distinction is dangerous, of course, in the way that any separation of form and content simplifies and makes less rich the poem, the paragraph, the sentence in question. But by way of comparison with his peers in their correspondence: Eliot and Pound give us direct news and gossip about the London literary world; Wallace Stevens takes us on long walks with him and tells us what he saw—later on he will explicate his own poems, often at tedious length. By contrast Frost's epistolary style is teasing, indirect, sometimes rather opaque, making us feel that perhaps we're missing something, the point maybe. In this he follows the style of his prose in the few essays he wrote: you never know quite which way he will jump, and sometimes you're not sure you've jumped with him in the right direction. What *is* the right direction, one asks?

In formulating his theory of poetry back in 1914, in England, he insisted, to his sounding-boards John Bartlett and Sidney Cox back in America, that sentence sounds, in and out of poetry, must "unmistakably" show a reader how to voice "the posture proper to the sentence": "Never if you can help it write down a sentence in which the voice will not know how to posture *specially*," he wrote Bartlett. But there may be some ambiguity here. Is Frost, as poet, mainly anxious to help the reader get the poem, the line, the special posture "right"? Or is it conceivable that he might also, even primarily, be interested in contriving, in his own voice, a posture so special as to confuse the reader—to leave him in the dust? In and out of the letters, from the beginning, there is an emphasis on wiliness ("ain't I wily," he once wrote); on his own complicated forethinking ("I am not undesigning"); and on collapsing presumed opposites together ("I am never so serious as when joking"). Think collaterally of the more than one occasion on which he held up "The Road Not Taken" as a tricky poem. Thompson says in his introduction to the letters that in this poem Frost was carrying himself in the manner of Edward Thomas, who on their walks in England kept regretting the road he had taken and thinking of the other one and what might have been. Thompson tells us that Frost sent the poem to Thomas in manuscript, hoping that "his friend would notice how the poem pivots ironically on the un-Frostian phrase, 'I shall be telling this with a sigh'." Edward Thomas missed it, says Thompson, because "the irony had been handled too slyly, too subtly," and he thinks Frost was similarly disappointed when

American readers missed the "pivotal irony" of the poem. Yet in Thompson's following paragraph he quotes Frost saying in a letter about his own writing, "I should like to be so subtle at this game as to seem to the casual person altogether obvious." And he indulged in what sounds like a boast to Untermeyer when he writes that "I bet not half a dozen people can tell who was hit and where he was hit by my Road Not Taken."

And of course it wasn't just a question of "The Road Not Taken" being a poem where Frost was too sly or subtle in his irony. Consider the final stanza of "Tree at my Window"

> That day she put our heads together
> Fate had her imagination about her,
> Your head so much concerned with outer,
> Mine with inner, weather.

Who would like to stand up and describe the special posture of "Fate had her imagination about her," to say just how serious or how humorous it is? Are seriousness and joking the same for Frost?

> They cannot look out far,
> They cannot look in deep,
> But when was that ever a bar
> To any watch they keep?

I needn't go into the difficulty critics and readers have had with *that* assertion—of just how to weigh it. The best Randall Jarrell could do was to address the "tone" of the last lines and immediately qualify that with "or rather, their careful suspension between several tones, as a piece of irony can be held in the air between powerful enough magnets." To say further how or why that suspension is "careful" was a task Jarrell didn't take on. I'm suggesting, in other words, that Frost's deepest impulse as writer of poems and prose, was (to use Jarrell's metaphor) suspended between the desire, on the one hand, not to be "caviare to the crowd," as Pound was—to reach out rather to all sorts and kinds of readers. But also, to be altogether unobvious to the casual—that is to most—readers: to hold back, to *not* say all he could an he would, to *not* unfold a tale that would tell all.

I.

In his *T. S. Eliot And Prejudice*, Christopher Ricks has a valuable comparison of Frost to Eliot by way of indicating the often undramatic quality of tone in Eliot's poetry. Ricks quotes Frost's 1913 4th of July letter home to Bartlett about the sound of sense, and after some examples of that sound ("You mean to tell me you can't read? I said no such thing. Well read then. You're not my teacher.") Frost writes "Those sounds are summoned by the audile imagination and they must be positive, strong, and definitely and unmistakeably indicated by the context. The reader must be at no loss to give his voice the posture proper to the sentence." Ricks calls this insistence "one half of the truth," and notes that although "Frost's poems are often less single-minded than this, as a commentator on poetry he is indeed single-minded." But Frost in his letters is many things besides a commentator on poetry, although he is never far from that subject, and one way of distinguishing his correspondence from that of his poetic contemporaries is to suggest how much doublemindedness there is in his writing. Consider a couple of sentences from letters to Susan Hayes Ward in 1894, after the magazine she edited (*The New York Independent*) had accepted "My Butterfly" for publication, the first such acceptance Frost had received. He thanks her profusely—"It is just such a letter...that I have been awaiting for two years"—then draws back, or moves in a more complicated direction: "Yet the consideration is hardly due me. Take my word for it that poem exaggerates my ability. You must spare my feelings when you come to read these others, for I haven't the courage to be a disappointment to anyone." What is the exact special posture of this? How "positive" and "strong" is its unmistakable tonal indication? "Take my word for it that poem exaggerates my ability"—what sort of "word" is this she's supposed to take? Does it help to call the word "tongue-in-cheek" or "ironical"? Not much, for what mainly comes across, especially in that oddly unexpected verb "exaggerates," is a cool elegance that is not unhumorous and that is both at variance with what the words literally say, yet created only through their distinctive way of saying. Spare my feelings, he warns her when she reads other work he is sending her ("Two of these are the returned poems and the other is no better"), since "I haven't the courage to be a disappointment to anyone." Is that what it takes to disappoint people—more courage than one has? Again irony, tongue-in-cheek, saying one thing while meaning another, are only the roughest handles to grab on to the felicity of that yoking of courage and disappointment. Six months or so later, back from his excursion in Virginia's Dismal Swamp, he thanks Susan Ward for printing "My Butterfly," then clears his throat and backs off into a new paragraph:

> Before proceeding further I perceive I must assume an attitude, or else endanger the coherency of my remarks,—for my natural attitude is one of enthusiasm verging on egotism and thus I always confused myself trying to be modest.

Part of this fussing is no more, perhaps, than the self-consciousness of a young man, sending off his wares for inspection by a person in a position to publish them. But the final sentence has the pleasure of an originality beyond nervousness: granted it's not uncommon for someone to admit he's enthusiastic, perhaps egotistical in that enthusiasm; but then the unexpected conclusions—"Thus I always confused myself trying to be modest." The only way, evidently, to be clear rather than confused is to assert yourself, egotistical as that way may be.

I have noted the inadequacy of ready-made labels like irony to deal with Frost's distinctive epistolary style. Since we may call that style, safely if vaguely, a humorous one, it's worth remembering what Frost in a letter had to say about humor as it bore on himself. The saying comes in a letter to Untermeyer, probably the correspondent who over the years, beginning in 1915 when Frost returned from England, called forth the poet's most extravagant and complicated performances. In a letter of 10 March 1924, Frost addressed himself to the meaning of "style" in prose or verse. It indicated "how the writer takes himself and what he is saying," and Frost proceeds to exemplify it by briefly and pungently characterizing the ways different writers like Stevenson, Swinburne, Emerson, Thoreau, Whitman, Carlyle ("whose way of taking himself simply infuriates me"), and Longfellow "took" themselves. Then a new paragraph:

> I own any form of humor shows fear and inferiority. Irony is simply a form of guardedness. So is a twinkle. It keeps the reader from criticism.... At bottom the world isn't a joke. We only joke about it to avoid an issue with someone to let someone know that we know he's there with his questions: to disarm him by seeming to have heard and done justice to his side of the standing argument. Humor is the most engaging cowardice. With it

> myself I have been able to hold some of my enemy in play far out of gunshot.

If asked to name, on the basis of these sentences, *Frost's* style—how he "took" himself—we could do it by lifting another sentence from the same letter, in which style is figured as "the mind skating circles round itself as it moves forward." "Style" is the way a writer "carries himself toward his ideas and deeds"; it is a product of "superfluity."

The vigorous skating round himself that goes on in Frost's letters, their "superfluity," is a virtuoso activity in which words are continually slipping out of their stable meanings at the command of the performer who puts new twists on them. In the sentence above ("I hold any form of humor shows fear or inferiority") words that usually have a less than admirable ring—especially for a tough guy like Frost—turn out to be necessary attributes of "any form of humor," and they join "irony" as the respectable constituents of a defensive style which, even as you scarcely notice it, turns into a subtle and effectively offensive one called "guardedness." The process seems wholly analogous to the moment at the end of his *Paris Review* interview when he muses on what's meant by "inspiration":

> ...it's just the same as when you feel a joke coming. You see somebody coming down the street that you're accustomed to abuse, and you feel it stirring in you, something to say as you pass each other.
>
> ....It's him coming toward you that gives you the animus, you know. When they want to know about inspiration, I tell them it's mostly animus.

To recap a bit: humor or irony is a way of showing "fear and inferiority"; it is a kind of "guardedness"; an "engaging cowardice" employed to hold the enemy "in play far out of gunshot." How much of this is "objective" thinking and how much is it a deeply subjective response to life, with its roots in Frost's biography? Surely it has much to do with his extreme wariness about other people—with his "overactive" imagination ("I am never not working," he loved to say), ever alert to the possibilities for embarrassment, for defeat, or perhaps victory, in human encounters ("You see somebody coming down the street whom you're accustomed to abuse"). It may have something to do with the years of relative isolation in his twenties when the shy and fiercely proud young man held himself and his gift apart from other people and from the world—that world where people seemed to be "disallowing" him, achieving more than him by graduating from college and establishing themselves in one or the other solid occupation. But Frost had, in his isolation, a vantage point: "And if by noon I have too much of these, / I have but to turn on my arm and lo, / The sunburned hillside sets my face aglow." With Elinor, he can share a vantage point on the world that is neglecting them, as in "In Neglect":

> They leave us so in the way we took
> As two in whom they were proved mistaken
> That we sit sometimes in a wayside nook
> With mischievous, vagrant, seraphic look
> And *try* if we cannot feel forsaken.

What a lovely way to keep the enemy in play and out of gunshot—to wield those three words that never before came within remote proximity of one another: "mischievous, vagrant, seraphic." Here is indeed inspiration, the animus well-breathed, as those adjectives brilliantly suggest the concentrated waywardness, the wandering mischief of Frost's humorous fantasies.

Sometimes those fantasies, as spun out in his correspondence, are so fiercely concentrated on undoing the enemy that it feels as if something like gunshot were in fact about to happen: the reader laughs, sort of, but feels contorted in so doing. Frost once wrote his eldest daughter, Lesley, who had been bothered by what he terms as some "co-occupants" of her New York City apartment. Frost provided free-of-charge advice on how to deal with them, "to set them back temporarily if not get rid of them entirely":

> You can get in a kerosene can a gallon of gasolene (price 36 cts) and pour, literally pour, it into every crack and corner of the wood work of the bed or cots and soak the canvas of them all along where it is nailed to the wood. Don't wet the mattresses: they are as uninhabited as the moon. You must do the deed very early in the day when no light or fire is lit in the room or going to be for a good many hours—that is till the gasolene has had time to evaporate and get out the windows. You can leave the windows open for the day. I say this only for your own comfort

> for the time being... You may have to buy a cheap kerosene can. It is the best thing to buy the gasolene in and to put the stuff on with. Don't spare it. Make the wood bubble. Go over the beds twice perhaps. Then open the windows and get out.

He adds in a final note, "This is the kind of letter I should hate to mail at the Franconia postoffice for fear Salome would open it for her amusement and keep it as a memorial for our private affairs." (He mailed it from the post office in Arlington, New Hampshire.) It took this reader some time to realize that the co-occupants were not obstreperous roommates, to be summarily dealt with, but stubborn bedbugs who would succumb only to liberally laid-on gasoline. Doubtless Frost's advice was good practical sense; yet isn't there a relish in his laying it out ("Don't spare it. Make the wood bubble") that goes beyond what a more ordinary father might have suggested his child should do? Frost, as father, delights in making mischief, in exuberantly, and with superfluity, imagining the end of such an insidious foe.

A quieter but no less deadly form of aggression occurs in a 1914 letter from England about the behavior of the Georgian poet W.H. Davies, who had been visiting Frost's friend Wilfrid Gibson. I've already referred to it in my book on Frost, but want to introduce it again here since it so perfectly expresses a central part of the Frostian epistolary temperament. He says that Davies had lately "disgusted" the Gibsons, then adds that

> His is the kind of egotism another man's egotism can't put up with. He was going from here to be with Conrad. He said that would be pleasant because Conrad knew his work *thoroughly*. After waiting long enough to obscure the point we asked him if he knew Conrad's work *thoroughly*. Oh no—was it good? We told him yes. He was glad we liked it.

There is a lot stirring, or rather bubbling, here. A less playful, more self-righteous spirit than Frost would have had Davies' egotism simply impossible to put up with, as if to say "you and I, reader, are not ourselves eogtistic but generously open to other people." But Frost surprises us with bringing in "another man's egotism," as if Davies' egotism were of the sort a mere ordinary egotist can't put up with. What's special about Davies' egotism? Perhaps it is his imperviousness to his betters, if not to Frost then surely to Joseph Conrad. Davies' patronizing of Conrad comes through by Frost wickedly repeating and italicizing the word "thoroughly," as in "he knows my work *thoroughly*," and there is also the surprise appearance of the altogether unobvious, unexpected verb "obscure," as in "after waiting long enough to obscure the point," suggesting that the trap set for Davies was of the most subtle kind, set by a plural "we"—although we're willing to blame Frost for all the inspiration. Then there is the fine, totally deadpan rendering of Davies' unawareness that Conrad might have a touch of egotism as well: "We asked him if he knew Conrad's work *thoroughly*. Oh no—was it good? We told him yes. He was glad we liked it." That last, mock-childish sentence, which gets the proper order of things all confused, is especially to be cherished. Extremely aggressive humor then, but at the same time delivered deadpan with an oddly muted, restrained distance about it, so as not to dignify Davies too much by assaulting him too directly, with too obvious a scornful tone of contempt. We remember Frost remarking in his notebooks about the cliché "dry humor" that it was "the kind of humor that doesn't seem to appreciate itself. I wish all literature were as dry in the same sense of the word," he wrote. One of the main ways of ensuring that this humorous play with W.H. Davies will be sufficiently "dry," is to suppress all "wet" feelings of obvious indignation and jealousy—to avoid such easily nameable special postures by making the tone more of a monotone, harder to get at, "cooler" than a heated rejoinder would have been. Frost never grew any more subtle at that game than in this letter home about a rival poet.

2.

Rarely in his letters did Frost address the subject of letter-writing; he complained to his former student Bartlett in 1916 that he had too many people to write to and would rather see them in the flesh, then added "Of course there's a whole lot about the art of writing that none of us there ever masters. We all remain duffers and properly dissatisfied with ourselves.... It is touch and go with any of us. Now we get it for a little run of sentences and now we don't." Getting "it" for that little run, being on what we call a roll, is what the poet aspires to, and letter-writing becomes something really satisfying, an "art," when it is analogously poetic—when the writer is "Make[ing] his own words as he goes" rather than depending on words already made "even if they be his own" (to Cox, 1914). One of the things that distinguishes Frost from his contemporaries, Eliot and Stevens and Pound, is that however dissatisfied he may be with his current academic affiliation at Amherst or Michigan or wherever, he invariably reaches out to the classroom as a place where, even though most of the time he and his students are "duffers" and properly dissatisfied with themselves, there can occur at moments something quite different, a little run of making words count. It is exciting to listen (and that is the right verb for it) to Frost, when, pursuing some point or argument in fairly ordinary ways, he suddenly rises to a different, indeed a higher plane, as he does in this letter to his Amherst colleague George Whicher. The apropos is Bread Loaf, and Frost is proposing some teaching of creative writing that (Thompson tells us) "paved the way for the Bread Loaf Writers' Conference in 1926." In the letter Frost makes various assertions about how the teacher should converse with his class, should turn from correcting grammar in red ink to "matching experience in black ink, experience of life and experience of art." Then this:

> The writing he has nothing to say to fails with him. The trouble with it is that it hasn't enough to it—of Heaven Earth Hell and the young author. The strength of the teacher's position lies in his waiting till he is come after. His society and audience are a privilege—and that is no pose. On the rare occasion when he goes after his pupils it will be to show them up not for what they aren't but for what they are. He will invade them to show them how much more they contain than they can write down; to show them their subject matter is where they came from and what in the last twenty years they have been doing.

I am moved by these sentences, partly because to my mind they are the assumption that underlay the Amherst course in freshman composition (taken and taught by me) designed by Theodore Baird, on whom Frost's influence was profound. One needn't assent to Frost's rule that students should be "gone after" only on the rare occasion; Baird went after them all the time. The crucial sentence is the one that says such invasion is for the purpose of showing students "how much more they contain than they can write down." But—and this Frost doesn't make explicit—writing that has something "to it" will attempt to express that "more," will be so bold as to contain "Heaven Earth Hell" as imagined by "the young author." I don't know any other modern poet who talks like this, or who would publish, in *The Atlantic Monthly* in 1951, a series of apothegms titled "Poetry and School," in which he treats the subject of how to deal with poetry in the classroom, indeed why it is *in* classrooms more than outside them. (I invariably begin my course in freshmen English—"Reading, Writing, Criticism"—with these declarations, such as "We go to college to be given one more chance to learn to read in case we haven't learned in High School. Once we have learned to read the rest can be trusted to add itself unto us." (Hanging around until you catch on was another way he put it.)

If I appear to be straying from my subject of Frost in his letters, I think the impression is only apparent. My aim is to suggest how Frost is a most interesting teacher in his letters and that his epistolary relation to his correspondents and to us can be usefully thought of as that of teacher to student or pupil or learner or ephebe, and that the nature of the instruction is extremely indirect, complex, poetic, as it seeks to show how much more there is to us than we realized. It may be of help to distinguish Frost's procedure from the tell-it-like-it-is one of Ezra Pound's. I am thinking of Pound's short manifesto, "The Teacher's Mission," not, to be sure, a letter, but no different from the kind of instruction furnished in the vigorous letters Pound wrote. He announces in his opening paragraph that "a nation's writers are the voltometers and steam-gauges of [a] nation's intellectual life," "recording instruments" that if they falsify reports can do great harm: "If you saw a man selling defective thermometers to a hospital, you would consider him a particularly vile kind of cheat," says Pound, then goes on to announce that this kind of cheating and falsifying has been going on for the last fifty years in America. He is there to blow the whistle, for he knows that "the mental life of a nation is no man's private property. The function of the teaching profession is to maintain the HEALTH OF THE NATIONAL MIND." He insists that it is only by comparing particular passages from artists that true knowledge may be gained, prejudices and shibboleths discarded, and a healthy society ensue—especially if (it is 1934) a vicious economic system is revamped.

In this and other essays and in much of the poetry of the *Cantos*, Pound's is a mind without ambiguity, a mind that believes there are no two ways about anything—except the right and the wrong one—and that he is there to extirpate the latter since he knows what the former is. The village explainer, said Gertrude Stein, good if you are a village, if not, not. Of course there was a lot of "village" in American literary culture, and Pound's explanations of and to it were often tonic, to say the least. But utterly unlike Frost's approach to things, as demonstrated quite wonderfully in the following passage from a letter to Sidney Cox, a disciple of Frost's who sometimes tried to get a little closer to the master than Frost preferred:

> ...I'd like to put it to you while you are still young and developing your procedure if you don't think a lot of things could be found to do in class besides debate and disagree. Clash is all very well for coming lawyers politicians and theologians. But I should think there must be a whole realm or plane above that—all sight and insight, perception, intuition, rapture....Having ideas that are neither pro nor con is the happy thing. Get up there high enough and the differences that make controversy become only the two legs of a body the weight of which is on one in one period on the other in the next. Democracy monarchy; puritanism paganism; form content; conservatism radicalism; systole diastole; rustic urbane; literary colloquial; work play. I should think too much of myself to let any teacher fool me into taking sides on any one of those oppositions.

I don't know what, if anything, Cox had said to provoke this train of thought; it surely has something to do with Frost's lingering battle with what he called "Mieklejaundice." Alexander Mieklejohn, the recent president of Amherst College, believed—as Frost saw it—in the replacing of "learning" by "thinking" and that—Frost had written Untermeyer two years previously—"by thinking [the students] meant stocking up with radical ideas, by learning they meant stocking up with conservative ideas." In that letter Frost said about one of his Amherst classes, "We reached an agreement that most of what they had regarded as thinking...was nothing but voting—taking sides on an issue they had nothing to do with laying down."

The letter to Cox develops a notion of what might go on in the liberal arts classroom besides dialectic, and here it seems to me Frost's recommendation is wholly relevant to what still happens, or doesn't happen, in our college classrooms at the end of the century. The title of one of his prose essays is "Education by Poetry," but this letter to Cox proposes something like Education *as* Poetry. It is very different not only from the instructive debate and disagreement that Meiklejohn promoted, or that a latter-day liberal philosopher like Martha Nussbaum espouses (she is for the classroom whose members confront one another with their different ideas and rationally work things out by active "thinking"). But different also from the Poundian method of instruction, in which a specimen from, say, Tennyson is placed next to one of, say, Donne, by way of illustrating something about one poet's superior use of image or diction.

Frost's aspiration is rather toward what I once called "Elevated Play," and this play takes place both in a good poem (as he conceived it) and in the classroom when "a little run of sentences" shared between teacher and students comes into being. One of Frost's favorite words for it is "performance," and the successful poem was "some sort of achievement in performance" that went along with, was the product of, a "feat of association." As he put it in the *Paris Review* interview, "All thought is a feat of association: having what's in front of you bring up something in your mind that you almost didn't know you knew. Putting this and that together. That click." In just how many classes was the click likely to occur? There is no unimpeachable testimony about Frost's classroom, but one suspects it was a rather disorderly place, a kind of Liberty Hall where on many days the students, and probably their teacher, would be hard-pressed to say just what happened and whether it profited those in attendance. But of course such "failure" in education, in teaching, is routine only for those who, like Frost, pitch their aspiration very high indeed—choose something like a star.

3.

In the space remaining I want to consider three moments in Frost's correspondence where the writer, the teacher, the wily veteran of holding other people—enemies but friends as well—in play and out of gunshot, has been himself seriously wounded, stricken by the death of his nearest and dearest. Between 1934 and 1940 he lost three members of his family, his wife Elinor and their children, son Carol and daughter Marjorie. The first to go was Marjorie, who after giving birth to a daughter caught an infection in the hospital and struggled for seven weeks until she died. Frost wrote Untermeyer shortly after the event, and I excerpt the letter:

> No death in war could more than match it for suffering and heroic endurance. Why all this talk in favor of peace? Peace has her victories over poor mortals no less merciless than war. Marge

> always said she would rather die in a gutter than in a hospital. But it was in a hospital she was caught to die after more than a hundred serum injections and blood transfusions....Never out of delirium for the last four weeks...The only way I could reach her was by putting my hand backward and forward between us as in counting out and saying with over-emphasis *You*—and—Me. The last time I did that, the day before she died, she smiled faintly and answered "All the same," frowned slightly and made it "Always the same."... Everything she said, however quaint and awry, was of an almost straining loftiness. It was as if her ruling passion must have been to be wise and good, or it could not have been so strong in death.... We thought to move heaven and earth—heaven with prayers and earth with money. We moved Nothing. And here we are Cadmus and Harmonia not yet placed safely in changed forms.

There are many things at work in this moving letter, the noblest I know written after such an event, but three of them are of particular note. Humorous play, undesirable in such a situation, gets only the briefest nod, in that bitter joke about war and peace. (The allusion is to Milton's "To the Lord General Cromwell"—"Peace hath her victories / No less renowned than war.") The letter strives to bring out Marjorie's heroism by noting the quality and tone of her speech, even in delirium: the correction of "all" to "always" (in "always the same") and the insistence on the elevated nature of her discourse, which "was of an almost straining loftiness." "Get up there high enough," Frost said about the classroom, and you will put that class into another realm, above controversy and disagreement. Marjorie Frost was straining toward that realm, and her father tries to help her with his posthumous words. Finally the man, the teacher, who has been able to move nothing, is left with only poetry as consolation, such as Callicles' beautiful lyric from Arnold's *Empedcles on Etna*:

> Far, far from here,
> The Adriatic breaks in a warm bay
> Above the green Illyrian hills; and there
> The sunshine in the happy glens is fair,
> And by the sea, and in the brakes.

There in those words live "two bright and aged snakes," Cadmus and Harmonia, "In breathless quiet, after all their ills." They had seen, "In Thebes, the billow of calamity / Over their own dear children roll'd, / Curse upon curse, pang upon pang." But unlike in the poem, Frost and Elinor are still in Thebes, "not yet placed safely in changed forms." The effort in this remarkable letter is finally toward a kind of sad self-instruction, one that ends with a feat of association—education by poetry, education *as* poetry—both futile and yet all there is to reach out to: only that.

Four years later, in March of 1938, Elinor Frost died of a heart attack and two weeks later her husband wrote the following words to his at that time good friend, Bernard DeVoto:

> I suppose love must always deceive. I'm afraid I deceived her a little in pretending for the sake of argument that I didn't think the world as bad a place as she did. My excuse was that I wanted to keep her a little happy for my own selfish pleasure. It is as if for the sake of argument she had sacrificed herself to give me this terrible answer and really bring me down in sorrow. She needn't have. I knew I never had a leg to stand on, and I should think I had said so in print.
>
> All the same I believe a lot of mitigating things, and anything I say against the universe must be taken with that qualification. I always shrank from hearing evil of poor little Edgar Allen Poe and my reason was when I come to search it out of my heart, that he wrote a prose poem out of those lovely old lines
>
> Stay for me there I will not fail
> To meet thee in the hollow vale.
>
> What is more he used a cadence caught from the Exequy to make the whole of his poem The Sleeper. Never mind that he couldn't be tender without being ghoulish. You have to remember he was little Edgar Allen Poe.

To be fair in representing this four-paragraph letter, it has an opening paragraph about Frost's loneliness and a closing one about arrangements for the funeral in Amherst. But the really interesting part is the two middle paragraphs I quoted, notable for the quite indirect way Frost conducts himself, first with the conceit that Elinor's death was a terrible answer to his own pretense that the world wasn't so bad a place as Elinor (an atheist) thought it was. "She needn't have" given him this terrible answer—needn't have died, as it were—since he knew the truth already. Then the business about Poe. Why, we might ask, as a more ordinary human being/letter writer might have done, didn't Frost just quote those two lines from King's "The Exequy" as illustrative of his private promise to Elinor—"Stay for me there; I will not fail / To meet thee in that hollow vale"? My, admittedly speculative, guess is this: that just as Poe "couldn't be tender without being ghoulish" (—some lines from Poe's "The Sleeper" read as follows

> My love, she sleeps! Oh may her sleep,
> As it is lasting, so be deep!
> Soft may the worms about her creep!

One of the worst triplets I know of)—so Frost couldn't be tender without being just the least bit wicked, or at least humorously debunking of the competition, of some other poet's attempt to deliver moving utterance in the face of death. It won't do for Frost simply to elevate himself and Elinor through the nobility of Henry King's lines; he needs as well to cast an ironic eye on something lower down the scale, on the bathetic attempt of "little Edgar Allen Poe" to rise to authentic feeling. At the beginning of the Poe paragraph, Frost reminds DeVoto that he, Frost, "believes a lot of mitigating things, and that anything [he] says against the universe must be taken with that qualification." If in these terms you believe a lot of mitigating things, then you are obliged to complicate and play around with any special posture of sorrow that might too nakedly and sincerely reveal your suffering soul. The effort at self-instruction is never more strongly made than in a seemingly final moment like this one in which, as we like to say, words can't express how... etc. But if poetry is the renewal of words, forever and forever, then expression is not to be given up on. "Humor is the most engaging cowardice," he had written, and even in these extreme moments of self-analysis something like humor shows its head. Or at least, some positive gesture of control, of mastery, in which the grief-stricken survivor may repose, momentarily, in a stay against confusion.

My final example is from a letter, again to Untermeyer, about Carol Frost's death by suicide (he shot himself). In the letter Frost writes "I took the wrong way with him. I tried many ways and every single one of them was wrong." He had tried to get his son to ease up on himself "and take life and farming off-hand." Frost then turns critically on his teacherly penchant: "Yesterday I was telling seven hundred Harvard freshmen how to live with books in college. Apparently nothing can stop us when we get going." But, he says, from now on he is "disqualified" from giving counsel. Then, following a description of Carol's son's heroic behavior in calling the police and standing by, Frost ends as follows:

> I failed to trick Carol or argue him into believing he was the least successful. That's what it came down to. He failed in farming and he failed in poetry (you may not have known). He was splendid with animals and little children. If only the emphasis could have been put on those. He should have lived with horses.

An absolutely astonishing thing, it has always seemed to me, to write about your dead son; but especially striking, or Frostian, in the way it recovers itself at the end, after castigating himself for failing in every way with that son and for pretending that he, Frost, can tell anyone how to live. Then to end the letter with that short, final pronouncement—"He should have lived with horses," "Never if you can help it write down a sentence in which the voice will not know how to posture *specially*," he said twenty-six years previously. I should hate to be challenged to describe the special posture of that last sentence about Carol, to weigh the exact tone in which it is to be said. Once again, Frost's practice was richer, more confusing, than his theory; and when, as with these three letters about the death of loved ones, the human being is most challenged to "say something" ("Say something we can take to heart and when alone repeat"), then the challenge to rise to something like poetry made itself poignantly felt. Poetry was a deed, he liked to say, and that old-fashioned word crops up tellingly in some final lines from a poem, and my conclusion today:

> Only where love and need are one,
> And the work is play for mortal stakes,
> Is the deed ever really done
> For heaven and the future's sakes.

—*New England Review*, Spring 2000.

The Letters of Robert Frost, Vol. 2

HERE IS VOLUME 2 of Robert Frost's letters, an enormous editorial project originally planned for four volumes, now for five. It covers the years 1920-1928, beginning with the end of his first stint of teaching at Amherst College (he began there in 1917) and ending as he was about to publish his fifth book of poems, *West-Running Brook.* The scope of this edition may be gauged by noting that previously Frost's letters from this period, as selected in different volumes by Lawrance Thompson and Louis Untermeyer, amounted to roughly 200 pages. In the new book there are 700 pages of letters, fully annotated, plus a glossary of correspondents and a chronology. Three of the four editors have written extensively about Frost: Donald Sheehy has published three long, penetrating essays about Frost's life; Mark Richardson has edited his poems for the Library of America as well as his complete prose with exhaustive notes; and Robert Hass has published a study of Frost and science. Exemplary is a wholly inadequate word to characterize their joint editorial enterprise. If you're curious about the scores of a baseball double header between the Red Sox and Cleveland (attended by Frost and his son-in-law in 1928), they are here in a footnote.

Frost once spoke of college as a game you played; these letters from the 1920s sketch out his continuing game with the academy: to the University of Michigan for a year as Fellow in Creative Arts; then back to Amherst for occasional appearances at the college; to Michigan again for a stretch, and eventually, in 1926, back at Amherst for ten weeks of teaching a year, settling into a relationship with the college that would last until 1938, when his wife Elinor died. The letters from the twenties are singularly lacking in interesting political or social comment on the American scene, except in its literary aspect. He brought contemporary poets to read at Michigan, often to overflow crowds; meanwhile the visits and readings he gave at colleges and universities were ever increasing, as was his own fame—a Pulitzer Prize in 1924 for the volume *New Hampshire*, and the steady accumulation of lyrics and narrative that he would bring together in his first Collected Poems in 1930.

A painful and recurrent concern in these letters, one that the editors treat strongly in their introduction, is the increasing ill-health of Frost's family. His wife having borne six children (two of whom died in infancy) suffered what Frost calls "a serious nervous collapse" in 1925, coinciding with the last of her miscarriages. There was the prolonged illness of his youngest daughter, Marjorie, who would die after childbirth in 1934. There was mental instability first in his sister Jeanie, institutionalized in 1920, later his daughter Irma, who would eventually suffer the same fate. And there was the growing distance between Frost and his son Carol, who took his own life in 1942. (Frost's own health miseries are minor: plenty of influenza and hay fever.) One of the revelations these letters afford is what a remarkable woman his oldest child Lesley was; along with the poet and anthologist Louis Untermeyer, she is the recipient of the richest of these letters.

In what prevailing manner are they rich? What kind of a letter writer was Frost and how does his correspondence stack up against acknowledged great literary letter writers—Keats surely, Byron or D.H Lawrence or Virginia Woolf perhaps? One of the innumerable striking entries in his Notebooks, published ten years ago, is a four-line poem:

> Nothing ever so sincere
> That unless it's out of sheer
> Mischief and a little queer
> It won't prove a bore to hear.

Poetry had an obligation to be unboring and, above all, to be something *heard*, to be mainly ear—rather than eye—read. It had to be something about which the listener couldn't say, oh yes, I've heard that one before. Finally, its "mischief" should be "sheer," created somehow for its own sake, for the sheer pleasure of committing it. This standard of performance is evident throughout the letters, not of course in every sentence, but frequently enough so that it come to seem a trademark of the Frostian style. When the youthful Frost had his first poem accepted by the editor, Susan Hayes Ward, he thanked her, then warned her: "Take my word for it, that poem exaggerates my ability. You must spare your feelings when you come to read these others, for I haven't the courage to be a disappointment to anyone." Anything but a straightforward way to say thanks. In one of his most interesting letters, to Untermeyer in 1924, he has "come to the conclusion that style in prose or verse is that which indicates how the writer takes himself and what he is saying." A writer's style is "the way he carries himself toward his ideas and deeds"; it is out of "superfluity...the mind skating circles round itself as it moves forward." After brief, pungent characterizations of the styles respectively of Emerson, Thoreau, Whitman, Stevenson, Longfellow, and Carlyle whose "way of taking himself simply infuriates me," he generalizes further: "I own any form of humor shows fear and inferiority.... Irony is simply a kind of guardedness. So is a twinkle... We only joke about [the world] to avoid an issue with some one; to let someone know that we know he's there with his questions: to disarm him by seeming to have heard and done justice to his side of the standing argument. Humor is the most engaging cowardice. With it myself I have been able to hold some of my enemies in play far out of gunshot." There is little room for anything "ever so sincere."

Taking these letters as a whole, it is not only "enemies" but presumed friends they aspire to hold in play. A prominent one, especially in the immediate years following Frost's first departure from Amherst College, was the man who brought him there in the first place, President Alexander Meiklejohn. It was in part out of very high-minded motives that Meiklejohn, in 1917, conceived the idea of having a poet on his faculty by way of uplifting education so as to make it more "philosophical." It was Meiklejohn's high-mindedness, perhaps above all else, that annoyed Frost, whose penchant was for more mixed motives in life. He put it to Untermeyer that "The boys had been made uncommonly interesting to themselves by Meiklejohn"—the very unobviousness of that way of putting it established Frost's playful critique of what he called "Mieklejaundice." The boys "fancied themselves as thinkers. At Amherst you thought while at other institutions you merely learned.... I found that by thinking they meant stocking up with radical ideas, by learning they meant stocking up with conservative ideas—a harmless distinction, bless their simple hearts." He mocks the radical educational idea that "the time was past for the teachers to teach the pupils. From now on it was the thing for the pupil to teach himself, using, as he saw fit, the teacher as an instrument." Frost taught two courses, one in "reading," one in "philosophy," but they came to the same thing:

> I was determined to have it out with my youngers and betters as to what thinking really was. We reached an agreement that most of what they had regarded as thinking, their own and other people's, was nothing but voting—taking sides on an issue they had nothing to do with laying down.

Perhaps his most eloquent description of what thinking in the classroom should be was made in a letter to Sidney Cox, a devoted former student of his at Pinkerton Academy. In the letter Frost sets himself against "clash" in the classroom; debating and disagreeing was well enough for "coming lawyers, politicians and theologians":

> But I should think there must be a whole realm or plane above that—all sight and insight, perception, intuition, rapture...Having ideas that are neither pro nor con is the happy thing. Get up there high enough and the differences that make controversy become only the two legs of a body the weight of which is on one in one period on the other in the next. Democracy monarchy; puritanism paganism; form content; conservatism radicalism; systole diastole; rustic urbane; literary colloquial; work play. I should think too much of myself to let any teacher fool me into taking sides on any one of those oppositions.

We have here, I think, the essence of Frost's "philosophy" of education, one in which the oppositional element is deeply engrained. In my *Lives of the Modern Poets* I titled the chapter on Frost "Elevated Play," a phrase than which I've found no better for suggesting his aim as a teacher, as someone with a distinctive style of "thinking."

It was of course not just Meiklejohn's philosophy of education that Frost set himself against, since there is a more general opposition to the whole idea and practice of higher education: "You know how I'm always at it against colleges in a vain attempt to reconcile myself with them." He is speaking apropos of dissatisfaction on the part of his daughter Lesley, whose stints at Wellesley, Barnard, and the University of Michigan were—like Frost's own at Dartmouth and Harvard—destined not to complete themselves. He notes wryly that his "line of talk isn't calculated to make her like any institution." He wrote Untermeyer of his continual fight with the "text book," which he would like to see "stripped to the bare text, freed entirely of 'busy work' improvement-play and teachers machinery." As with other social and literary conventions he wants to make the school as "un-schoollike" as possible. In later years he was not above suggesting to dissatisfied students that it wasn't their fault but the institution's and they would do well to clear out of colleges for someplace less school-like. "Hanging around until you catch on," was his favorite slogan for what students should aspire to in college, and often, as in his own case and his daughter's, the hanging around shouldn't last too long.

His "conspiracy to de-formalize education" had a positive aim, although, as with other "positive" proposals by Frost, it was loosely formulated. He speaks more than once of trying to "get a little more American literature directly out of the colleges," which couldn't be done by "exercises to be blue-penciled for details by teachers." The aim was rather in the direction of what he calls "absolute literature," and his only recommendation for its furtherance was a vague one and on the negative side: it should eschew "mechanical proficiency and compulsory exercises." Instead—and here Frost becomes vague, and we must rely on the testimony of one of his colleagues at Amherst, George Whicher, who in an article described Frost's teaching method in the advanced composition course both he and Frost taught. Whicher says about Frost: "His first care in the writing course was to preserve freedom of action for his students, respecting perhaps too highly in some cases the impetus that carried them into it. He invited, provoked, teased, and shamed them into writing, but was chary of employing compulsion." One guesses that the percentage of success to failure with the students was a low one, but that didn't bother Frost. When, before he went to England for the first time, he used to assign Milton's *Comus* to his classes, one suspects that they weren't instructed about Milton's intentions and meanings in such a remote (even frivolous, Frost might say) piece of writing but rather introduced to the writing itself, whatever that might mean. It could only "mean" when one or another student saw or heard or felt something and tried to put words to it. On at least one occasion he went even further in stripping classroom education of its materials, as when he wrote Mark DeWolfe Howe that "It would be just like me sometime to try what withholding the whole subjects of writing and reading for a while would do for literature in college... I don't mean I should desert the poor children entirely with poetry—for good and all. I just shouldn't be so forward with it as some of us are now." The lines from his little ditty come again to mind: "Nothing... unless it's out of sheer mischief and a little queer" would make teaching, education, somehow unboring.

"Having ideas that are neither pro nor con is the happy thing," he wrote in praise of the elevated play he aspired to. When he failed to "get up there high enough" the results are less happy, as when he takes offense at how Mark Van Doren, an admirer of Frost's poems, may be under-representing him in an anthology or representing him by not quite the right poems: "Dear Van Doren: I confess a choice so perfunctory and slighting hurts my feelings...If such is the best you naturally do with or for me, what do you say if I stay out of this anthology and turn my thoughts elsewhere?" Not much play in this petulance. (He later stepped down from his high horse and apologized to Van Doren.) Occasionally he takes too heavy a hand with something that offends his moral sensibility. When Untermeyer divorces, marries another woman, then remarries the first Frost calls him out: "How much better if you had been a staid orthodox Jew and never had run wild after a super wisdom that doesn't exist. You are back now where you started from and not one bit improved in mind or spirit. The whole experiment has been a waste of time and energy." How did Frost come to know with such apparent certainty the state of Louis Untermeyer's soul? In a similar mode he writes to Lesley, cautioning her to avoid their sometime friend Raymond Holden: "He's been talking all the bold bad stuff of the books he derives his poetry from. He is no sort of person for youthful folly to trifle with." In another letter he notes the absence of any erotic element in Christ's language: "Is he even a little Pagan? Isn't he pretty nearly all Puritan for better or worse?" The answer is, definitely for better, and it suits Frost's highly un-Pagan picture of himself. No wonder he fully disliked Paris and the French when he and Elinor took Marjorie on an ill-fated visit to Europe, hoping to improve her health. In Paris he finds not beauty but "deceitful hate all around us." Although he did like French bread, "the wine doesn't mean much to us." To borrow an epithet from one of his poem, Frost was "Puritan Yankee through and through." But perhaps such examples of an all-too-human Frost come as a relief from the ideal thinker who wants to remain above the fray.

There is little interesting commentary in these letters about his contemporaries, or indeed predecessors, although the number of quiet allusions to mainly nineteenth-century English poems is remarkable. He was surely not generous in his judgments of the modern American poets with whom he was being grouped in anthologies and critical essays. Carl Sandburg was "an artificial and studied ruffian," whom Frost addressed in a letter as "You old ballad-monger." He tiptoed around E. A. Robinson pretty carefully—there was some competition there. When Amy Lowell died he wrote Untermeyer that nobody minded her "outrageousness": "In life she didn't know where the feelings were to hurt them any more than in poetry she knew where they were to touch them." Sarah Teasdale and Conrad Aiken ("Comrad Aching") receive some approval. The one American writer who gets unqualified praise is Willa Cather, whom he called "A No 1" and about whose fine story "Coming, Aphrodite" he declared, "We have had no such short story...Every stroke of it to the very last. I wept for the sheer perfection." (Of course Cather had previously expressed admiration for *North of Boston.*) As for the poems he published during these years, a fairly severe culling still produces a list of the best ones like the following: from *New Hampshire*—"A Star in a Stone-Boat," "The Witch of Coos," "Stopping By Woods on a Snowy Evening" (which he himself calls "flawless"), "For Once, Then, Something," "The Onset," "To Earthward," "Two Look at Two," and "The Need of Being Versed in Country Things"; from *West-Running Brook*—the title poem, along with "Spring Pools," "Once by the Pacific," "Acceptance," "Tree at My Window," and "Acquainted With the Night." Add to that such tiny gems as "Fire and Ice," "Nothing Gold Can Stay," and "Fireflies in the Garden."

When Frost published *New Hampshire* in 1923, the year after Eliot's *The Waste Land,* he divided the volume into two sections, "Notes" and "Grace Notes," and peppered individual poems with footnotes referring them to other poems in the book. Eliot was on his mind. In January of that year he wrote to John Erskine: "Such news reaches me from the great world as that common sense is now considered plebean [sic] and any sense at all only less so: the aristocrat will spurn both this season; an American poet living in England has made an anthology of the Best Lines in Poetry. He has run the lines loosely together in a sort of narrative and copyrighted them so that anyone using them again will have to enclose them in double quotation marks." Frost was perhaps unaware that the American poet living in England had recently written a London Letter for the *Dial* that concluded a brief survey of American poets with "Mr Frost seems the nearest equivalent to an English poet, specializing in torpor; his verse, it is regretfully said, is uninteresting, and what is uninteresting is unreadable, and what is unreadable is not read. There that is done." Indeed, and done in a mischievous mock-solemn way, different from Frost's way, but equally devious.

Now almost a century later, as this significant batch of Frost letters appears, there is a concurrent one of Eliot's (Vol. 6) edited by John Haffenden with a fullness equal to the Frost volume. Never such epistolary treasures again.

—*Hopkins Review*, Fall 2016.

Poetry and Pressure: *The Letters of Robert Frost, Vol. 3*

The Letters of Robert Frost
Volume 3. 1929-1936. Edited by Mark Richardson,
Donald Sheehy, Robert Bernard Hass, and Henry Atmore.
Belknap Press of Harvard U.P.

"ONCE IN AWHILE I meet someone who has read me. It did him good. I mean it served him right." A way of identifying these terse sentences would be to name some poets of the modern era who could not have written them: W. B. Yeats and T. S. Eliot will do for starters, helping to set off the distinctive voice of Robert Frost. Had the quotation ended with "It did him good," one might assume a feisty, self-justifying voice behind it; but when that voice adds "I mean it served him right," we're less certain just what to call it. Playful would be a place to start and a fair way to characterize most of the letters Frost wrote in his life, now displayed in the third of this five-volume correspondence, masterfully edited within an inch of its life by Mark Richardson and three fellow scholars. The seven years represented, 1929-1936, weigh in at 800 pages and would surely, if Frost had seen them, have made him wonder whether it had indeed served him right.

The editors describe previous volumes of these letters as being "about the making of Frost as a man of letters" and the new one as about Frost as "a made man." Compared to the earlier volumes, we hear much less of the poet expostulating about the centrality of sentence sounds ("the sound of sense") and the importance of registering the "special posture" each line must exhibit. He is once again a member of the Amherst College faculty but required to be on campus for only three months of the year; thus the lectures and readings at various colleges and universities—what Frost liked to call his "barding around"—were unabated. What's most continuous with earlier letters is a predilection for the playful: "Great thought, delicate thought, sinister thought, but in any case, playful thought. It must be a play of thought to be a poem." At times the play is pure, untouched by anything delicate or sinister, as when he assures the author of a guidebook to Vermont that he has read about every town once and some twice and advises him, "Next time put in more elevations. Nothing is so uplifting as the heights of small towns. The town of Peacham did me good."

If there is a downside, and I think there is, to this penchant for the playful, it has to do with Frost's occasional self-congratulation at something he has done or said. "Aint I wiley?" he asks Louis Untermeyer, the most appreciative audience for his performances of wiliness, and we may answer, Yes indeed, perhaps overmuch so. But the wiliness is grounded in something deep and defensive, a resolve never to give away too much of himself on any occasion. On one hand he didn't want a "success d'estime" ("it butters no parsnips"), therefore would reach out to all sorts of readers, not just the literary elite. On the other hand he didn't want to make himself too available: "I have written to keep the over curious out of the secret places of my mind both in my verse and in my letters to such as you." (The "you" here was Sidney Cox, a younger scholar eager to celebrate his teacher.)

Frost's insistence, memorably stated in a letter of 1929, was that "something has to be kept back for pressure and to anybody puzzled to know what I should suggest that for a beginning it might as well be his friends, wife, children, and self." No free verser, he believed that poetry was "measured feet" but "more important still it is a measured amount of all we could say an we would." All the more striking then are moments in the correspondence when his experience was such that it could not be held back for pressure, but issued rather in words and sentences testing the limits of his measuring. Not surprisingly they were often occasions involving family members and the presence of death: the passing of his dog, Winnie; the grave loss of his and Elinor's youngest child, Marjorie. He wrote his son Carol about the disastrous mistake he had made in trying to treat the dog, who had gotten a face of porcupine quills, with chloroform. He gave her an overdose, causing Winnie's death: "That spoils this place for me forever; I shall never come here again." He wishes Carol had been there to help him judge the correct dosage. No teasing, no wiliness, no playful thought in this stark account of a mistake.

More grim was the death of Marjorie Frost from puerperal fever, the first of three family deaths (his wife Elinor's and son's to come) Frost experienced within the years 1934–1940. He began a poignant account of it to Untermeyer with "The noblest of us all is dead and has taken our hearts out of the world with her." After years of ill health (tuberculosis), Marjorie married and had a child, only to be fatally stricken: "No death in war could more than match it for suffering and heroic endurance. Why all this talk in favor of peace? Peace has her victory over poor mortals no less merciless than war." Delirious in her final four weeks, she was barely able to speak, but her father summoned up movingly expressive language to salute her when she did: "Everything she said however quaint and awry was of an almost straining loftiness." This is a poet's language, quaint and awry.

Moved to sudden anger, Frost curses the doctors for, so he thought, neglecting scientific precautions, then in an elevated three sentences completes the letter: "We thought to move heaven and death—heaven with prayers and earth with money. We moved nothing. And here we are Cadmus and Harmonia not yet placed safely in changed forms." The allusion is to Matthew Arnold's lines about an aged couple who, after their earthly woes, were transformed into "two bright and aged snakes," a transformation not yet granted to Frost and Elinor. Here it seems nothing has been kept back for pressure, even as the superb sad rightness of Arnold's elegy is called into play.

The full weight of Frost's family deaths would not be felt in his poems until *A Witness Tree* in 1942, but his sixth book, *A Further Range*, published during the last year of these letters, is full of strong poems of surprising variety. A short list gives us familiar ones like "Desert Places," "Neither Out Far Nor In Deep," "Design," "Provide, Provide," "The Strong are Saying Nothing Until They See"; less familiar ones like "The Bearer of Evil Tidings" and the miraculous "Iris By Night"; as well as a number of fine specimens of light verse: "A Record Stride," "A Drumlin Woodchuck," and "Departmental." He had earlier expressed a wish about his own writing, "I should like to be so subtle at this game as to seem to the casual person altogether obvious." Now when, as he put it, "Reputation is a cumulative congestion," his poetic devotion to the unobvious was never stronger.

—Originally published in *The Wall Street Journal*, April 9, 2021 as "'The Letters of Robert Frost' Review: Poetry and Pressure."

A Witness Tree and Frost's Biography

IN A 1975 ESSAY, where I proposed Frost's "The Wind and the Rain" as his best "unknown" poem, I also claimed that the opening ten poems in *A Witness Tree*, 1942 ("The Wind and the Rain" is one of them) constitute the most impressive sequence of poems to be found anywhere in the poet's work. The sequence, I wrote, contained "extremes of delicate tenderness and of shocking brutality," and its pervasive melancholy reached a depth not hitherto encountered, or to be encountered again, in Frost. Two accounts of the biographical circumstances out of which *A Witness Tree* emerged have caused me and perhaps others to think again about that book, especially its opening sequence, and about the degree to which a poet's art can be more fully understood and appreciated when we learn more about the life experiences that surround and motivate it. My comments here are directed toward clarifying, or at least exploring further, these matters of literary and biographical criticism.

I.

I should begin by acknowledging with gratitude the first of these two accounts, Donald Sheehy's 1990 essay, "Refiguring Love: Robert Frost in Crisis, 1938-1942," by far the most subtle and penetrating treatment of Frost's life in the years following his wife Elinor's death in 1938, up through the publication of *A Witness Tree* in 1942. Those years include, most saliently, his relationship with Kathleen Morrison, officially his secretary, unofficially and surely his lover, and the most important "other" in his life in those four post-1938 years. During them, Frost composed some of the best poems in *A Witness Tree,* also his great essay "The Figure a Poem Makes" that prefaced his *Complete Poems* (1949). Mr. Sheehy's claim for the opening sequence in *A Witness Tree* is similar to mine, but sets it more richly within the biographical nexus:

> Taken in its entirety, the opening section of *A Witness Tree* is a major triumph of Frost's career, rivaled in its sustained power and human complexity only by *North of Boston.* To read it exclusively as a record of personal experience is, of course, to diminish its poetic accomplishment, but to approach it without recognizing it to be a poetic chapter of personal crisis and resolution is finally to devalue the emotional and psychological achievement that it represents. If a career is a progress both public and private, then for no poet more than for Frost were the two moments so inextricably linked.

This is admirably and tactfully said, and it invites us to investigate more fully the extent to which it's possible to read this sequence "as a record of personal experience."

The other recent effort to make a case for *A Witness Tree* in its biographical circumstances is to be found in Jeffery Meyers's 1996 biography of Frost, whose most revelatory chapter is one that treats Frost's relations with Kay Morrison. What Sheehy's essay did with tact and complication, Meyers approaches in his typically blunt, free-swinging way, providing us with a you-are-there glimpse of the poet and his new love. In a key paragraph he describes the consummation of their relationship, and the single footnote to this paragraph refers us to Robert Newdick's unfinished biography of Frost—in which Frost spoke to Newdick about being "fearful" of the "arrangement with Kay"; also, more germanely, we are referred to Lawrance Thompson's unpublished "Notes on Frost." It is presumably the latter source, unless Meyers is inventing things, that enables him to write as follows: "Troubled and excited by their long walks in the woods, [Frost] took along condoms (which he had been reluctant to use with Elinor)." There follows, and in quotation marks, "Then Frost began making passionate love to her and found that she was willing.…All he had to do was to take off her drawers and consummate an urge that seemed mutual." Meyers makes things even more exciting by alluding to a figure from "The Figure a Poem Makes": "Frost rode on her own melting." He concludes the paragraphs with two sentences I am unable to fathom: "Frost wrote that no one could object to being legally wed when the marriage was consummated naked in bed. But it is an entirely different matter when you have sex out of doors with no clothes off but drawers."

At the conclusion of this chapter about Kay Morrison—whose love affairs with Bernard DeVoto, a hired man named Stafford Dragon, and with Thompson himself are detailed—Meyers writes three-and-a-half pages in which he reveals "the real meaning of *A Witness Tree.*" Of course such a phrase as "real meaning" should in itself be enough to alert readers that some activity other than sensitive criticism of lyric poetry is going on. As usual. Meyers is of no two minds in his judgments, telling us that the first ten poems of *A Witness Tree* under the rubric "One or Two," take up "the question of whether Frost will be alone or joined with Kay." (Meyers neglects to mention that Frost's previous collection, *A Further Range* [1936], organized its poems under the rubrics "Taken Doubly" and "Taken Singly.") "The ten poems express, directly or indirectly," Meyers goes on, "his love for Kay." Meyers thinks that the first of them, "The Silken Tent" "describes, with the greatest possible delicacy, the conflict between Kay's bondage and freedom as she is pulled, loosely by Ted in marriage or tightly by Frost in love." By way of indicating an aspect of the poem's great delicacy, Meyers instances Frost's use of the word "guys" ("So that in guys it gently sways at ease") as "a triple pun on ropes, mockery, and men." So much for delicacy. Among other poems mentioned by the biographer is "The Most of It," which "describes Frost's longing for and response to Kay." Presumably Frost identified with the great buck who "creates an orgasmic waterfall, so that his mate can make The Most of It." As for "Never Again Would Birds' Song Be the Same," its final line—"And to do that to birds was why she came"—"concludes on a bold sexual pun," suggesting that "as the lady's voice intensified the birds' song, so Kay's sexual passion inspired the words that made this poem."

"The poem must resist the intelligence / Almost successfully," wrote Wallace Stevens, and Frost himself either as man or poet had no wish to be too easily found out. In a letter of 1929 he addressed the question of how much personal material should go into one's poems:

> Everybody knows something has to be kept back for pressure and to anybody puzzled to know what I should suggest that for a beginning it might as well be his friends, wife, children, and self....Poetry is measured in more senses than one: it is

> measured feet but more important still it is a measured amount of all we could say an we would. We shall be judged finally by the delicacy of our feeling of where to stop short.

The trouble with Meyers's account of these *Witness Tree* poems is that it doesn't know where or when to stop short. The poems don't resist his intelligence "almost successfully"; indeed they don't resist it at all. Or so he presumes, insofar as their real and true meaning can be grasped and stated as easily and quickly as it takes to desubtilize them by plugging their lines and imagined situations into real-life equivalents named "Kay," or "orgasmic waterfall." The question remains, what exactly has one understood by so penetrating the poems' language in order to extract their real meanings? The answer is, I'm afraid, not very much. And even Meyers would probably agree that establishing the crucial biographical importance of the love between Frost and Kay Morrison does not mean perforce that we must put a high value on the poems supposedly resulting from it. We might also remind ourselves that *A Further Range,* dedicated to Elinor Frost, contained poems as major to the Frost canon as "Two Tramps in Mud Time," "Desert Places," "The Strong Are Saying Nothing," "Neither Out Far Nor In Deep," "Design," "Provide, Provide," and the lovely, underappreciated "Iris by Night." It is not as if Frost in the 1930s had entered or declined into some rut in which he did no more than rework old themes or perform his bardlike functions as public entertainer.

Yet the sequence in *A Witness Tree* is something special. After two epigraph-like and rather enigmatic short poems, "Beech" and "Sycamore," we have the following: "The Silken Tent," "All Revelation," "Happiness Makes Up in Height for What It Lacks in Length," "Come In," "I Could Give All to Time," "Carpe Diem," "The Wind and the Rain," "The Most of It," "Never Again Would Birds' Song Be the Same," and "The Subverted Flower." After this sequence the final four poems in "One or Two" are a falling-off, although "The Quest of the Purple-Fringed," written much earlier, is exquisite. Perhaps the use of that adjective about this poem in praise of the orchis (or rather, as George Monteiro has suggested, the gentian), may suggest the difference between it and the earlier ten poems:

> I felt the chill of the meadow underfoot,
> But the sun overhead;

And snatches of verse and song of scenes like this
I sung or said.

I skirted the margin alders for miles and miles
In a sweeping line.
The day was the day by every flower that blooms,
But I saw no sign.

Yet further I went to be before the scythe,
For the grass was high;
Till I saw the path where the slender fox had come
And gone panting by.

Then at last and following him I found—
In the very hour
When the color flushed to the petals it must have been—
The far-sought flower.

There stood the purple spires with no breath of air
Nor headlong bee
To disturb their perfect poise the livelong day
'Neath the alder tree.

I only knelt and putting the boughs aside
Looked, or at most
Counted them all to the buds in the copse's depth
That were pale as a ghost.

Then I arose and silently wandered home,
And I for one
Said that the fall might come and whirl of leaves,
For summer was done.

With reference to the man's discovery of the flower he has been seeking, Frank Lentricchia called it "the purest celebratory moment in Frost's poetry," and surely it is a lovely one, a lyric instance of song that ends itself as fully as Frost ever ended any poem. It doesn't invite a search for some key that might unlock it; it is not a "conflicted" poem, and if, as Frost claimed, everything written is as good as it is dramatic, I take "The Quest of the Purple-Fringed" to be a small exception to that rule. Or at least its dramatic component—in the sense of some argument or complication going on between voices in the poem—is small: it has an "I" whom we can trust, who is telling us a small story of discovery that has a beginning, middle, and end. It *settles,* admittedly in a slightly melancholy way, rather than unsettles; in this it is distinguished from the earlier sequence in *A Witness Tree.*

Those ten poems are neatly divided in half, five of them with an "I" speaking out of a dramatic situation whose level of realization varies, though in none of them is it as strongly located in place and time as is "The Quest of the Purple-Fringed," or as it was in earlier Frost poems like "The Tuft of Flowers," "The Wood-Pile," or "Two Look at Two." Perhaps the most conventionally "dramatic" of the first-person poems from "One or Two" is "Come In," with its familiar prop of man confronting dark woods ("Into My Own" began all that) and debating whether or not to enter them. What's most familiar about "Come In" is the play of tone by which the speaker declines the thrushes' blandishment, first by making much of their song, although in a way that hedges slightly—"Almost like a call to come in / To the dark and lament"—then more emphatically declining the invitation in two stages: "But no, I was out for stars: / I would not come in," followed by the admission that it wasn't an invitation at all—"I meant not even if asked, / And I hadn't been." Joseph Brodsky made much of the poem, in a line-by-line exposition, but ended up with translating, disappointingly, the title into a meaning—"I am afraid, the expression 'come in' means die"—rather than pointing out how Frost the trickster once more, in the language of "One Step Backward Taken," "saved myself from going." For all its cleverness, I find "Come In" perhaps the most predictable poem in the sequence.

Of course, thinking sequentially about the ten poems isn't an inevitable or even necessary way of proceeding: they can be read individually, without regard to juxtapositions; or they can be put with poems from earlier volumes by way of establishing thematic and other relationships. But if we care at all about Frost's literary career with its order of published volumes, and if we take seriously the order in which, within the individual volume, Frost arranged the poems, then there appears to be visible a grouping of these ten poems by way of how they approach subject and reader. The first two, "The Silken Tent" and "All Revelation," are impersonal pronouncements that propose universal or mythic, revelatory disclosures. They are followed by five more personal disclosures, especially as concerned with the lyric speaker's feelings about present and past, time, change, and death. Four of these five are told in the first person; "Carpe Diem," told in the third person, nevertheless belongs with the others in tone and theme. Then follow "The Most of It," "Never Again Would Birds' Song…," and "The Subverted Flower": large, parable-like declarations that refuse to declare themselves quickly or unambiguously.

As for how these poems have been valued, relative to one another, the nod goes clearly to the third-person ones, which tend to get anthologized. (Interestingly enough, Randall Jarrell, in "To the Laodiceans," where he made lists of Frost's best and second-best poems, included only "The Most of It" and "I Could Give All To Time.") Richard Poirier has made the strongest case for the closing three poems, claiming that they suggest, as did Frost's earliest ones in *A Boy's Will,* "That consciousness is determined in part by the way one 'reads' the response of nature to human sound." He also claims that by placing "Never Again…" between "The Most of It" and "The Subverted Flower," "Frost once again revealed his deep commitment to married love as a precondition for discovering human 'embodiments' in nature." Poirier is eloquent about both "The Most of It" and "Never Again…" and his phrase, in referring to "The Most of It," about that poem's "large but wavering mythological context" suggests to me that, especially with reference to the second adjective, the formulation may be of use in thinking about not just "The Most of It" but the whole *Witness Tree* sequence.

"Wavering"—restless, playing or moving to and fro, swaying, hesitating, faltering, unsettled in opinion—these filial relatives in the "wavering" family have often been invoked by readers of Frost who are responding to the moral and human doubleness that informs his situations and concerns. The principle of wavering informs the last poem from Frost's earlier volume *Mountain Interval* (1916), "The Sound of the Trees":

> I wonder about the trees.
> Why do we wish to bear
> Forever the noise of these
> More than another noise
> So close to our dwelling place?

We suffer them by the day
Till we lose all measure of pace,
And fixity in our joys,
And acquire a listening air.
They are that that talks of going
But never gets away;
And that talks no less for knowing,
As it grows wiser and older,
That now it means to stay.
My feet tug at the floor
And my head sways to my shoulder
Sometimes when I watch trees sway,
From the window or the door.
I shall set forth for somewhere,
I shall make the reckless choice
Some day when they are in voice
And tossing so as to scare
The white clouds over them on.
I shall have less to say,
But I shall be gone.

From the beginning of his career, it was not only the sound of trees but more centrally the sound of sense that the real poet cultivated and the good ear—reader attended to, having acquired a listening air. There is no diminishment of this commitment to sound in the *Witness Tree* poems; indeed, the more we reread them, the more familiar we become with their "content," the more we marvel at the rhythmic life and variety of their sentence sounds. And the more they add up to an achieved "wavering," from one poem to the next and within individual poems. Which makes biographical accountings for them, such as Meyers's of how "Kay" inspired this one, or how that one is "about" Frost and her, less and less to the point.

2.

By way of demonstration, I shall make some remarks about the prosodic rhythms of some of these poems, neglecting—perhaps to the point of folly—their content, my purpose being no more or less than to bring out the strange originality, even for the always original Frost, of their aural inventiveness. In "The Silken Tent," we have an Elizabethan sonnet, consisting of a single sentence which, like the tent's central cedar pole, is "loosely bound," at least to the extent where Judith Oster, at the outset of her rigorously exhaustive grammatical analysis of it, admits that "the sentence comes perilously close to going out of control with the multiplication of subordinate clauses." Attempts to paraphrase "The Silken Tent," by way of unpacking its content, inevitably feel lame and uninteresting and tend to sound like this one: "The ties to 'everything on earth the compass round' reveals her awareness and concern for all people and the whole scope of experience." Let us call it rather a poem that's extremely beautiful as you perform it, say it aloud, but from which there is nothing to take away, at least at least not thoughts about either a woman or a tent. In fact, you could even say there's no woman in the poem, and no tent either. For "The Silken Tent" is fictive music played out through a grammar complicated and elusive enough so as to provide no easy and direct way out to the world, to action, to human beings, to a woman—whether she is named Elinor Frost or Kathleen Morrison. In his preface to *King Jasper* Frost once considered the question of how or whether a poem leads to action. "Surely art can be considered good only as it prompts to action," says a young man to Frost. "How soon, I asked him. But there is danger of undue levity in teasing the young."

"All Revelation," which Reuben Brower writes well about in his still useful book, *The Poetry of Robert Frost,* is an especially challenging poem, certainly one I've never spoken about with confidence. In calling it Frost's "most symbolist poem," Brower seems to acknowledge the air of equivocation that characterizes it. Brower calls the final line—"All revelation has been ours"—an achieved answer "to the doubts and wonders expressed in the exclamation that concludes the second stanza—"Strange apparition of the mind!" But though he thinks "All Revelation" is "Frost's most vigorous answer to the larger question of the relation between mind and reality," he immediately qualifies the claim by finding an "irony" that remains in "asserting so limited a revelation." And he warns us not to suppose Frost "has reached a firm conclusion or final position in this or any poem."

This lack of a firm position is of course what so annoyed Yvor Winters about Frost's poetry generally, and though few of us are likely to accept his strictures on Frost's limitations as a poet, Winters identified something crucial to the poetry. It may be indicated by some words from a letter Frost wrote to Leonidas Payne in answer to Payne's question whether, in

"Mending Wall," Frost's intention was fulfilled "with the characters portrayed and the atmosphere of the place." "I should be sorry," wrote Frost in reply, "if a single one of my poems stopped with either of those things—stopped anywhere in fact. My poems...are all set to trip the reader head foremost into the boundless." He went on in the same letter to speak of his "innate mischievousness," a mischievousness that we find in programmatically playful poems like "Mending Wall" or "Departmental," but just as much in the lyric soundings of affirmation—the large declarations in *A Witness Tree* about "countless silken ties of love and thought," or of how "All revelation has been ours." A reader who doesn't "trip" over them, not just on a first or second reading but permanently, won't be propelled into the boundless, a place where it's not reassuring to be, but which is our true and real destination in Frost's best work.

In "I Could Give All to Time," fifth poem in the sequence, a propelling into something like the boundless occurs in the third stanza, two earlier ones having described the inexorable leveling action of "Time" on all things. Now the man, just because he knows all about Time's effects, is impelled to resist them:

> I could give all to Time except—except
> What I myself have held. But why declare
> The things forbidden that while the Customs slept
> I have crossed to Safety with? For I am There,
> And what I would not part with I have kept.

In that final stanza we see those capital letters, hear that ringing human affirmation (which Randall Jarrell compared to the affirmation at the close of Yeats's "Dialogue of Self and Soul"), but get tripped up when we attempt to specify or analyze exactly *what* has been declared. We are left instead with the mischievous, double-edged Customs metaphor and the unparticularized "what" of the final line—"And what I would not part with I have kept."

In that same essay of Jarrell's on Frost, he speaks of how some Frost poems might be considered "slight," yet says that the sigh we give after we read them isn't a slight one. In these terms, perhaps the two slightest poems in the sequence are "Happiness Makes Up in Height for What It Lacks in Length," and "Carpe Diem." Both are slim poems to the eye, twenty-four and twenty-six lines long, respectively, written in trimeter—"Happiness," in trimeter couplets; "Carpe Diem," unrhymed. Trimeter tends to be "monotonous," says *The Princeton Encyclopedia of Poetic Terms,* and its "tripping" potential, especially in couplets, might seem to make for triviality rather than for lyric depth. Yet Yeats uses it—without couplets—in some of his finest verse: in "Easter, 1916," "The Tower," part 3, and "In Memory of Eva Gore-Booth and Con Markiewicz." Frost had exploited trimeter with success in "The Sound of the Trees," and in "Happiness..." he also manages to portray a wavering and meditative imagination at work, arriving at "wisdom" over the course of, through the figure of, the poem ("It begins in delight and ends in wisdom. The figure is the same as for love"—"The Figure a Poem Makes"). He achieves his effects, in this poem, mainly by playing the sense units against the couplet rhyme and overriding the couplet's closure. It is an excellent meter for poems designed to "trip the reader," since it has in its feel a "tripping" rhythm, reluctant (in Frost's words) to "stop anywhere":

> Oh, stormy stormy world,
> The days you were not swirled
> Around with mist and cloud,
> Or wrapped as in a shroud,
> And the sun's brilliant ball
> Was not in part or all
> Obscured from mortal view—
> Were days so very few
> I can but wonder whence
> I get the lasting sense
> Of so much warmth and light.
> If my mistrust is right
> It may be altogether
> From one day's perfect weather,
> When starting clear at dawn,
> The day swept clearly on
> To finish clear at eve.
> I verily believe
> My fair impression may
> Be all from that one day
> No shadow crossed but ours
> As through its blazing flowers

> We went from house to wood
> For change of solitude.

It is a poem of three sentences, the first completing itself with line eleven, the second with line seventeen, then sweeping on to end the third in line twenty-four. As with the way the couplets succeed one another, there's a sense of irregularity about the sentence units, and both these qualities help to create the illusion of a mind exploring the past, rather than owning an attitude toward it all made up in advance:

> I verily believe
> My fair impression may
> Be all from that one day
> No shadow crossed but ours
> As through its blazing flowers
> We went from house to wood
> For change of solitude.

No punctuation at the ends of lines; slightly off rhymes like "ours / flowers" and "wood / solitude": it is an example of what Milton in the note he added to *Paradise Lost* called "the sense variously drawn out from one Verse into another." In Frost's words from "The Figure a Poem Makes," a "clarification of life" has been achieved, but just barely, and not one, as he put it, "such as sects and cults are founded on."

Similarly with "Carpe Diem," which Poirier treats sketchily and rather condescendingly as "inadequate to the mixed complications it proposes to sort out." On the contrary, it seems to me a highly adequate way of thinking about time present and time past, and as with "Happiness...," its adequacy—call it rather its beauty—is intimately connected with the movement of its verse. Instead of rhyming couplets, each line has a feminine ending (stress on the penultimate syllable) that contributes to the irregularity and informality of rhythm. There is also a playful jamming-up of words that echo, sometimes duplicate, one another—both within and at the ends of lines—perhaps by way of suggesting the crowding, confusing present that defeats our imagination. The poem opens with a rather creaky personification, "Age," who takes it upon himself to instruct a pair of youthful lovers (though not to their faces) on how to seize the day. After

Age does his number, Frost takes over the poem and instructs Age on the way things happen in real life, rather than in the commonplaces and conventions of literary wisdom. Simple enough, but it is made complicated and complexly satisfying by the way the language is worked:

> Age saw two quiet children
> Go loving by at twilight,
> He knew not whether homeward,
> Or outward from the village,
> Or (chimes were ringing) churchyard.
> He waited (they were strangers)
> Till they were out of hearing
> To bid them both be happy.
> "Be happy, happy, happy,
> And seize the day of pleasure."
> The age-long theme is Age's.
> 'Twas Age imposed on poems
> Their gather-roses burden
> To warn against the danger
> That overtaken lovers
> From being overflooded
> With happiness should have it
> And yet not know they have it.
> But bid life seize the present?
> It lives less in the present
> Than in the future always,
> And less in both together
> Than in the past. The present
> Is too much for the senses,
> Too crowding, too confusing—
> Too present to imagine.

Three "happy"s succeeding one another in a line is almost enough in itself to demonstrate the fatuity of Age's advice, and immediately after he says his little piece, Frost plays with Age's personified status by turning it back on him—"The age-long theme is Age's"—before delivering a seven-line, unpunctuated sentence that makes a tricky, quite subtle sound of sense:

'Twas Age imposed on poems
Their gather-roses burden
To warn against the danger
That overtaken lovers
From being overflooded
With happiness should have it
And yet not know they have it.

The play with "overtaken / overflooded," the repetition at line ends of "have it," guarantees that Frost's sense will be sounder than Age's simple "Be happy, happy, happy." The play continues in the poem's final eight lines—another sentence—with "the present" concluding three of the lines and introducing something of an aural vertigo ("Too crowding, too confusing") from which we emerge only in the final line. There "present," now no longer "the present," becomes instead an adjective nested within the line and replaced at its end with the weighted verb "imagine." One thinks, by contrast, of the weighty, toneless annunciation of Eliot in the opening lines of "Burnt Norton"—"Time present and time past / Are both perhaps present in time future, / And time future contained in time past." Indeed a comparison between Eliot and Frost could well be conducted by juxtaposing "Carpe Diem" and the beginning of "Burnt Norton" ("He plays Eucharist and I play Euchre," Frost once said about his rival).

No wonder then that Frost critics often look up from the analytical task, clear their throats, and admit how difficult it is to perform that task without heavy-handedness. Even so resourceful an interpreter as Poirier says at one point that some of Frost's poems are beyond us, not quite understandable. A recent essay on the poet by Jason Mauro speaks of how hard Frost makes us work, how the reader "must strain to keep things from splitting apart," and notes that Frost's genius "works at teasing out the duplicitous, complex nature of any utterance, any sentence, any word." Judith Oster, before launching her commentary on "The Most of It," says "This is a poem that eludes any definite interpretation or response." This elusiveness, which I believe to be part of the greatness of these *Witness Tree* poems, is there in "The Most of It" not despite but because of its forthright, declarative sequence of assertions, right down to "And that was all"—which says everything, and nothing in particular. It is there as well in "Never Again Would Birds' Song Be the Same," through the opposite of declarative forthrightness, in a sonnet that begins, cagily, "He would declare and could himself believe," then follows such conditionals with subtle qualifiers like "Admittedly," "Be that as may be," "Moreover," and "probably."

As for "The Subverted Flower," final poem in the sequence, Frost liked to say—in his "devilish" way and while not reading the poem aloud—that it was about "frigidity in women." The poem may have originated from an incident involving him and Elinor, though Poirier suggests that it is more a nightmare, a symbolic dream-enactment of something terrible. Meyers says that it "obliquely describes their passionate sex life" but doesn't demonstrate how it does so "obliquely." An important part of that obliqueness I attribute to its meter, which is again trimeter (not the four-stressed line Poirier hears), here rhymed in an irregular, off-balanced way that gives it the shimmering strangeness of fairy tale (I quote the poem's second half):

> It was then her mother's call
> From inside the garden wall
> Made her steal a look of fear
> To see if he could hear
> And would pounce to end it all
> Before her mother came.
> She looked and saw the shame:
> A hand hung like a paw,
> An arm worked like a saw
> As if to be persuasive,
> An ingratiating laugh
> That cut the snout in half,
> An eye become evasive.
> A girl could only see
> That a flower had marred a man,
> But what she could not see
> Was that the flower might be
> Other than base and fetid:
> That the flower had done but part,
> And what the flower began
> Her own too meager heart
> Had terribly completed.
> She looked and saw the worst.
> And the dog or what it was,
> Obeying bestial laws,

A coward save at night,
Turned from the place and ran.
She heard him stumble first
And use his hands in flight.
She heard him bark outright.
And oh, for one so young
The bitter words she spit
Like some tenacious bit
That will not leave the tongue.
She plucked her lips for it,
And still the horror clung.
Her mother wiped the foam
From her chin, picked up her comb
And drew her backward home.

Brower, in his remarks on the poem, says that the girl's horrified "discovery" of her lover's sexuality is rendered with some of D. H. Lawrence's hard purity. Yet when he quotes to illustrate this, Brower omits the very lines that are to me supremely and relentlessly memorable:

A girl could only see
That a flower had marred a man,
But what she could not see
Was that the flower might be
Other than base and fetid:
That the flower had done but part,
And what the flower began
Her own too meager heart
Had terribly completed.

In one of his best formulations, Frost has said that there should be more than disagreement and debate in a classroom: "Clash is all very well for coming lawyers, politicians and theologians. But I should think there must be a whole realm or plane above that—all sight and insight, perception, intuition, rapture.... Get up there high enough and the differences that make controversy become only the two legs of a body." I have written before about Frost's "elevated play," and these lines from "The Subverted

Flower," for all the terror of their content, are a great instance of both elevation and play, in the face of the unspeakable. At such a moment, and in these poems from the section of *A Witness Tree* most clearly connected to Frost's life experiences of love and death, he reaches the realm or plane where a reader, rather than explaining things biographically or otherwise, must prepare to be tripped head foremost into the boundless.

—*The Cambridge Companion to Robert Frost,* edited by Robert Faggen (New York: Cambridge University Press, 2001).

West of Boston: Robert Frost

I ENCOUNTERED HIM FIRST when I was a sophomore at Amherst College in the fall of 1950—not at one of the public readings he gave each year to overflow crowds in Johnson Chapel, but in the living room of a fraternity to which I'd recently become pledged. Accompanied by a member of the English department, Robert Frost came to spend a couple of hours with the brothers of Phi Alpha Psi, who turned out for the occasion dressed up in their gray flannel slacks, scuffed white bucks, button-down collars, and striped ties (*de rigueur*). He read poems to us for a while and talked about them and life generally. I can't remember anything he said, probably because I had in mind a question to put to him. When it came time for such, I asked him about his poem "Bereft," which we had studied that fall in an introductory course in critical reading. "Where had I heard this wind before / Change like this to a deeper roar?" it began, and concluded this way:

> Word I was in the house alone
> Somehow must have gotten abroad,
> Word I was in my life alone,
> Word I had no one left but God.

Fresh from Johnson City, New York, and beginning to have doubts about my confident Episcopalian faith, I asked the poet just how much that "God" of the poem's final line amounted to. "Where are you when you have no one left but God?" I said, imitating a member of the English department who had suggested that in such a situation you were more or less nowhere.

Frost didn't answer the question but rather gave me a little lecture, kind but firm, about how poets draw a line over which they won't step, and how my question was the sort of one that invited him to step over that line, and how he wasn't going to step over it. I subsided, aware that I had been taken down a bit, though not scolded too severely. But later one of my fraternity mates—a rather pompous fellow, I thought—took me to task: hadn't I realized that we were *not* supposed to ask Mr. Frost direct questions about what lines from his poetry did or didn't mean? How could I have been so crass?

After that I remember almost nothing about Frost during my undergraduate years at Amherst. (I do remember one evening at another fraternity where the assembled students asked him too much about baseball—they had been clued in that he was in favor of baseball.) He made himself available at the Lord Jeffery Inn during certain hours for individual visits, but I would never have dared go. I didn't think of myself (and quite rightly) as a poet; indeed, I was majoring in philosophy rather than English. But when I left Amherst for graduate school I carried along the green volume of *Complete Poems* (1949) and grew as much or more attached to them as to those of any poet, ancient or modern. Eventually I undertook a doctoral dissertation on him and decided—since I was then at Harvard and Frost had a residence on Brewster Street in Cambridge—to write and request a private chat. With much fussing and twisting I penned the letter, posted it, and never received a reply. So I reminded myself, a bit ruefully, that the important thing about a poet was his poetry and that Frost was a public figure with better things to do than answer letters from eager graduate students.

Little did I expect that I would soon have that public figure on my hands during one of his two-week biyearly stays at Amherst College. I had accepted a job in the English department there and was asked, the fall that I arrived, to take charge of Frost's social schedule—to see that he knew with whom he was having lunch or dinner on each particular day, field any requests or complaints, and generally check in on him in the mornings to talk over the night before and the shape of the new day. (Was I not writing a dissertation on his poetry? Who better to do these things?) Our first meeting was agreeable enough. Though he teased me a bit about writing on him, he didn't seem annoyed by the fact ("I don't read criticism," he insisted more than once). The moment that remains vividly in memory, though, came at the end of an evening when my wife and I had been invited to have dinner with him and one or two others at the home of the widow of a professor (George Frisbie Whicher) with whom Frost had been friends. We had a drink or so before dinner and Frost asked for some rum, into which he put sugar, explaining that sugar was good for you and also that there was a colonial air about the beverage that he approved of. Dinner and the talk afterward—mostly by him—were pleasant enough (I got him to talk a bit about Santayana), and as things drew to a close Frost suggested we walk back to the inn.

It was a splendid October night, leaves most satisfyingly in evidence, and as we crunched through them up Amity Street—which felt at that moment like the most beautiful street in the world—poetry was the subject. Somehow we got on Browning, a poet I'd had a terrible time reading in graduate school and was pretty sure was Browning's fault. Suddenly Frost began to quote some verses I had never before heard:

> The fancy I had to-day,
> Fancy which turned a fear!
> I swam far out in the bay,
> Since waves laughed warm and clear.
>
> I lay and looked at the sun,
> The noon-sun looked at me:
> Between us two, no one
> Live creature, that I could see.

He went on quoting and I could follow well enough to register the arrival of a live creature, indeed a butterfly:

> A handbreadth over head!
> All of the sea my own,
> It owned the sky instead;
> Both of us were alone.

There was something thrilling about the way he said that line "Both of us were alone." What was it—an early poem of Frost's I'd never read? No, he said, it was Browning. But what poem, I wanted to know. He suggested I look it up, perhaps because he couldn't remember the title, perhaps because he wanted to make me earn it.

By this time we had come to the inn and I prepared to see him to the door and continue on my way toward what was sometimes referred to as "the compound," a college housing project in which young instructors resided. I didn't know then that Frost would initiate his ritual of prolonging the evening: "I'll walk a ways with you in your direction," he offered, and we rounded the Beta corner and continued on to Chi Phi. "Do you want to go back?—I'll walk you back," I offered, and we headed toward the inn. There were at least one or two more shorter turns, and by the time the talk was over and I got home, it was late. Frost liked to stay up until 2 a.m. or so, especially if he had someone to talk to. I, on the other hand, was teaching two sections of Freshman Composition which met every day, Monday through Saturday, and with a set of papers to be graded and handed back for each class. A slight conflict of interest there, and if my interest in Frost prevailed I still had to get the papers back on time. When I got home I looked for the Browning, couldn't find it, then discovered it next day in a complete edition of his poetry under the title "Amphibian," prologue to a late, lengthy, and not appealing operation· called, of all things, *Fifine at the Fair.* As I read "Amphibian" through, I discovered a later stanza Frost hadn't quoted:

> Emancipate through passion
> And thought, with sea for sky,
> We substitute, in a fashion,
> For Heaven—poetry.

It hit home, since substituting poetry for Heaven was what, in a fashion, I had been trying to do for years. As was later the case with James Shirley's "The glories of our blood and state," or William Collins's "How Sleep the Brave," or Edwin Arlington Robinson's "The Sheaves," Browning's little poem meant and means a lot to me largely because it was Frost who literally passed along the word—something more sustaining than the "Word I had no one left but God."

Looking back from the vantage point of almost thirty years, those evenings and readings blend into the undifferentiated, though I rarely remember being bored or wishing I were anywhere else. I do remember things about food and drink—for example, that we tended to serve him chicken or beef when he came to supper at our house. We didn't offer him rum, but he would have a bourbon and water with some added sugar (sugar is good for you). When he gave his public reading in the chapel he ate nothing before; afterward, in the kitchen of the president's house, he had scrambled eggs, toast, and milk. At one point I even became aware that not everybody in the world, even in Amherst, loved Mr. Frost—at least didn't love to have him around in all situations. At the English department cocktail party, a yearly institution to which Frost was once brought by a senior faculty member, a younger, rather unruly colleague who had (like the rest of us) had a few, felt constrained by his presence and growled at me, "Get that old man out of here." Frost must have felt somewhat out of place, not enough the center of attention, because on leaving rather early he cast his eye about us all and said rather threateningly to the professor who had brought him, "Get rid of them all! Fire 'em!" We assured ourselves, after he left, that he had just been teasing and wouldn't decide to push the suggestion further. Anyway, I survived.

A couple of additional pictures, the first of them remaining fondly in the mind's eye. My infant son was brought in to be introduced to the old man. Frost was eighty-six years old and my son about three weeks old; the poet kindly paid him some attention, taking one of his tiny hands in his hoary one, playing with the fingers for a few seconds. Words don't get the picture into very good focus. The last time I saw him was after he had been ill with pneumonia. He said he was tired, and the business manager of the college (who had come along with Frost to our house after a reception) suggested to him loudly—Frost being selectively deaf—that he might move to Amherst and settle down for good. "Why, you could live in this house," he offered, as my wife and I shared a moment of concern. But the most vivid recollection, along with that late walk up Amity Street, comes from the time when, at the end of his annual spring visit, he suddenly decided he wanted to go back to Cambridge. I volunteered to drive him, even cancelled a composition class to do it, while to my wife fell the uneasy task of calling up the people with whom he was to have had dinner that night and explaining to them why Frost wouldn't be showing up. At that time we owned a 1952 Dodge on its last legs that burned oil like crazy. To save money I carried along a can of oil in the car and was always prepared, should smoke begin to issue freely from the exhaust, to step out on Route 2, raise the hood, and pour it in. So was I also prepared to change a tire. But I was prepared neither to change a tire nor pour in oil with America's first poet looking on in amusement or dismay from the front seat. Crossing my fingers, I checked the oil, kicked the tires, and we proceeded without incident to Cambridge.

As I drove along I told him that I hoped to turn my recently finished dissertation into a book about his poetry, and that a commercial publisher had shown interest (that was all they showed). Frost was less than enthusiastic about the idea: "Keep it around," he advised. "Deepen it." At the time it was just what I didn't want to hear, though of course he was right. When we got to Cambridge he suggested lunch at a restaurant. Where should we go? Why, to the Commander Hotel, a Cambridge spot somewhat out of the graduate student run of things. We were seated in fine style. Shouldn't we have a cocktail, he said, and shouldn't it be a daiquiri? One of my less favorite drinks, but I accepted with pleasure and agreed that sugar was a good thing. Afterward we proceeded to his house, and though I had always looked down on autograph seekers, I asked him to write something in my old copy of *Complete Poems.* There was no index to this edition, as he found out while trying to locate a particular poem. So the inscription, when he slowly and laboriously finished it, read "To William Pritchard: Thanks for sight of this old edition without index of titles and first lines." He signed and dated it, then added underneath, as if in afterthought, "And for the ride from Amherst to Cambridge he made pleasant." Driving home I felt about as pleasant as I've ever managed to feel.

—*Yale Review*, June 1987.

Frost and Edward Thomas

After learning that Edward Thomas had been killed in the battle of Arras in France, 1917, Robert Frost wrote to his widow, paying his tribute to "the bravest and best of any men you and I have ever known." Although he finds nothing to "regret" in Thomas's noble sacrifice, he wishes that Thomas could have "saved his life without so wholly losing it." For Frost wanted to "tell him something," "that he was a poet." The following November Frost wrote Wilbur Cross, editor of *The Yale Review*, explaining or excusing his "failure to do anything about Thomas in print":

> I find he was too near me. Some time I shall write about him. Perhaps it will come to me to write in verse. As yet I feel too much the loss of the best friend I ever had. And by that I don't mean I am overwhelmed with grief. Something in me refuses to take the risk—angrily refuses to take the risk—of seeming to use a grief for literary purposes. When I care less, I can do more.

This letter is unmistakably Frost's in its complicated way of accounting for not having put words to his friend's death. He rejects the common notion that, having lost such a friend, he would be overwhelmed with grief, thus rendered wordless. No, Frost's was a resistance, an angry resistance to the risk that whatever poem he wrote would be promoting "literary purposes" over the grief that lay behind it. Thus the curt summation: "When I care less, I can do more."

The first "more" he did for Thomas was, three years later, to publish the poem "To E.T.":

> I slumbered with your poems on my breast
> Spread open as I dropped them half-read through

Like dove-wings on a figure on a tomb
To see, if in a dream they brought of you,

I might not have the chance I missed in life
Through some delay, and tell you to your face
First soldier, and then poet, and then both,
Who died a soldier-poet of your race.

I meant, you meant, that nothing should remain
Unsaid between us, brother, and this remained—
And one thing more that was not then to say
The Victory for what it lost and gained.

You went to meet the shell's embrace of fire
On Vimy Ridge, and when you fell that day
The war seemed over more for you than me,
But now for me than you—the other way.

How over, though, for even me who knew
The foe thrust back unsafe beyond the Rhine,
If I was not to speak of it to you
And see you pleased once more with words of mine.

Five quatrains rhyming ABCB except for the final one with its ABAB—just a shade more complete in its rhyming figure. Reading it aloud, or typing it out as I have just done, makes one aware of its complications as a little story: "We meant, you and I, to leave nothing unsaid between us. But I didn't get the chance to call you a true soldier-poet; nor, because you were killed, did I ever get the chance to speak about the "Victory" you laid down your life for. When you were killed, the war (of course) was over for you; now, looking at the consequences of that war, I lament that we couldn't have talked about it together." This awkward attempt to chart the poem's "argument" is made more awkward because of the clipped, laconic, often monosyllabic style of Frost's lines.

"To E.T." is notable among Frost's other poem since, as Tim Kendall reminds us, it is the only elegy he ever wrote for a named individual.[1] It

1. Tim Kendall. *The Art of Robert Frost.* Yale University Press, 2012.

also stands out, I think, because of the specific name of a battlefield, Vimy Ridge, and later the allusion to the river Rhine, such naming of places—certainly of European ones—being very unlike Frost's usual procedures. Then there is the rather odd line about "The foe thrust back unsafe beyond the Rhine." Did he have anything in mind about a world situation, or was it that "Rhine" was a good rhyme with "mine"? My sense is that "To E.T." begins gracefully and poignantly, with the slumbering poet attempting through his dream to come to acceptable terms with his friend's death. But the final stanza winds things up in a way that is less than satisfying, playing with how the war is "over" yet not over for the still-troubled poet-elegist:

> How over, though, for even me who knew
> The foe thrust back unsafe beyond the Rhine,
> If I were not to speak of it to you
> And see you pleased once more with words of mine?

The closing two monosyllabic lines in their ingenuity detract from rather than expand the poet's sympathetic question, and is there something the least bit unsettling about Frost ending with "words of mine," that would have pleased the dead Thomas if he hadn't died? Tim Kendall is right to speak of a "tonal instability" in the poem, and that instability has everything to do with Frost's still conflicted feelings about Thomas's death, wanting yet not quite wanting to write about it.

By contrast, there is no such instability in "A Soldier," which substitutes a wholly impersonal presence for the fallen Thomas of the earlier poem. "A Soldier" is a professional performance in a traditional mode, a Shakespearean sonnet, three ABBA quatrains and a concluding couplet. Reuben Brower calls it a "metaphysical sonnet," alluding to the central presence of a "conceit" in it:

> He is that fallen lance that lies as hurled,
> That lies unlifted now, come dew, come rust,
> But still lies pointed as it plowed the dust.
> If we who sight along it round the world,
> See nothing worthy to have been its mark,
> It is because like men we look too near,
> Forgetting that as fitted to the sphere,

Our missiles always make too short an arc.
They fall, they rip the grass, they intersect
The curve of earth, and striking, break their own;
They make us cringe for metal-point on stone.
But this we know, the obstacle that checked
And tripped the body, shot the spirit on
Further than target ever showed or shone.

This is a portrait of The Unknown Soldier, stripped of any human, identificatory qualities, transformed into a fallen lance in the dust. There is a somewhat chilly remoteness about the "we" who both misperceive the true nature of human missiles, which always fall short of their projected target as they "intersect" the earth and break their own arc. This "we" in the early part of the sonnet is , like all men, short-sighted, but by the final three lines has gained in assurance and tonal power:

But this we know, the obstacle that checked
And tripped the body, shot the spirit on,
Further than target ever shown or shone.

Here "we" is the poet Frost, speaking for all men and professing a faith that exhibits what his favorite philosopher, William James, called "the Will to Believe." The belief is asserted importantly through the rush of "s" sounds in the final two lines, from "shot" to "spirit" to "shown" to "shone." That final word, ending the poem, the past participle of "shine," gives a slightly archaic and enhanced richness to the inexpressible range of the spirit's reach. How much more is there to say about this kind of knowledge, ultimate in its effect? Frost may have converted his caring less about Thomas's death into doing more. But the "doing" in this perfect little sonnet is achieved apart from any particular human figure, place, or deed.

If "A Soldier" had turned out to be Frost's final words in poetry about Thomas's death, they would have been incomplete, substituting the neatly turned out "metaphysical" poem for something more intimate, personal. But we only see "A Soldier" as thus incomplete because we have been given a vivid example of such completeness in the beautiful "Iris By Night." Published in 1936, it is a curiously neglected Frost poem, never a candidate for the anthologies and much too complicated in its rhyme and movement to be easily memorizable (compare "Neither Out Far Nor In Deep" or "Stopping By Woods On A Snowy Evening). It is also, so this reader finds, extremely difficult to rise adequately to in print, since its aural range and nuance can only be suggested by the spoken word. With "Iris By Night," one yearns for the classroom, where it can be read aloud, pausing and resaying, correcting a possible missaying of a particular run of lines while attempting to keep the whole somehow in the ear. It is a poem of uneven length (31 lines) with an elaborate rhyme scheme that often surprises by challenging us with the unexpected. Its rhymes employ fourteen of the available twenty-two opening letters of the alphabet; its pattern of sentence length is varied, informing the lines as follows: 3, 5, 1, 3, 4, 3, 3, 6, 3—nine sentences, the longest of which occurring appropriately at the poem's climax. Instead of quoting it entire, I shall paraphrase its first half (16 lines), then quote and attempt to praise the marvelous second half.

In "Iris By Night" Frost and his friend (the unnamed Edward Thomas) are headed home in the early evening after a climb in the Malvern hills ("the last wet fields and dripping hedges home"). Suddenly something out of the ordinary happens, a "moment of confusing light" that is compared to such an occurrence in classical legend, then an access of light ("a paste of pigment in our eyes"), a moon, and a scene "so watery as to seem submarine." In this scene the two men are "saturated, drowned," the pressure of the air turned to "water weight." A new sentence beginning with the leading conjunction "Then" introduces the outcome of this strange, even overwhelming moment:

> Then a small rainbow like a trellis gate,
> A very small moon-made prismatic bow,
> Stood closely over us through which to go,
> And then we were vouchsafed the miracle
> That never yet to other two befell
> And I alone of us have lived to tell.
> A wonder! Bow and rainbow as it bent,
> Instead of moving with us as we went,
> (To keep the pots of gold from being found)
> It lifted from is dewy pediment
> Its two mote-swimming, many-colored ends,
> And gathered them together in a ring.
> And we stood in it softly circled round

> From all division time or foe can bring
> In a relation of elected friends.

In "To E.T." the Frost hopes to see in a dream of Thomas the chance he missed in life to tell his friend that he was a soldier and a poet. That telling was to remain un-related. Now, the shared moment of mystery and wonder on the Malvern hills twenty years earlier constitutes the "miracle" that they two alone were witness to. In "A Soldier" the narration is virtually toneless, the slight heightening of voice in "But this we know" not disrupting the overall evenness of presentation. Now, the exclamatory "A wonder!" at the beginning of a line does a great deal of tonal work, taking the two men to a place higher than the Malvern hill they were descending.

Earlier I spoke of the elaborate rhyme scheme, a sometime feature of Frost's works that has not been enough remarked on. The early "October" from *A Boy's Will* demonstrates how various a rhyming pattern he could make in twenty-one lines: "The Exposed Nest," from *Mountain Interval,* is another example of the resourcefulness he brought to making lines rhyme irregularly and sometimes harken back through the rhyme word to a much earlier partner. Chrisopher Ricks comments tellingly on the relation between rhyme and friendship, with Frost and Thomas in mind:

> In their art, both Frost and Thomas enjoyed the conditions in which rhymes were friends, not only friends to the poets' art but friends to one another, to their fellow-rhymes. Rhyme is like friendship in that it is only by being reciprocated that it constitutes rhyme.

"Iris By Night" has a "G" rhyme in lines 12 and 13; the word is then dropped but surprisingly picked up again in lines 25 and 29, almost at the end of the poem. It would take an ear more trained than probably exists to detect such a surprising recurrence; only through eye-counting can this one in "Iris By Night" be registered. Here the "G" rhyme completes itself three lines from the poem's end—"And we stood in it softly circled round"—and may vouch for the miraculous completion of the wonder that has befallen the favored men.

In his overall excellent book on Frost, Richard Poirier is wholly dismissive of "Iris By Night," calling it a " garden club evocation" and mistakenly supposing that the rainbow "encircles a group, including Frost."[2,3] I presume such a response to the poem would center on the moment of "miracle" in which the two ends of the rainbow are gathered together in the ring that circles and eternizes the two men. Casting about for a literary moment analogous to this one, I thought of Hardy's great poem from the "Poems of 1912-13" sequence, "At Castle Boterel," perhaps the best of those many fine poems. It records a memory of Hardy and his young wife-to-be, he and an accompanying "girlish form" as they climb the hill. Hardy muses on the remembered scene:

What we did as we climbed, and what we talked of
  Matters not much, nor to what it led,—
Something that life will not be balked of
  Without rude reason till hope is dead.
    And feeling fled.

It filled but a minute. But was there ever
  An hour of such quality, since or before,
In this hill's story? To one mind never,
  Though it has been climbed, foot-swift, foot-sore
    By thousands more.

Primeval rocks form the road's steep border,
  And much have they faced there, first and last
Of the transitory in Earth's long order;
  But what they record in colour and cast
    Is—that we two passed.

And to me, though Time's unflinching rigour,
  In mindless rote, has ruled from sight
The substance now, one phantom figure
  Remains on the slope, as when that night
    Saw us alight.

2. Christopher Ricks. "Afterword," in *Elected Friends: Robert Frost and Edward Thomas To One Another,* ed. Matthew Spencer. Handsel Books. 2003
3. Richard Poirier. *Robert Frost: The Work of Knowing.* Oxford University Press, 1977

Donald Davie has written well about the force of this declaration: "The crucial word is 'quality'—a time of such *quality.* For the qualitative has no existence outside of a mind that registers it. And quality is therefore invulnerable to time, since the 'rote' by which Time works is mindless."[4] Oddly enough, Frost had almost nothing to say about Hardy's poetry, and I somehow doubt that he was even aware of "At Castle Boterel." Nevertheless, the two affirmations are strikingly at the center of their respective poems.

We may recall Frost's declaration in the letter explaining why he hadn't yet written anything about Thomas's death: "When I care less, I can do more." That "more" is most handsomely and movingly apparent in the complicated melody of "Iris By Night."

—Originally published in *Dymock Poets and Friends*,
No. 17, 2018 as "Frost and Thomas."

4. Donald Davie. "Hardy's Virgilian Purples," in *With The Grain.* Carcanet. U.K. 1998

Frost's Mischievous Grip

PART OF MY TITLE is taken from a letter Robert Frost wrote home from England on Christmas Day of 1912, just a few months after he had settled with his family outside London, and preparatory to publishing his first book of poems, *A Boy's Will* in 1913. In this Christmas Day letter to a school principal in New Hampshire under whom Frost had taught, and who disapproved of his decision to seek his literary fortune in England, Frost pokes fun at the un-New England-like mild English winter, then builds to the following announcement:

> We have had ice (a few times) on the rain barrel if that constitutes winter. And one morning early in December the papers were out with scare heads like this:
>
> ENGLAND IN THE GRIP OF FROST
>
> I accept the omen, says I, I accept the omen. Better so than that Frost should be in the grip of England.

If I had to choose one favorite, single illustration of his peculiar genius as a writer, this is the one I'd choose, and for a number of reasons, closely related. There is the immediately auditory aspect of it, the way you have to adjust your ear to the parenthetical ("a few times") after "We have had ice (a few times"), and the way those "scare heads" should ring out: *England in The Grip of Frost*, followed by the heroic, or mock-heroic, "I accept the omen, says I, I accept the omen." There is a constant edge on the tone of each assertion, so as to insure that nothing can be taken straight, nothing can be heard as wholeheartedly sincere. Consider the American condescension to English weather in "if that constitutes winter" (referring to ice on the rain barrel, evidently a pitiful phenomenon); or the making silly of those headlines by calling them "scare heads"; and of course the final "better so," in which Frost's grip proves stronger than England's.

In line with these observations is a central one about the performer's willingness—and Frost is very much a performer in this bid for delighted applause from his audience—to put himself on stage front and center: to turn the unthinking language of publicity and convenience—a dead metaphor in which something is "in the grip of" something else—into an extremely personal, bold, and witty act of verbal aggression: "Better so than that Frost should be in the grip of England." One of his many fertile definitions of poetry was that it is "organized violence upon language." The violence and the organization in this grip-of-Frost letter reminds us that he wrote more "poetry" than that which is arranged in lines of verse.

His recently published notebooks provide innumerable instances of such organized violence upon language. In a more colloquial way, he described the activity of poetry as "Pushing Things Around," and one of his notebook items is so titled: "Pushing Things Around—things & people. It may be affectionately or hatefully. It may be affectionately & still roughly and the more roughly the better. But whether affectionately or hatefully it is always playfully." Or so he would like to have us see his own "pushing around," whether done in affection or with malice aforethought. A similar bid for inclusiveness and unity can be found in the final stanza of his "Two Tramps in Mud Time," which insists that

> Only where love and need are one
> And the work is play for mortal stakes
> Is the deed ever really done
> For heaven and the future's sakes.

This notion of play, of poetry as a kind of play, fascinated him, and he kept returning to ring changes on the things he could say about it, as in this notebook item: "Play no matter how deep has got to be so playful that the audience is left in doubt whether it is deep or shallow." The item is another undermining of the romantic, Shelleyan notion of poetry as a sincere attempt to say straight out, from the heart or the soul, what the poet really deeply means. Such attempted sincerity is what Shelley suffers from in "To a Skylark":

We look before and after
And pine for what is not
Our sincerest laughter
With some pain is fraught
Our sweetest songs are those that tell of saddest thought.

The notion of a "sincerest laughter" would have been, for Frost, something to have a laugh about, and he might have characterized Shelley's insistence that such laughter always "With some pain is fraught" as a species of sublime belly-aching. Shelley's play here isn't deep enough, since—in Frost's term—the audience is in absolutely no doubt that it is supposed to be very deep indeed. In a similar spirit, Frost provided his own definition and revivification of the cliché, "dry humor": "Dry humor is the kind that doesn't seem to appreciate itself. I wish all literature were as dry in the same sense of the word." He would squeeze out of literature, out of poetry, out of what he called playing around, the pushing around of things and people, all "wet" feelings of self-reverence, self-appreciation, self-importance. He would make singing not the brilliant, joyous, impossibly un-human song of Shelley's skylark, who, up there in the intense inane, "Pourest thy full heart / In profuse sounds of unpremeditated art"—but something different, the sort of singing done by the oven bird in Frost's poem of that title:

There is a singer everyone has heard,
Loud, a mid-summer and a mid-wood bird,
Who makes the solid tree trunks sound again.
He says that leaves are old and that for flowers
Mid-summer is to spring as one to ten.
He says the early petal-fall is past
When pear and cherry bloom went down in showers
On sunny days a moment overcast;
And comes that other fall we name the fall.
He says the highway dust is over all.
The bird would cease and be as other birds
But that he knows in singing not to sing.
The question that he frames in all but words
Is what to make of a diminished thing.

The Oven Bird sings from mid-summer on into fall, no, doesn't sing but rather "He *says* the early petal fall is past"; "He *says* the highway dust is over all" (audiences at Frost's readings of his poetry remember that he always told them, "I'm gonna *say* a few poems for ya"). Why, with such a pedestrian message—as if we didn't know it already—does the oven bird go on producing his special brand of song?

> The bird would cease and be as other birds
> But that he knows in singing not to sing.
> The question that he frames in all but words
> Is what to make of a diminished thing.

This is a bird who sees, or says, double, who—as Frost himself defined the nature of metaphor—says one thing while meaning another, who "knows in singing not to sing." He is, in other words, a potentially ironic bird, could he find the words he "all but" frames his question in. (And he is in fact a rather pedagogical as well as a playful bird—indeed, the oven bird's song has been rendered in words as "Teacher, Teacher.") "The question is, is it right to educate young people by shock. They are an undeniable temptation to teachers," wrote Frost in one of his notebooks, at the end of a little educative dialogue between a man and a boy titled "Crash there goes another young ideal." The oven bird's way of teaching, like the poem's, is gentler, perhaps subtler, as it concerns itself with helping us know what to make of a diminished thing, especially after the inflated thing made of it—made of life—by a romantic poet like Shelley.

Frost's playfulness was in part a response to the American poetry he saw being published when, at the end of the nineteenth century, he began to send his own poems to magazines. The dominant American note was that of heavy, indeed lugubrious, sincerity, an uplifted "noble" strain of edification, a monotonous monotone in which fine sentiments were droned out. These poems have now largely disappeared from an anthology such as the *Oxford Book of American Verse,* but in 1927, when Bliss Carman put his edition of the book together, they were still very much present. Here is part of a typical one, by Amelia Josephine Burr (most of the poets had three names), b. 1878:

> Because I have loved life, I shall have no sorrow to die.
> I have sent up my gladness on wings, to be lost in the blue of the sky.

> I have run and leaped with the rain, I have taken the wind to my
> breast
> My cheek like a drowsy child to the face of the earth I have pressed.
> Because I have loved life, I shall have no sorrow to die.

This from "A Song of Living." But Frost wrote in his notebook the following four-liner:

> Nothing ever so sincere
> That unless it's out of sheer
> Mischief and a little queer
> It won't prove a bore to hear.

For him, above all else, literature had to be un-boring, and since it was something to *hear*—to ear-read more than eye-read (as he put it)—it had better be "a little queer," something just enough out of the ordinary so that one couldn't say, "Oh, I've heard *that* before."

As in this ditty from Frost's notebook, it's important that the mischief be "sheer mischief," contrived not so much so as to discomfit someone in particular, but for its own sake rather, for the "sheer" pleasure of committing it. His four-line poem makes mischief essential to the whole enterprise of writing poetry, and on another occasion—in an interview conducted near the end of his life—he speculated on the nature of poetic inspiration. Where did it come from, what was it?

> Young people wonder about that, don't they? But I tell them it's just the same as when you feel a joke coming. You see somebody coming down the street that you're accustomed to abuse, and you feel it rising in you, something to say as you pass each other. Coming over him the same way. And where do these thoughts come from? Where does a thought? Something does it to you. It's him coming toward you that gives you the animus, you know. When they want to know about inspiration, I tell them it's mostly animus.

Whether called inspiration or animus, it is as native to the spirit as breathing, and just as "sheer" as mischief should be. Why does the mower in "The Tuft of Flowers" leave that one small tuft spared from his scythe's otherwise even relentlessness? The speaker who discovers the flowers tries, at the end of the poem, to answer this question:

> The mower in the dew had loved them thus,
> By leaving them to flourish, not for us
>
> Nor yet to draw one thought of ours to him,
> But from sheer morning gladness at the brim.

And he goes on to draw something further from the act:

> The butterfly and I had lit upon,
> Nevertheless, a message from the dawn,
>
> That made me hear the wakening birds around,
> And hear his long scythe whispering to the ground,
>
> And feel a spirit kindred to my own;
> So that henceforth I worked no more alone;
>
> But glad with him, I worked as with his aid,
> And weary, sought at noon with him the shade,
>
> And dreaming, as it were, held brotherly speech
> With one whose thought I had not hoped to reach.
>
> "Men work together," I told him from the heart,
> Whether they work together or apart.

He discovers that somebody else in the world has done something out of a motive that is "sheer," uncontaminated by altruism or self-regard, humanitarian sentiment or prideful exhibitionism. In speaking about the poem Frost was eager to say that it was written against the idea that when people did things like write poems or spare flowers, all they were doing was "showin' off." It was thus against "exhibitionism." He spoke in a similar manner about the virtue of memorizing a poem just *for itself*, the virtue in being able to say or write out the lines correctly, with punctuation and line-endings gotten right.

Here are a few of the ways Frost liked to talk about what poetry was or did: it was organized violence upon language, the grip of a powerful imagination; it pushed words and things and people around, sometimes roughly, but always playfully; it was play for mortal stakes, play that was so playful an audience would be unable to say whether it was deep or shallow; it exhibited a dry humor with so much of the "wet" squeezed out of it that people who labeled it "dry humor"—as if they knew what *that* really meant—were not quite getting it; it was knowing in singing not to sing; it was ironic and, in a certain sense, insincere; it was "a little queer"—sheer mischief practiced for its own sake, its only justification that it should be un-boring. What consequences do these ways of talking about poetry have for the poems Frost wrote? Or rather, assuming that similar impulses and aspirations informed both the poems and his "theories" about poetry, what is it that remains compelling, and fascinating, and maybe finally, not quite understandable about his poems?

We know the ways in which, compared to other modern poets, he is *easy* to read and understand. No arcane references, as in Ezra Pound; no systematic keys to history and personality such as W. B. Yeat's *A Vision* is sometimes thought to provide for Yeats's later poetry; no whirling surrealistic excess or related dependence on the dictionary, as with Hart Crane or Wallace Stevens; no toneless, cryptic, allusive rumination, as in some of T. S. Eliot. You don't need annotation to help you read "Birches" or "Mending Wall." And yet. Frost's difficulty—what keeps us going back and back to the poems—is nevertheless formidable and real, and it has, so I believe, everything to do with his mischief. He reaches out to us, offers us something—an attitude toward life, a bit of wisdom culled from experience, a formulation, a gesture at least, a turn of phrase, something heard that won't be forgotten. Yet as "he" reaches out (but is there a "he" there, or rather a dance of words?) we find it hard to know just how to take him, how seriously or how humorously ("I am never more serious than when joking," he kept insisting)—with what degree of engagement and in precisely what mood, to respond to his invitations.

Consider "The Vantage Point," an early sonnet from his first book of poems:

> If tired of trees I seek again mankind,
>   Well I know where to hie me—in the dawn,
>   To a slope where the cattle keep the lawn.

There amid lolling juniper reclined,
Myself unseen, I see in white defined
        Far off the homes of men, and farther still,
        The graves of men on an opposing hill,
Living or dead, whichever are to mind.

And if by noon I have too much of these,
        I have but to turn on my arm, and lo,
        The sun-burned hillside sets my face aglow,
My breathing shakes the bluet like a breeze,
        I smell the earth, I smell the bruised plant,
        I look into the crater of the ant.

Here the momentary seeker, once again, of mankind, is careful not to come too close, as he reclines there on the slope under the juniper, unseen but all-seeing, whether his object be the homes or the graves of men—"Living or dead, whichever are to mind." The sonnet's octave establishes him in position, then the sestet provides him with an out, in case he has had too much of a good thing. All he need do, so it seems, is to make one of those "turns" so important in Frost's poetry: "And if by noon I have too much of these, / I have but to turn on my arm, and lo"—all sorts of wonders follow, as this telescope turned microscope conducts extraordinarily sensitive commerce with the hillside, the bluet, the bruised plant, and—in a fine, witty phrase— "the crater of the ant."

In this charming, graceful poem from *A Boy's Will*, Frost had already become expert at achieving what he was to call "the sound of sense," the special postures of speech appropriate to different moments in his poems. For example, note the contrast in sound and movement of voice when he is carefully concealed— "There amid lolling juniper reclined, / Myself unseen, I see in white defined / Far off..." (a very involuted and elaborate movement of words), with the sestet in which, after turning on his arm with "and lo," there is the immediacy of direct sensation, expressed in assertive, declaratory, uncomplex sentences:

The sun-burned hillside sets my face aglow,
My breathing shakes the bluet like a breeze.
I smell the earth, I smell the bruisèd plant [verb repeats]
I look into the crater of the ant.

But this very charm and grace make "The Vantage Point" that much more difficult to speak of, to make claims for, without sounding pompous and solemn. A voice may whisper to us, isn't Frost just playing around in this little poem? What does he mean, that by turning on his arm he can have it all differently, bid goodbye once more to mankind and exult in the smells and sights of the natural world? How much of this poem is but "sheer mischief" shaped into the neat figure of a sonnet? And is that enough to make significant poetry? How seriously do we weigh it?

One of his most popular poems, a favorite one for him to read aloud, is similarly useful as example of his peculiar kind of difficulty. "Mending Wall" also contains the most important use of the word "mischief"—"Spring is the mischief in me"—in his poetry. Discussion of the poem has sometimes been conducted at the level of what it tells us about Frost's beliefs—was he For or Against Walls? Yet as he himself remarked more than once, the two sides both get stated in the poem: "Something there is that doesn't love a wall" but also "Good fences make good neighbors," each given equal time, stated twice. Rather than grasping at "meaning" we might instead take pleasure in listening to the developing sequence of sentence sounds, sometimes unmistakably clear, as when early in the poem our speaker refers to the "gaps" made by the frost that has spilled the upper boulders. He isn't talking about man-made intervention, as with the over-eager hunters, but of natural process: "The gaps *I* mean. No one has seen them made or heard them made." Here one must say, "The gaps *I* mean" with just that vocal inflection, and there is pleasure in getting it right, a pleasure out of proportion to the importance, the "meaning" of what's being said. It is a sheer pleasure.

But for all the precision and its attendant pleasure in how things are said, "Mending Wall" is finally more than a little elusive, even as it entertains us so deftly. My sense of the elusive culminates in the last eighteen lines of the poem that come after the neighbor has uttered his saying for the first time: "Good fences make good neighbors." The speaker-narrator, a questioner of such accepted, unexamined truths, perhaps a poet with the "mischief" in him, imagines that he might shake up his neighbor by making some rational distinctions, asking why and to what purpose this act of barrier-erecting is being performed:

> Spring is the mischief in me, and I wonder
> If I could put a notion in his head:

> '*Why* do they make good neighbors? Isn't it
> Where there are cows? But here there are no cows.
> Before I built a wall I'd ask to know
> What I was walling in or walling out,
> And to whom I was like to give offense.
> Something there is that doesn't love a wall,
> That wants it down.'

Here he warms to the task, as we can tell from the tonal expressivenesss of his voice, in its mixture of righteous questioning of shibboleths, with its extension of the "wall" to notions of "walling" in or out, and with the thoughtful, "liberal," regard for the feelings of others in "to whom I was like to give offense" consideration. Finally he is moved to quote himself but with a difference—"*Some*thing there is that doesn't love a wall, / That wants it down."

But what makes the poem Frost's rather than someone else's is the way it sets up and then refuses to be satisfied with an exposure of the neighbor's blindness. Is it in fact blindness, or something our clever narrator can't quite see to the bottom of? The poem's ending raises these questions, as it moves from a playful tone to one harder to characterize:

> I could say "Elves" to him
> But it's not elves exactly, and I'd rather
> He said it for himself. I see him there
> Bringing a stone grasped firmly by the top
> In each hand, like an old-stone savage armed.
> He moves in darkness as it seems to me,
> Not of woods only and the shade of trees.
> He will not go behind his father's saying,
> And he likes having thought of it so well
> He says again, "Good fences make good neighbors."

It ends humorously, with the thinking and the repeating of his father's saying, in a moment of imagined self-satisfaction. But before that, as the "I" sees him there—wherever "there" is, not just at some real wall but as in a dream vision ("in my mind's eye, Horatio")—the man is heroically "armed" like a prehistoric old-stone figure from another world. And indeed "he moves in darkness...Not of woods only and the shade of trees"—the very expression of this dark vision gives its subject dignity, depth, mystery. So the poem might be said to have discovered something about that subject it didn't know at the beginning. Frost's work as a whole should similarly be seen as experimental and exploratory of human character—of life.

Yet it is experimental and exploratory only by virtue of the depth of its play. His power as a lyric poet is seen in the boldness and beauty with which he dares to play with nature, with time, with the course of things—the way he dares to ask for suspensions in the flux that we all know can't be suspended. But the lyric poet won't take this knowledge for an answer, as he declares at the end of "Reluctance"—

> Ah, when to the heart of man
> Was it ever less than a treason
> To go with the drift of things
> To yield with a grace to reason,
> And bow and accept the end,
> Of a love or a season.

Instead he will try, through the power of his own song, to enchant the enchanting atmosphere of an October morning:

> O hushed October morning mild,
> Thy leaves have ripened to the fall;
> Tomorrow's wind, if it be wild,
> Should waste them all.
> The crows above the forest call;
> Tomorrow they may form and go.
> O hushed October morning mild,
> Begin the hours of this day slow.
> Make the day seem to us less brief.
> Hearts not averse to being beguiled,
> Beguile us in the way you know.
> Release one leaf at break of day;
> At noon release another leaf;
> One from our trees, one far away.
> Retard the sun with gentle mist;
> Enchant the land with amethyst.
> Slow, slow!

For the grapes' sake, if they were all,
Whose leaves already are burnt with frost,
Whose clustered fruit must else be lost—
For the grapes' sake along the wall.

Run your eye and ear down the final words in the lines and note the pattern of recurrence in the rhymes (sometimes words rhyming with themselves) of this artful sound-system: "mild / fall / wild / all / call / go / mild / slow / brief / beguiled / know / day / leaf / away / mist / amethyst / slow / all / frost / lost / wall. Perhaps the key moment in the little poem occurs in that extraordinary two-word two-syllable line of exclamation: "Slow, slow!" which acts out the "retard" just previously called for on the part of nature. Really it is but another sort of mischief, pretending that you can conduct things so elegantly, with your rhyme pattern, that, as it were, the October morning will follow your beat.

It depends how seriously you take those "as if" moments, when time and change and death are suddenly crossed and arrested by the play of words—the sound, the music of poetry. That Frost took them more seriously than anything else in life I think there is no doubt, and his most eloquent statement of the matter may be found at the inclusion of his preface to a volume by the recently dead American poet, Edwin Arlington Robinson. Robinson's sadness, Frost said, was solid, not just a "fishing for ministration and consolation." Frost ends his preface with a playful gloss on two lines from one of Robinson's poems:

Give us immedicable woes—woes that nothing can be
done for—woes flat and final. And then to play.
The play's the thing. Play's the thing. All virtue
in "as if".

As if the last of days
Were fading and all wars were done.

As if they were. As if, as if!

(To think for a moment of Auden: poetry makes nothing happen, yet it is a way of happening we can't do without.)

Frost's gestures of play, those "as if" moments so central to his practice as a poet, challenge us as readers to respond accurately and sensitively, but to be cautious in attributing large, important, symbolic significances to small poems, like "I Could Give All to Time," from later in his career:

> To Time it never seems that he is brave
> To set himself against the peaks of snow
> To lay them level with the running wave
> Nor is he overjoyed when they lie low,
> But only grave, contemplative and grave.
>
> What now is inland shall be ocean isle,
> Then eddies playing round a sunken reef
> Like the curl at the corner of a smile
> And I could share Time's lack of joy or grief
> At such a planetary change of style.
>
> I could give all to Time except—except
> What I myself have held. But why declare
> The things forbidden that while the Customs slept
> I have crossed to Safety with? For I am There,
> And what I would not part with I have kept.

This is a poem about how the speaker "could" do something if he chose to, and about how Time, his antagonist has—for all his power—no such choice: there is no "conditional" to Time, who does not think of himself as brave or joyful as he performs his feetings of leveling and eroding. You might repeat yourself when trying to describe what Time is like—not this, or that, "But only grave, contemplative and grave." In the face of such massive, perhaps boring, imperturbability, the speaker "could" try to sound like a dispassionate pronouncer of the fact of continental drift over eons of "grave" time: "What now is inland shall be ocean isle, / Then eddies playing round a sunken reef." He *could* do that imitation of Time speaking (if Time could speak, since he's also weak on words), except that something like mischief breaks in. Talk about "eddies playing" and just like that he is reminded of something, the way human beings, unlike Time, are reminded of something by something else: "Then eddies playing round a sunken reef / Like the curl at the corner of a smile," and not only reminded of something else but saying it out, *sounding* it with a distinct, uncontemplative and un-grave lilt: "Like the curl at the corner of a smile." Having said so much the speaker becomes bolder, collapses the "grave" passionless objectivity of Time toward its own works into a witty and memorable way of summing them up—"such a planetary change of style."

But it is the last stanza that is boldest and most extreme, with its heavy capitalization and ingenious metaphor of Time now mesmerized into a drowsing Customs official who has failed to catch the clever smuggler, slipped by with his undeclared goods. "I could give all to time except—except / What I myself have held." In the very saying there is deviousness, as when Frost remarks about "freedom" in his essay "The Figure a Poem makes":

> Political freedom is nothing to me. I bestow it right and left. All I would keep for myself is the freedom of my material—the condition of body and mind now and then to summons aptly from the vast chaos of all I have lived through.

"The Figure a Poem makes" as well as "I Could Give All To Time" were written when the vast chaos Frost had lived through included most notably the recent deaths of his daughter, Marjorie, and his wife, Elinor; his son Carol's suicide lay just ahead. As in the essay Frost makes the meaningless bestowal, left and right, of political freedom, so in the poem he allows as how he "could give all to Time," "except" everything that matters—like the ability to "summons aptly" in a poem. "I could give all to Time except"—and here we have a most expressive and tonally powerful dash—"except what I myself have held." Held on to, held back, held as principle in the face of political or domestic struggle? This "idea" we've already seen in the early "Reluctance"—"Ah when to the heart of man / Was it ever less than a treason / To go with the drift of things"—except that the reluctance is now louder and more playful in the way it flaunts what it presumes to get away with, especially in those capital letters: "Customs," "Safety," and "There." The great critic of Frost, Randall Jarrell, spoke of the ending of this poem as "calm and rapturous certainty," calling it "transfiguring." But with its commonplace words, flat rhymes, and almost awkward enjambment ("that while the Customs slept / I have crossed to Safety with"—imagine, ending with a preposition!) that ending may sound more mischievous than "transfiguring."

One of my favorite poems of his ("An Answer"), is only two lines long and might serve as a motto for some of the kinds of mischief we've been considering:

> But Islands of the Blessèd, bless you, son,
> I never came upon a blessèd one.

What other modern poet could have written or proudly published this perfect example of the playful turning of a word so as to squeeze new meanings and attitudes out of it. The capitalized poetic reverence of "Islands of the Blessèd" turns into the uncertain directive, "Bless you, son," then into the ironic vernacular of line two, "I never came upon a blessèd one," where the word means something like blasted or cursed, cursèd. What does this poem tell us about Frost's ultimate beliefs? Was he, finally, deep down, a religious man, a believer? Or was he sceptic and mocker? Neither, or both? When asked in an interview about the notion of poetry as communication Frost responded, "What do I want to communicate but what a *hell* of a good time I had writing it?" This is the answer communicated by "An Answer," and his career as a whole.

An appropriate place to end this presentation of Frost as a poet of mischievous play is a poem published when he was in his seventies, which came to figure for some readers as his ultimate statement about ultimate things—Frost's testament to posterity. It is titled, in a testamentary way, "Directive," and is spoken by a voice we may think of as that of an experienced guide who proposes to "us," to the reader, to a "you" out there somewhere, a journey "Back out of all this now too much for us." Under this guide's expert direction we are to travel a road back through time and place, through a nature whose "wearings" go back to "an enormous Glacier / That braced his feet against the Arctic Pole." The guide invites us to "make up a cheering song" about the life that once was and is now no more ("How someone's road home from work this once was"), but in imagination only:

> Back out of all this now too much for us,
> Back in a time made simple by the loss
> Of detail, burned, dissolved, and broken off
> Like graveyard marble sculpture in the weather,
> There is a house that is no more a house
> Upon a farm that is no more a farm

And in a town that is no more a town.
The road there, if you'll let a guide direct you
Who only has at heart your getting lost,
May seem as if it should have been a quarry—
Great monlolithic knees the former town
Long since gave up pretense of keeping covered.
And there's a story in a book about it:
Besides the wear of iron wagon wheels
The ledges show lines ruled southeast northwest,
The chisel work of an enormous Glacier
That braced his feet against the Arctic Pole.
You must not mind a certain coolness from him
Still said to haunt this side of Panther Mountain.
Nor need you mind the serial ordeal
Of being watched from forty cellar holes
As if by eye pairs out of forty firkins.
As for the woods' excitement over you
That sends light rustle rushes to their leaves,
Charge that to upstart inexperience.
Where were they all not twenty years ago?
They think too much of having shaded out
A few old pecker-fretted apple trees.
Make yourself up a cheering song of how
Someone's road home from work this once was,
Who may be just ahead of you on foot
Or creaking with a buggy load of grain.
The height of the adventure is the height
Of country where two village cultures faded
Into each other. Both of them are lost.

The point seems to be that we must become well-lost to the ordinary world, the "now too much for us" we are escaping, so as to reach "the height of the adventure," by attaining a place where two lost villages faded into one another. Here is the second half of the poem, the end or the beginning of something:

And if you're lost enough to find yourself
By now, pull in your ladder road behind you

And put a sign up CLOSED to all but me.
Then make yourself at home. The only field
Now left's no bigger than a harness gall.
First there's the children's house of make believe,
Some shattered dishes underneath a pine,
The playthings in the playhouse of the children.
Weep for what little things could make them glad.
Then for the house that is no more a house,
But only a belilaced cellar hole,
Now slowly closing like a dent in dough.
This was no playhouse but a house in earnest.
Your destination and your destiny's
A brook that was the water of the house,
Cold as a spring as yet so near its source,
Too lofty and original to rage.
(We know the valley streams that when aroused
Will leave their tatters hung on barb and thorn.)
I have kept hidden in the instep arch
Of an old cedar at the waterside
A broken drinking goblet like the Grail
Under a spell so the wrong ones can't find it,
So can't get saved, as Saint Mark says they mustn't.
(I stole the goblet from the children's playhouse.)
Here are your waters and your watering place.
Drink and be whole again beyond confusion.

More than once, in print and in the classroom, I have tried to give an account of these final lines and invariably have been dissatisfied with my effort. Could it be that this is not merely my readerly inadequacy, but that the lines themselves are highly resistant, even invulnerable, to an account of them that would fix with precision their exact manner and weight of utterance? As a guide, they only have at heart our getting lost, and I do get lost, well-lost, when, for example, I am instructed to pull in my ladder road and put a sign up "Closed, to all but me." To whom? Who is this person speaking? Is he a "person" or something else? Then I am directed to observe those shattered dishes, the children's playthings in their playhouse, and in a single parenthetical line am invited to "Weep for what little things could make them glad." How do I do that? Why and for whom am

I to weep? Then there is the house, no more a house, weirdly, unsettlingly described as "slowly closing like a dent in dough," and I am told that "This was no playhouse but a house in earnest." Have I not, by this time, lost my bearings sufficiently, so that distinguishing between true and imaginary, "real" house and playhouse, is impossible?

Then there is the concluding offer of the goblet, not the Holy Grail, but a "broken drinking goblet like the grail," under the guide's private spell so that the "wrong ones can't find it, / So can't get saved," unlike us, presumably, who are by now the "right" ones if we've followed directions. Then a parenthetical confidence, that "I stole the goblet from the children's playhouse": as with the earlier advice about how we should "weep" for the children, we wonder whether the parenthesis heightens the pathos or discounts it somewhat, ironically qualifying it. How are we to know, when the poem concludes with two final directives, not easy to take in: "Here are your waters and your watering place. / Drink and be whole again beyond confusion"? One of Frost's most famous definitions of poetry, and perhaps his best one, was that it is "a momentary stay against confusion." Is to be "whole again beyond confusion" something grander than anything poetry can provide? Is it a wholeness available only in fantasy, in make-believe, in—as it were—playhouse time? How are we to judge the character of this guide? An inspired prophet? A trickster/wizard/magician? A crafty teller of Tall Tales to innocent readers?

Here we come up against, for a final time, Frost's peculiar difficulty, his challenge to readers, one at least equal to though distinct from that of some other modern poets. I think particularly of Yeats, of T. S. Eliot, of Wallace Stevens, and the way their poems deal with salvationist, ultimate concerns. I think of the end of Eliot's last quartet, "Little Gidding":

> We shall not cease from exploration
> And the end of all our exploring
> Will be to arrive where we started
> And know the place for the first time.

The gravity of tone, the solemn, almost liturgical manner of presentation has no room for mischief. Nor do the final lines of Stevens's "Sunday Morning," which invite us to embrace the grandeur and beauty of nature, which endures even as we perish: "Deer walk upon our mountains, and the quail / Whistle about us their spontaneous cries." Eliot and Stevens, not to mention Yeats, offer their readers versions of paradise and do so unambiguously: this, finally, is the way things are, their poems assert.

With Frost the case is different, even in the late "Directive," where he may have felt the temptation to speak more grandly and unequivocally than was his wont. The habit of years, however, told against such unequivocality—the little refrain still ran in his head: "Nothing ever so sincere / That unless it's out of / Sheer mischief and a little queer, / It won't prove a bore to hear." For is there not something more than a little queer about the end of "Directive," with its solemn-faced, indeed priestly offering of the salvatory waters and the promise of wholeness to be gained from drinking them out of this special goblet? "Play's the thing. All virtue in As If," and here, perhaps, is an especially ingenious bit of play, as with a wave of his hand and the magical words "be whole again," our guide bestows salvation upon us. Perhaps this bestowal is akin, in its large, vague impressiveness, to the bestowal of political freedom right and left he spoke of in "The Figure a Poem Makes," or perhaps it is like his easy claim that "I Could Give All to Time" only followed by that significant "except." Is it not, perhaps, also a sadly ironic acceptance of the fact that poetry makes nothing happen—that it is *only* a way of happening? Yet those to whom "only" means not just "Oh, that's all?" but means also what is unique, singular, excellent, and rare (as in E. M. Forster's "Only connect")—those readers may accept the goblet and drink of the waters in the spirit with which they are offered, in the grip of Frost once more.

—Originally delivered as a talk at the Jones Library in Amherst, Massachusetts as part of the ALA's Frost Literary Landmark Celebration, October 21, 2009.

Part II: Eliot

T. S. Eliot: A Revaluation

FOR HIS GRADUATION EXERCISES at Smith Academy in St. Louis, Thomas Stearns Eliot composed and recited a poem of fourteen rhymed stanzas in which appropriately lofty and inspiring sentiments were uttered about youth, age, the road of life, sons departing the school to which they would return—changed but still loyal. Most grandly, about the modern world:

> Great duties call—the twentieth century
> More grandly dowered than those which came before,
> Summons—who knows what time may hold in store.

Five years or so later, having graduated from Harvard and having read some French poets, notably Jules Laforgue, Eliot was writing lines like the following:

> Wipe your hand across your mouth, and laugh;
> The worlds revolve like ancient women
> Gathering fuel in vacant lots.

From an expansive, large-souled looker into the future and what it held for mankind's great destiny, he had become an imagistic ironist, still making grand and mysterious gestures ("The worlds revolve like ancient women / Gathering fuel") but now in an unillusioned manner. It was the "modern" note, the note that initially strikes a reader picking up Eliot's poetry.

Or so it struck this reader when as an undergraduate I read to myself and read aloud the opening lines of "The Love Song of J. Alfred Prufrock": "Let us go then, you and I, / When the evening is spread out against the sky / Like a patient etherised upon a table." "You and I"—who are we and what sort of relationship is this? "When the evening is spread out against the sky"—when exactly does that occur and how can one tell? "Like a patient etherised upon a table"—how is the evening "like" an etherised patient and what does such a likeness portend? In fact, I didn't ask these questions, didn't pause and shake my head in dismay over them, but instead read on, either pretending the difficulties were only temporary and would be resolved, or electing to hear what the poet would say next, what new strange collocation of details would puzzle and excite. Sure enough, within a few lines occurs the infamous couplet—"In the room the women come and go, / Talking of Michelangelo"; utterly memorable, but what did it mean? That whatever sort of women they are in whatever sort of room, coming and going, they are, all of them, talking of Michelangelo. But what are they saying and what does it have to do with the "sawdust restaurants with oyster shells" just preceding, or the patient etherised upon a table with which we began? Is it an unworthy thing to do, to talk of Michelangelo—horribly superficial perhaps? But we are told nothing of how the talk is conducted, in what accents or at what level of perception; no more than with the sawdust restaurants and oyster shells are we given clear signals on how to regard the talking women. But we remember the couplet in which they appear.

Or so thinks one of the "we" who learned to read poetry during the age of Eliot, an age that began in the early 1920s when "Prufrock," *The Waste Land*, and a number of influential critical essays had given him a reputation as the significant poet-critic of his time. That significance only widened until his death in 1965, even though after *Four Quartets* (1943) he had ceased almost entirely to write poetry. To a college student in the 1950s, Eliot's name was magic, the source of profound wisdom about the chaos of modern civilization and the difficulties—the impossibilities—of successful communication between human beings. Even as we struggled in our lives, sometimes with pretty good results, to know and love some other people, Eliot's work was there as a great looming warning, a grim shaking of the head at the vanity and fragility of human wishes and aspirations. "Between the idea and the reality…Falls the shadow," he told us in "The Hollow Men," and the words reverberated. And while his poetry was revered as a source of disenchanted wisdom about life, his critical and historical pronouncements in *The Sacred Wood* and *Selected Essays,* his valuations and comparisons of writers past and present, were deployed in countless undergraduate and graduate English papers. Notions of tradition, or the dissociated sensibility that had overtaken English poetry in the seventeenth century, or the "objective correlative" that Shakespeare in *Hamlet* was unable to discover—these Eliotic formulations were invoked by way of giving authority to whatever argument we were attempting to make. Less important to us were the later attempts at social and religious polemic—the books about culture (*Notes towards the Definition of Culture*) and religion (*The Idea of a Christian Society*) where Eliot spelled out, with maximum qualification and circumspection, his exclusionary notions of life in a world he said was "worm-eaten with liberalism." Nor, despite the popular success of *The Cocktail Party*, did the plays command our lively attention. It was the small body of poems and a selection of essays from a much wider spread of prose writings that constituted his powerful appeal.

The question is whether the appeal is still felt by teachers and students in the last decade of this century. (I am assuming there does not exist a younger nonacademic reading public for Eliot's writings.) His death coincided with a time when American poets were becoming more responsive to William Carlos Williams's experiments in the American grain, than to the "classical" values Eliot espoused and the, by then, too-familiar poems that had made his reputation. And as Wallace Stevens's body of work became increasingly influential, as—under the critical authority of Harold Bloom and Helen Vendler—Stevens's status as our most important poet was asserted, Eliot's reputation enjoyed no comparable enriching. In fact there was a perceptible decline in the capacity of his poetry to make a difference in people's lives. His centennial was celebrated in 1988, and the novelist Cynthia Ozick, writing in *The New Yorker* the following year, put the matter in a way that, though excessive and needlessly melodramatic, is accurate in its estimation of how the winds have been blowing:

> In the early seventies, it was still possible to uncover, here and there, a tenacious English Department offering a vestigial graduate seminar given over to the study of Eliot. But by the close of the eighties only "The Love Song of J. Alfred Prufrock" appears to have survived the indifference of the schools—as two or three pages in the anthologies, a fleeting assignment for high-school seniors and college freshmen. "Prufrock," and "Prufrock" alone, is what the latest generations know (barely know); not "The Hollow Men," not "La Figlia che Piange," not "Ash-Wednesday"—not even "The Waste Land." Never "Four

> Quartets." And the mammoth prophetic presence of T. S. Eliot himself—that immortal, sovereign rock—the latest generation do not know at all. (In *Art and Folly,* 1993)

Having herself been one of the generation that eagerly discovered Eliot, Ozick feels saddened by the loss; but she is also unhappy at the reactionary nature of Eliot's political and social attitudes, and she ends her essay by informing us solemnly that it is our "unsparing obligation to dismiss the reactionary Eliot," even as we will probably miss forever "the golden cape of our youth, the power and prestige of high art."

Ozick's conclusion is put forth in a more self-important tone than Eliot used about himself (he once told an audience that since he had a reputation for "affecting pedantic precision" he should not like to lose it). But even more misguided is her attempt to make Eliot less disagreeable to the liberal conscience by telling us we must "dismiss" his reactionary opinions. Surely the business of a good reader consists in something other than condemning qualities in a writer that don't square with certifiably correct morals and politics. If we are uneasy about some or all of Eliot's references to Jews—about, say, his pronouncement in *After Strange Gods* (1934) that since a traditional society needs to be homogeneous, "reasons of race and religion combine to make any large number of free-thinking Jews undesirable"—we should analyze and judge the remark by putting it in relation to comparable assertions and ideas in Eliot's prose and verse. Dismissing it is no more called for than embracing it, and the same may be said of controversial and disturbing moments in the writings of (among others) Milton, Tolstoy, and D. H. Lawrence. It may even be the case that a great writer's power is commensurate with his power to offend.

But I am less interested in quarreling with Ozick than in qualifying her assumption that "the latest generation" doesn't at all know Eliot's poetry. Without asking which poet it is the latest generation knows *well,* it can be said that over the years and right up through a just-completed semester, numbers of students have read Eliot with me in courses called Modern Poetry, Modern British Poetry, and Modern American Poetry, and that these students have found him no less difficult nor less interesting than they find Yeats or Stevens, Robert Lowell, or Elizabeth Bishop. Ozick's reading of the world-cultural poetry barometer that registers who's high and who's low must be corrected by the insistence that at least at one college—and I suspect at many more—Eliot is alive and well, his poems, and to some extent his criticism, seriously and satisfyingly engaged with by members of the latest generation.

My attempt in the following pages is to speak not as an impartial, objective observer of the poetry scene, as this century nears its termination, but rather as a critic and teacher who values and is moved by Eliot's work as a whole and who finds parts of it to be of supreme literary quality. While I don't mean to tag certain poems as exclusively the ones in which that quality can be found, I shall mainly focus on three of them from different stages in Eliot's career—"The Love Song of J. Alfred Prufrock," *The Waste Land,* and *Four Quartets*—and on the criticism he wrote in the years roughly from 1917 to 1922.

"Prufrock," with the help of Ezra Pound, was first published in *Poetry* in 1915, but it was written in 1910-11, the year Eliot spent abroad, mainly in Paris. It is often pointed out that, as with "Portrait of a Lady," written during the same period, its milieu is Boston. Yet "Prufrock" is the sort of poem that refuses to be located in one topographical cityscape or another, and in fact Eliot's biographer, Peter Ackroyd, terms the "yellow fog" in the poem a St. Louis one. Its landscape is for want of a better word psychological, and in the poem's moment of greatest feeling its protagonist wonders if "it would have been worth it, after all" to have made some large annunciation to the woman, the "she" who lolls and entertains him amidst marmalade and cups of tea. "After" (a key reiterated word in the poem) these and many other pieces of worldly furniture are enumerated, Prufrock suddenly exclaims

> It is impossible to say just what I mean!
> But as if a magic lantern threw the nerves in patterns on a screen:

To say "just" what you mean would be presumably to move beyond the excitements and inadequacies of metaphor into the realm of truth where words mean precisely what they say—a world exactly contrary to the poetic one Eliot creates.

It is as if we were to look at a series of nerve patterns and as if somehow these constituted not a composite visual shape but a musical performance, indeed a love song. "Prufrock" has no plot, no narrative with a beginning, middle, and end; its characters aren't characters but nervous ghosts who mysteriously appear and disappear as elusively as the yellow fog that slides along its street. In the course of various formulations, or half-formulations, the "I" who tells us he has "known" just about everything decides that he doesn't dare disturb the universe, that he shouldn't "presume" to begin to do anything, that probably he "should have been a pair of ragged claws," that he is not a prophet (even if he's seen his own slightly balding head brought in on a platter), that he really can't manage to pass as either a Lazarus or a Hamlet figure, that he's "almost" (but not quite?) ridiculous, almost (capitalized) "the Fool." Finally, that the mermaids won't sing to him whether he eats a peach and wears white flannel trousers or whether he doesn't. What I'm suggesting by this cavalier assembling of the "facts" about J. Alfred Prufrock is that there aren't any facts, that the "content" of the poem is really a hoax—or rather an occasion for a voice to make haunting music out of them.

To hear that music one must read the poem aloud to a friend, to a class of students, or declaim it silently to the listener within. I can think of no single piece of writing more wholly dependent for its effect on the "performance" that R. P. Blackmur once said was the only way to know literature "afresh"—"in reading and seeing and hearing what is actually in it at this place and this time." For example, one of the important ways Eliot exercises a hold on our ears is to make sequences out of repetitions that don't quite repeat, as in the three quietly lengthening verse paragraphs (from six lines to seven to eight) in the middle of the poem beginning with "For I have known them all already, known them all." Recall the closing questions in each unit: "So how should I presume?..."And how should I presume?"; "And how should I begin?" (that last one preceded by "And should I then presume?"). Or recall the echoing "And would it have been worth it after all?..."Would it have been worth while," and the co-presence, but in varying patterns, of other echoes echoing: "I am Lazarus, come from the dead, / Come back to tell you all, I shall tell you all"; "That is not what I meant at all. / That is not it, at all." What in a reading aloud is heard as ingeniously melodic, subtly compelling, refuses to be carried over into the sentences of a quoting critic at his typewriter.

A contemporary English critic, Barbara Everett, once wrote that the voice in "Prufrock" (it makes more sense to say *in* "Prufrock" the poem rather than of Prufrock the character) manages to hold us through its spellbinder's charm. This spell, though, is very much an aural one, depending less upon any sense or point about life that is made—beyond the general declaration of weary futility, of having come too late and missed out on everything—but rather on the seductive drawn-out repetitions, the music of consonantal and vowel echoings. Indeed the theme of weary futility is contradicted by the vitality of the verbal, aural performance. An example from the first of two tercets about the mermaids which end the poem:

> I have seen them riding seaward on the waves
> Combing the white hair of the waves blown back
> When the wind blows the water white and black.

This is really not so much a vision as it is something heard, from "seen" to "seaward," from "waves" to "white" to "waves" to "when" to "wind" to "water" to "white"; from "blown back" to "blows…black"—an auditory tour de force surely. For all Eliot's explicitly acknowledged debt in "Prufrock" and the other early poems to Laforgue ("My early vers libre, of course, was started under the endeavor to practice the same form as Laforgue. This meant merely rhyming lines of irregular length, with the rhymes coming in irregular places"), it is the English Tennyson of "The Lotus Eaters" these lines recall:

> …but evermore
> Most weary seemed the sea, weary the oar,
> Weary the wandering fields of barren foam.

And rather than asking exactly what the mermaids are doing out there (aside from "combing"), we experience the doing as an effect registered memorably by someone who has "lingered in the chambers of the sea," as Eliot did in the echo chambers of this poem. The astonishing thing about "Prufrock" is of course how it has continued to speak to the most unlikely readers. Or maybe there is no such thing as an unlikely reader: writing about teaching literature in a community college, Clara Clairborne Park remembers one of her students telling her "I must have read that poem fifty times…I *am* J. Alfred Prufrock." Such is the power of "a piece of rhythmical grumbling"—Eliot's own phrase about *The Waste Land,* but even more applicable to "Prufrock"—to cast a spell over the responsive ear.

Prufrock and Other Observations was published in 1917. Some of the other observations include, most significantly, "Portrait of a Lady"—probably completed before "Prufrock"—and "La Figlia che Piange." (All three poems involve the central presence of a woman.) "Portrait" is clever and adept at striking off the weary cadences of the lady ("So intimate, this Chopin, that I think his soul / Should be resurrected only among friends") and in opposing them with the furtive, guilty, self-lacerating consciousness of the speaker, an Eliot-like young man who nervously resists being drawn into her orbit. Yet as a poem it now seems less stirring, more dated than "Prufrock." Pound called the latter poem, rather inaccurately, a "portrait satire on futility," but the label might be more justly applied to "Portrait of a Lady" in its probing of the young man's paralyzed responses: "Not knowing what to feel or if I understand / Or whether wise or foolish, tardy or too soon..." The line breaks off in an ellipsis, and there is a sense in which the poem does so as well, ending upon two unanswered questions.

A more affecting poem, and rather more mysterious than "Portrait" both in its impulse and its outcome, is the beautiful "La Figlia che Piange." As with "Portrait" and "Prufrock," romantic materials are disguised or displaced by a modernist rearrangement of situation, one not clearly set forth but subjected to fluid definition and redefinition. The opening stanza features an unnamed, unspecified young woman alluded to by the epigraph from the *Aeneid, "O quam te memorem virgo."* In Virgil, Aeneas asks Venus, disguised as an ordinary girl, how he should address her. In Eliot's poem the woman is told to "Stand," to "Lean," to "Weave, weave the sunlight in your hair," to "Clasp your flowers to you with a pained surprise,"—as if she were an actress being coached into presenting the most effective romantic posture.

But the second stanza unsettles this scenario by introducing an "I" who tells how he "would have" had the grieving maiden stand, and how he "would have had" her lover take leave of her. Halfway through the stanza he seems to speak as a lover rather than a detached choreographer, when he says that "I should find...Some way we both should understand." This doubling of the speaker may be a way of insinuating into "La Figlia" the kinds of hesitations and confusions present, in both "Prufrock" and "Portrait," toward the attractive woman who makes a claim on the protagonist that is both desired and feared. Finally, in stanza three, the "I" tells us that his imagination has been compelled by the woman, "Many days and many hours," and that he wonders "how they should have been together!"—presumably if he had not interfered with *their* scene. Yet by this point in the poem, as the speaker wonders and opines that "I should have lost a gesture and a pose," we must be lost as well, for Eliot has not provided us with any stabilized dramatic situation nor drawn out any clear meaning or implication from the scene. "La Figlia" looks forward to Eliot's major work in that its narrative consciousness is no more or less elusive than it will be in *The Waste Land.* Part of that elusiveness, as well as attractiveness, has to do with the poem's aural richness, its unexpectedly occurring rhymes, its incantatory hieratic repetitions. For all the distance there is between "La Figlia che Piange" and an early poem of Wallace Stevens's like "Peter Quince at the Clavier," or an early poem of Robert Frost's like "October," they can be grouped under the slogan Frost formulated about reading when, in a letter of 1914, he laid it down that "*The ear does it.* The ear is the only true writer and the only true reader." It was a principle that Eliot's poems would consistently embody, right down to the charming one he wrote to Walter de la Mare in 1948—which ended by praising de la Mare for "the delicate, invisible web you wove— / The inexplicable mystery of sound."

In "The Frontiers of Criticism," Eliot's 1956 lecture delivered to fourteen thousand people gathered in the gymnasium at the University of Minnesota, he said, in a typically self-deprecatory disclaimer, "I fail to see any critical movement which can be said to derive from myself." Perhaps the disclaimer is not so much self-deprecatory as a proud fending off of those who come after Eliot the true original: how could you think (we might conceive him saying) that *I* can be held responsible for this or that critical procedure or movement? In fact, for all the academic recycling of Eliotic terms that occurred in the 1940s and 1950s, Eliot's critical convictions and principles do not take kindly to being passed along. We may speak of some critic as a Poundian or Leavisite or a follower of Yvor Winters (Wintersian?) but never as an Eliotian, or even a follower of Eliot. This has to do with the absence in Eliot of a systematic critical method ("the only method is to be very intelligent," he said in his preface to *The Sacred Wood*) or a prescribed routine for conducting literary analysis that we find, to one degree or another, in Pound and Leavis and Winters. As for Eliot's much-used terms which have had such a strong, even notorious, life, they have by now all been thoroughly and adversely criticized; no critic today would use "dissociation of sensibility" or "objective correlative" without the most elaborate qualification.

Still, Eliot remains the major poet-critic of our century, taking a rightful place in the line from Ben Jonson to Dryden, Samuel Johnson, Coleridge, and Matthew Arnold. The last named was felt by Eliot as his immediate predecessor whose work, while it deserved much respect, had also to be firmly placed in perspective. So in introducing his first volume of criticism,

The Sacred Wood, Eliot saluted Arnold's plea for a criticism that would complement and make more self-aware the work of poets. He agrees with Arnold that this work had not been sufficiently done for the Romantic poets, nor, by implication, for those who were currently writing in English one hundred years later. But he wishes also that Arnold had been more of a practical critic; that he had, in Eliot's examples, taken it upon himself to compare Thackeray with Flaubert, or analyzed Dickens and compared him with George Eliot and Stendhal. Instead Arnold spent too much of his time "attacking the uncritical" and concerned himself more with matters of culture, society, and religion than with literary ones. About which Eliot remarks, adducing his contemporaries H. G. Wells and G. K. Chesterton, "The temptation, to any man who is interested in ideas and primarily in literature, is to put literature into the corner until he has cleaned up the whole country first." So his judgment was that Arnold was more a "propagandist for criticism" than a critic.

Eliot didn't begin by attempting to clean up the whole country; in fact it was not until after his assuming editorship of *The Criterion* in 1922—and especially after his conversion to Anglo-Catholicism in 1927—that his interest shifted from the comparison and analysis of individual writers and literary works to (in words from his preface to the second, 1928, edition of *The Sacred Wood*) "the relation of poetry to the spiritual and social life of its time and of other times." His most productive, most brilliant years as a "pure" critic of literature were the ones in which his creative work flowered—from the publication of *Prufrock and Other Observations* in 1917 to *The Waste Land* in 1922. After that, although he wrote a number of fine essays about particular writers (perhaps most notably about Dante, Samuel Johnson, Byron, Tennyson, and Yeats), those for which he is most strongly remembered had their birth within a fairly small range of years. (A list of them would include essays on Marlowe, Jonson, *Hamlet,* Philip Massinger, the Metaphysicals, Marvell, Dryden, Blake, and Swinburne.)

Often in the briefest of compasses, Eliot can make a brilliant redirection of our sense of a writer. For example, the Swinburne essay is only six pages long but they are pages in which, as he says approvingly about Aristotle in "The Perfect Critic," Eliot is "swiftly operating the analysis of sensation to the point of principle and definition." In a series of lightning-like comparisons of lines from Swinburne's verse with lines from Thomas Campion, Shakespeare, and Shelley, he establishes his point about how Swinburne's genius was to identify meaning and sound, to present "emotion" that is "never particular, never in direct line of vision, never focussed"—emotion reinforced by "expansion." A moment from these comparisons may suggest Eliot's typical operation in his essays and reviews. He is about to compare Swinburne with Shakespeare, then with Wordsworth:

> It is, in fact, the word that gives him the thrill, not the object. When you take to pieces any verse of Swinburne, you find always that the object was not there—only the word. Compare
>
> Snowdrops that plead for pardon
> And pine for fright
>
> with the daffodils that come before the swallow dares. The snow-drop of Swinburne disappears, the daffodil of Shakespeare remains. The swallow of Shakespeare remains in the verse of *Macbeth;* the bird of Wordsworth
>
> Breaking the silence of the seas
>
> remains; the swallow of "Itylus" disappears.

This is dazzling, virtually sleight-of-hand. Fully to register these comparisons a reader would have to remember Swinburne's "Before the Mirror" (whence the snowdrops), then lines from Act 4 of *The Winter's Tale* about the daffodils, then think of the "temple-haunting martlet" (the "swallow" in *Macbeth* which Duncan invokes as he prepares to enter Macbeth's castle), then Wordsworth's nightingale in "The Solitary Reaper," and finally the evanescence of Swinburne's swallow ("Swallow, my sister, O sister swallow"). Whether readers are able or likely to do all this even as they ponder the convincingness of Eliot's comparisons is wholly doubtful. More likely we may just nod agreement, impressed by the breezy authority with which the critic proceeds to his conclusion that in Swinburne's verse "the meaning is merely the hallucination of meaning, because language, uprooted, has adapted itself to an independent life of atmospheric nourishment."

Eliot's practical criticism, as instanced in this particularly telescoped example of it, is seldom or never a matter of patient analysis of a poem, but of provocative assertion and invitations to compare one poem or series of lines with another. It is invigorating to read him partly because the twists of his discourse (not typically a soberly conducted "argument") have the surprise and originality of poetry itself. He likes to strew difficulties in the paths of his readers and himself—anything to make things other than cut and dried. In the following sentences from a never-reprinted *Athenaeum* review of 1919, "The Education of Taste," he sets out the difficulties that lie in the way of the practicing critic who must make decisions about how to operate:

> To communicate impressions is difficult; to communicate a coordinated system of impressions is more difficult; to theorize demands vast ingenuity, and to avoid theorizing requires vast honesty. Also there is the generality, which is usually a substitute for both impression and theory.

The neat movement here from theorizing to the avoidance of theorizing, then the capping reference to "generality" in which earlier terms like impression and honesty are brought back, has the force of true wit, Oscar Wilde crossed by Matthew Arnold.

Eliot is especially vigilant toward well-known literary terms a naive, insufficiently disillusioned poet or critic might rely on—terms like "technique." In prefacing the second edition of *The Sacred Wood* he takes us around the mulberry bush by beginning with a definition of poetry that—like Swift's definition of good prose as "proper words in proper places"—says everything and not much of anything in particular. Poetry, he writes, consists of "excellent words in excellent arrangement and excellent metre." But what more can be said?

> That is what is called the technique of verse. But we observe that we cannot define even the technique of verse; we cannot say at what point "technique" begins or where it ends; and if we add to it a "technique of feeling," that glib phrase will carry us only a little farther. We can only say that a poem, in some sense, has its own life.

In other words there is no shortcut, indeed no road through to certainty in literary matters. We can only say that "in some sense" a poem has its own life; or we can say, in Eliot's echo of Bishop Butler, that in considering poetry "we must consider it primarily as poetry and not another thing." Or, in that same playful preface to *The Sacred Wood,* we may agree that poetry is "a superior amusement." Is that a sufficient definition? Not at all:

> I do not mean an amusement for superior people. I call it an amusement, an amusement *pour distraire les honnêtes gens,* not because that is a true definition, but because if you call it anything else you are likely to call it something still more false. If we think of the nature of amusement, then poetry is not amusing; but if we think of anything else that poetry may seem to be, we are led into far greater difficulties.

Such sidestepping and ducking have their perils, and in his later prose Eliot would succumb to them, as in the often lugubrious fussings of *Notes towards the Definition of Culture.* But they also tease and refresh our minds in salutary ways.

Eliot performed similar services with regard to words like tradition, rhetoric, satire—perhaps most importantly to "wit," the promotion of which quality into a major one for great poetry may be his most forceful contribution to literary criticism. In "Andrew Marvell" (1921) he made a memorable attempt to define, even as he deprecated the possibility of clearly defining it, the quality of wit that distinguished Marvell's work and that, over the course of subsequent centuries, had been nearly absent from English poetry. Eliot's account claims that the seventeenth century took the "high" style developed in Marlowe and Jonson and separated it into qualities of wit and magniloquence. While allowing that the terms are fluid, and that the style of Marvell, Cowley, Milton, and others often showed these qualities blended, he attempts to distinguish Caroline wit from what followed it:

> The wit of the Caroline poets is not the wit of Shakespeare, and it is not the wit of Dryden, the great master of contempt, or of Pope, the great master of hatred, or of Swift, the great master of disgust. What is meant is some quality which is common to the songs in *Comus* and Cowley's Anacreontics and Marvell's Horatian Ode. It is more than a technical accomplishment, or the vocabulary and syntax of an epoch; it is, what we have designated tentatively as wit, a tough reasonableness beneath the slight lyric grace. You cannot find it in Shelley or Keats or Wordsworth; you cannot find more than an echo of it in Landor, still less in Tennyson or Browning; and among contemporaries Mr. Yeats is an Irishman and Mr. Hardy is a modern Englishman—

> that is to say, Mr. Hardy is without it and Mr. Yeats is outside of the tradition altogether.

It can be found, he goes on to add, in Laforgue and Gautier, two poets Eliot had managed to make use of in his own work during the decade that had just concluded itself.

Such an account is itself a specimen of wit, right down to the lyric grace of naming those three great masters of contempt, hatred, and disgust, and the tough reasonableness—or so it pretends to be—of excluding both Hardy and Yeats from any consideration in these terms. Like most exciting passages in Eliot's criticism, we read and silently correct its overstatements: we *can* find wit in some of Keats, even in Shelley occasionally; we know that the dismissal of Yeats and Hardy is too sweeping, unfair. But as Eliot's friend Wyndham Lewis reminds us, satire is always unfair, and Eliot's early criticism is never far from a satiric—or at least a mischievously subversive—perspective on things. "Someone said: 'The dead writers are remote from us because we *know* so much more than they did.' Precisely, and they are that which we know." These sentences from "Tradition and the Individual Talent" might be turned upon Eliot's own criticism insofar as its formulations have entered the bloodstream of later generations of readers who were helped to become critics by having to move beyond the Eliot criticism that they knew.

I have been suggesting that the challenge and pleasure of reading Eliot's essays and reviews lie somewhere else than in extracting doctrines or key terms from them. Nor should we take his comparings of writers and passages as the basis for a systematic account of English literature. At least two of his successors, F. R. Leavis in *Revaluation* (1936) and Cleanth Brooks in *Modern Poetry and the Tradition* (1939), wrote lively books that took Eliot's inadequate responses to nineteenth-century English poetry as a warrant for their ignoring, or largely demeaning, the work of Romantic and Victorian poets, even as Leavis and Brooks exalted the Metaphysicals and admired Eliot for the way his poems had reestablished connection with seventeenth-century wit.

In the introduction to a selection from Eliot's prose, Frank Kermode usefully quotes a remark from a 1935 letter to Stephen Spender: "You don't," said Eliot, "really criticize any author to whom you have never surrendered yourself.... Even just the bewildering minute counts; you have to give yourself up, and then recover yourself, and the third moment is having something to say, before you have wholly forgotten both surrender and recovery." Kermode points out that this insistence on the primacy of "surrender" to a poet, a poem, a line (the "bewildering minute" referred to here is Eliot's allusion to lines from Tourneur's *The Revenger's Tragedy*), is the opposite of constructing a system, then bringing it to bear on a particular object—"reading to prove one's own point," Kermode calls it. Such an emphasis on surrender perhaps accounts for the scorn Eliot felt for Matthew Arnold's insistence that poetry was a "criticism of life." This was a way of speaking, Eliot said scornfully, "than which no phrase can sound more frigid to anyone who has felt the full surprise and elevation of a new experience of poetry." The surprise and elevation demanded nothing less than surrender, then demanded—in the subsequent "recovery"—a correspondingly fresh and unordinary way of "having something to say." It was here that Eliot's supreme originality as reader and writer made itself felt.

With the publication of the first volume of Eliot's letters, reaching to the end of 1922, we have a rich particular sense of what we knew only in outline before: that his marriage to Vivien Haigh-Wood in 1915 became progressively more painful and that both his health and hers worsened. In his case a "breakdown" occurred in 1921 when he took rest cures first in Margate, then in Lausanne, Switzerland, even as he was finishing *The Waste Land.* Epistolary Eliot was able at times to take a sardonically humorous perspective on his problems, saying that he felt himself to be "living in one of Dostoyevsky's novels, you see, not in one of Jane Austen's," or assuring a correspondent that his health wasn't all that bad: "My teeth are falling to pieces, I have to wear spectacles to read, and from time to time I am contorted with rheumatism—otherwise I am pretty well." Meanwhile Vivien was writing his mother about the deplorable condition of "Tom's" wardrobe ("his old underwear is still thick and in *fair* condition, but it needs *incessant darning.* Darning alone takes me hours out of the week"), especially his lack of pyjamas: "He is still worse provided with pyjamas than anything.... He is very rough with his pyjamas, and shirts—tears them unmercifully."

It is of interest then to contemplate this hapless creature (as Eliot and his wife present him to others) carrying out brilliantly various public roles in the years 1917-1921: working efficiently in the colonial and foreign department of Lloyds Bank, teaching night school and extension courses in English literature, turning out enormous amounts of journalism for the *Egoist* and *Athenaeum,* and (in his spare time, one might say) assembling a second volume of verse, *Poems 1920,* consisting of "Gerontion" and a number of poems in quatrains. He praised Wyndham Lewis's *Tarr* when it appeared in 1918 for the "active unpleasantness" of its style, and something of that style permeates the quatrain poems, not only in their references in "Burbank with a Baedeker..." to "the Jew" and to Bleistein himself—"Chicago, Semite, Viennese"—but in the milieus of the two Sweeney poems ("The epileptic on the bed / Waiting until the shriek subsides") and the "rank" feline smell distilled by Grishkin in "Whispers of Immortality." The best of these poems may be the most humorous one, "The Hippopotamus," about how the church inevitably capitulates to worldly considerations while the hippo ascends to heaven:

> He shall be washed as white as snow,
> By all the martyr'd virgins kist,
> While the True Church remains below
> Wrapt in the old miasmal mist.

By contrast "A Cooking Egg," one of the most impenetrable of them, has the dubious distinction of having generated a seemingly endless debate in the pages of a learned journal on such matters as the identity of a character named Pipit (it was never satisfactorily explained). The quatrain poems share the quality of being highly memorizable, and they possess arresting individual lines. But they don't add up to a body of work we return to frequently. "In my experience everyone except the fools seem to be warped and stunted," wrote Eliot in 1919; in the quatrain poems he made "fools" like Sweeney or Grishkin or Bleistein the subject of scrupulous caricatural attention. These and their counterparts would perform in *The Waste Land* and in the uncompleted "Sweeney Agonistes" from the late 1920s. But a more important role was reserved for the "warped and stunted," the Gerontion- or Tiresias-like protagonist who has foresuffered all, whose existence is characterized by aridity and deliquescence, and whose head is filled with marvelous lines and cadences from earlier poets.

"Gerontion" is Eliot's bleakest, chilliest, most inaccessible poem, virtually "unreadable" by the procedures we use to read more conventional works. It is Eliot at his most complicatedly and concentratedly allusive, as well as his most elusive. What are we to make of a monologue (if it is that) which in seeming to draw itself together near the end proffers the following sentiment—"I would meet you upon this honestly"—in which there is no credible "I," in which the "you" doesn't exist, and in which the adverb "honestly" can't be credited as accurately modifying any credible verb? The referential currency of such a line is about equal to that possessed by the figures—no more than names, really—who momentarily surface in the poem, then just as mysteriously disappear, as Hakagawa bows among the Titians, as Madame de Tornquist shifts the candles, and as Fräulein von Kulp turns in the hall, one hand on the door. Gerontion, whoever "he" may be, puts it thus: "Vacant shuttles weave the wind." The weaving and unweaving of verbal patterns in Eliot's most relentlessly verbal poem has the effect, so it seems to this reader, of rendering the large windy portents about Christianity and history less rather than more intelligible. As always in Eliot, there are wonderfully memorable lines, especially those from the section about history that begins "After such knowledge, what forgiveness?" But they don't contribute to a meditation that sustains itself in moral content as well as in rhetorical flourish. "Whenever a character in Shakespeare makes a direct appeal to us," Eliot wrote in " 'Rhetoric' and Poetic Drama," "we are either the victims of our own sentiment, or we are in the presence of a vicious rhetoric." That he was aware of this assertion in relation to "Gerontion" or that he set out to have the poem's speaker expose himself as fraudulent, is conceivable, yet doubtful. We should remember that he seriously considered using the poem as prologue to *The Waste Land,* desisting only when Pound told him he mustn't.

I should prefer to think that the harassed Eliot—caught in a painful marriage, overworked, plagued by bad teeth and eyesight, contorted by rheumatism, pyjamas falling to pieces, living in, as it were, a novel by Dostoyevsky—cheered himself up by seeing himself in the dramatic light of a poem, as he said Othello was really cheering himself up in his speech before he stabs himself:

> He is endeavouring to escape reality, he has ceased to think about Desdemona, and he is thinking about himself.... Othello succeeds in turning himself into a pathetic figure, by adopting an *aesthetic* rather than a moral attitude, dramatizing himself against his environment. He takes in the spectator, but the human motive is primarily to take in himself.

The question is perhaps whether either Gerontion or "Gerontion" succeeds in taking *us* in, without the five acts of tortuous dramatic development Shakespeare subjects Othello to and that makes his final end so moving. My answer is that, brilliant as the poem is, it lacks the humor and humanity of "Prufrock." And that for all its evocation of aridity, of "Thoughts of a dry brain in a dry season," it fails to take us in, to take hold of us the way Eliot was about to do in *The Waste Land.*

But how does *The Waste Land* "take hold"? Not so many years ago it seemed important to try to loosen the poem from the interpretive structures critics had attached to it; there was so much "scaffolding"—to use Cleanth Brooks's word about what his own influential essay on the poem provided—that it was all but impossible to see the object the scaffolding surrounded. Now, much of that surrounding material has fallen away, or has become so inert that it's simply no longer of interest. Few critics these days deal with the poem by applying the Fisher King legend, Jessie Weston's *From Ritual to Romance,* or Frazer's *The Golden Bough.* It was of course Eliot himself, in his introductory note, who attached these books and legends to the poem; but the notes to *The Waste Land* are a kind of playful poetry themselves. It is Eliot's superior amusement, for example, to remind us that the hermit-thrush in "What the Thunder Said" is "*Turdus aonalaschkae pallasii,*" that he's heard it in Quebec Province, and that "Its 'water-dripping song' is justly celebrated." Eliot's notes, if not taken too seriously, are harmless and sometimes amusing. But other sorts of notes or glosses adhering to the poem, whether they exist in, say, *The Norton Anthology of Modern Poetry,* or in the mind of an individual reader, can be more insidious, more inhibiting to creative, responsive reading. I am thinking of a gloss such as Norton gives to the Baudelaire allusion at the end of part I, "The Burial of the Dead": "*You: hypocrite lecteur!—mon semblable,—mon frère!*" After identifying the source, the editor says that "with this line Baudelaire and Eliot assault the reader and draw him accusingly into the same plight as themselves." The problem with this assertion is, of course, that after reading the footnote no sensible reader is going to feel the least bit assaulted. It's just one more allusion to store untroubled in the mind and then read on. Or consider the moment when the narrator, regarding the morning crowd flowing over London Bridge, suddenly recognizes someone named Stetson and addresses him as "You who were with me in the ships at Mylae!" The anthology note identifies Mylae as a battle in the first Punic War between Rome and Carthage, then says: "It merges with the First World War, in which the speaker and Stetson fought; both wars are seen as pointless and futile." This is an example of an editorial anxiety to fill in the blanks that the poem so carefully does *not* fill in: we are told neither that these figures fought in the First World War, nor that the war was pointless. And if—as Eliot's own note claims—all the poem's "characters" merge into Tiresias, it's hard to see how, being blind, he could have fought in any war.

Samuel Johnson's wisdom about notes should be remembered, when in his editorial preface to Shakespeare he wrote "Particular passages are cleared by notes, but the general effect of the work is weakened. The mind is refrigerated by interruption; the thoughts are diverted from the principal subject. . . ." A poem such as *The Waste Land,* just as much as a Shakespeare play, suffers when the reading of it is constantly interrupted by a recurrence to notes or their equivalent. What we need to work at instead is keeping the poem moving, paying attention to the sequence; above all, listening to the voices—for it is voices in motion that make up the poem's substance. Again, Johnson's advice to the reader of Shakespeare is wholly appropriate to reading Eliot: "Let him read on through brightness and obscurity, through integrity and corruption; let him preserve his comprehension of the dialogue and his interest in the fable. And when the pleasures of novelty have ceased, let him attempt exactness, and read the commentators."

Another way of putting it is Wyndham Lewis's way when, decades ago, he said about Joyce's *Ulysses,* recently published, that "No one who looks *at* it will ever want to look *behind* it." Lewis was paying grudging tribute to the incredibly rich surface Joyce's book presents to the reader. And Eliot himself in his essay of 1923, "*Ulysses:* Order and Myth," said that Joyce had given him "all the surprise, delight, and terror that I can require." We may presume that these qualities emanated from looking at and listening to the surface of *Ulysses,* rather than from probing the depths of Joyce's thought or discovering deep meanings supposedly hidden in his book. During the time he wrote *The Waste Land,* Eliot was preoccupied with what he called, in his 1919 essay on Ben Jonson, "poetry of the surface." Many of the things he admired in Jonson's dramatic art he named in terms that could equally well apply to the art of *The Waste Land:* "simplified characters," a "flat distortion" in the drawing, "an art of caricature," "a brutality, a lack of sentiment, a polished surface, a handling of large bold designs in brilliant colours"—one could go on. "We cannot call a man's work superficial when it is the creation of a world; a man cannot be accused of dealing superficially with the world which he himself has created; the superficies *is* the world," wrote Eliot, summing it all up by calling Jonson's drama "a titanic show." The phrase would not be amiss as a collective name for the different "shows" of which *The Waste Land* is composed, whether as conducted at Madame Sosostris's or on London Bridge, or round behind the gashouse, or in the typist's flat.

The challenge lies in saying something relevant and appropriate to these surfaces without saying too much, without foisting a burden of "meaning" on the poem (as do explanatory footnotes, often) that makes it merely portentous. Consider the marvelous and scary utterances of the "neurasthenic" woman, as she is sometimes referred to, in the first section of part 2, "A Game of Chess." "Under the brush, her hair / Spread out in fiery points / Glowed into words, then would be savagely still," as she implores the faceless narrator to "Speak to me," to "Think." Vivien Eliot, who must have been in her husband's mind when he wrote these lines, was reduced to a single marginal response to those words as they appeared in *The Waste Land* manuscript—"Wonderful!" There was no more that needed to be said, and a similar enthusiastic exclamation might be made to the woman in the pub (in the second half of "A Game of Chess") as she runs on about what she told Lil about how to treat her husband Albert, who has been in the army and wants a good time: "And if you don't give it him, there's other will, I said. / Oh is there, she said. Something o' that, I said." Neither of these women should be understood as representing or embodying some large important symbolic value—some truth about modern civilization. For if we insist on making the characters representative of something "more," something deeper, we run the risk of missing out on surface intensities, memorable accents and associations—what Lil's friend and critic, referring to the hot gammon Lil and Albert served her, calls "the beauty of it hot." Shakespeare comes to mind again and the critical habit of treating his plays (particularly the last ones) as symbolic utterances, large spiritual meanings about ultimate things. Yet the surface of these plays is so much more active, complex, and just plain interesting than what supposedly lies behind it, that to translate language and events into other terms is simply to dilute and enfeeble them.

Blackmur's name for what Eliot gave us in *The Waste Land* was "sensual metaphysics." In a provocative comment from his Library of Congress lectures (*Anni Mirabiles*, 1921-1925) he confronted the surreal nightmare passage in part 5, "What the Thunder Said," in which "a woman drew her long black hair out tight," in which the towers turn upside down and the bats crawl downward "down a blackened wall" and voices sing "out of empty cisterns and exhausted wells":

> The exegetes tell us, and it is true, that we are in Chapel Perilous and the Perilous Cemetery is no doubt near at hand, and it may be as one of the exegetes says that we hear something like the voice of John the Baptist in the last line. But for myself, I muse and merge and ache and find myself feeling with the very senses of my thought greetings and cries from all the senses that are.

Testimony such as this risks being no more than a fancier version of the professor in the classroom assuring his students how deeply he is moved by a passage; but we can risk it, in the interests of opening up rather than shutting down the poem.

The most challenging of recent reconsiderations of *The Waste Land* is to be found in Christopher Ricks's *T. S. Eliot and Prejudice,* which doesn't address the poem as a whole but selects the openings of part 1 and part 5 with a view to demonstrating how Eliot's poetry is a principled refusal to strike and maintain clear, dramatic postures—the unmistakable postures of sentence sounds that Robert Frost said poetry should provide. As Ricks shows in patient detail, Eliot's openings—"April is the cruelest month" and "After the torchlight red on sweaty faces"—are memorable ones, but the sequences these lines initiate are anything but clearly marked: "The force of this opening [he is speaking of the "April" one] is in its combination of unmistakable directness with all these lurking possibilities of mistaking its direction." For all their differences of vocabulary and emphasis, both Blackmur and Ricks prefer to respond to the volatile surface intensities of language rather than the stable meanings some critics have presumed to lie underneath them. My own experience in teaching the poem is that, if you read it aloud and ask what people hear in it—anywhere in the five parts—the variety of responses, most of them cogent and relevant, will prove *The Waste Land* to be a work eminently hospitable to divergent reading possibilities, and full of—in Ricks's phrase—"lurking possibilities of mistaking its direction." These qualities make the poem still vibrant after seven decades of interpretation; my procedure here has been, accordingly, not to offer another one but to consider the question of and the necessity for "interpretation."

An essay on Eliot's work that ignores the part of it produced between *The Waste Land* and "Burnt Norton," first of *Four Quartets,* and indeed that says nothing about the plays or the criticism as they appeared in the 1930s and beyond, can have no pretense at responsible coverage. My excuse, apart from the usual limitations of space, is that some of Eliot's poems from this period, original and distinct as they are, seem to me not particularly to invite further commentary. I am thinking especially of "Ash-Wednesday," in its combination of ritual invocation and private muttering; also of the exquisitely cadenced "Marina." These and the "Ariel" poems are interesting mainly for the way they attempt, with varying degrees of success, to open up channels to a "reality" which, in the language of "Burnt Norton," we are told human kind cannot bear very much of. This opening up of channels is performed so impressively in the *Quartets* that by contrast the earlier "Ash-Wednesday" often seems flashy and desperate in some of its strategies. I am thinking, for example, of the verbal contortions that mar part 5 of that poem, ones in which even though the rhyming extravagances are deliberate—"Where shall the word be found, where will the word / Resound?" or "not on the mainland, in the desert or the rain land," or most egregiously "No place of grace for those who avoid the face,"—the effect is too much that of a zany prophet crying out his message, advising us to beware.

Four Quartets has many strategies for opening itself and the reader to "reality," some of them more subtle and engaging than others. Yet if it is true, as Henry James insisted it was in "The Art of Fiction," that "Art lives upon discussion, upon experiment, upon curiosity, upon variety of attempt, upon the exchange of views and the comparison of standpoints," then *Four Quartets* may be the least living poem in Eliot's oeuvre, justifying Cynthia Ozick's statement that the latest generation "never" reads it. Even with the publication in 1978 of Helen Gardner's fine study of the poem's composition, the relative absence of exchange of views, of lively argument about the poem's status, has persisted. Commentators are agreed, for the most part, that it is a mixture of very private and very public poetry, and that as a result its texture is extremely uneven. The question is whether such unevenness is a fault in the poem or the source of its power and beauty.

Donald Davie's way of distinguishing, broadly, the two kinds of characteristic poetry in the *Quartets* is to call one "the sonorous opulence of Mallarmé," the other a "prosaicism so homespun as to be, from time to time, positively 'prosey' or 'prosing.'" And he adds that Eliot's famous line about how "The poetry does not matter" is directed at the second, prosaic pole. But the statement about poetry not mattering occurs in the second section of "East Coker," part 2, after the Mallarméan opalescence of "What is the late November doing / With the disturbance of the spring." That lyric having concluded itself, there is a blank space after which a voice intones:

> That was a way of putting it—not very satisfactory;
> A periphrastic study in a worn-out poetical fashion.

and we are told that "one" is still left with the "intolerable wrestle / With words and meanings" and that "The poetry does not matter." It is an extravagant thing for a poet who has spent his life wrestling with words and meanings to say, and it surely has just as much reference—perhaps more—to the "poetical" Mallarmé-like passages in the poem as to the prosaic ones it might be seen as rationalizing or justifying. At the same time, the claim about poetry not mattering shouldn't be taken too solemnly, as commentators sometimes do when they compare Eliot's work to the late Beethoven quartets which also, it is said, try to get "beyond" music (as Eliot would get beyond poetry). In fact the differences between listening to Beethoven and reading Eliot are a lot more apparent and significant than the similarities. Let us say rather that they may be compared only to the extent that, despite the innovative, unconventional gestures these artists make in tonality and rhetoric, each remains intractably committed to his medium—Beethoven to music, Eliot to words.

Ten years after he completed "Little Gidding," Eliot published "The Three Voices of Poetry," an essay that contains a number of interesting formulations about the creative act, the most relevant to our purposes being one he uses to distinguish two of these voices—the first and most important of which is that of the poet when he is primarily not attempting "to communicate with anything at all." Eliot draws on Gottfried Benn's lecture *"Probleme der Lyrik"* but prefers to use the term "meditative verse" rather than "lyric" for this first voice. It (the first voice) originates from something germinating in the poet for which he must find words; it is nothing so definite as an idea, not even an emotion—it is what Eliot calls an "obscure impulse," and he says the following about the poet's relation to that impulse:

> He does not know what he has to say until he has said it, and in the effort to say it he is not concerned with making other people understand anything. He is not concerned, at this stage, with other people at all: only with finding the right words or, anyhow the least wrong words...he is going to all that trouble, not in order to communicate with anyone, but to gain relief from acute discomfort.

The Waste Land, we remember, was in Eliot's term just a piece of rhythmical grumbling in which various obscure impulses causing active discomfort (a nervous collapse, say) eventually found their way into an order of right—or at least the least wrong—words.

It may be objected that *Four Quartets* is not *The Waste Land,* and that its impulse is less an impulse than an idea, expressed by Eliot in a number of ways over the post-wasteland years: that we lived in a society worm-eaten with liberalism; that the modern world was no longer capable of entertaining the "higher dream," as Dante had; that "The world is trying the experiment of attempting to form a civilized but non-Christian mentality—an experiment which will fail but only after which failure can the world be saved from suicide." That is, *Four Quartets* seems to have issued from an Eliot, or from a part of him, very much concerned with making other people understand that something terribly wrong had happened to the world, and that the poet's task was to warn them of what had happened and to inspire them with the possibilities of another kind of happening.

My contention is that if *Four Quartets* were such a poem, concerned with giving poetic expression to the sentiments Eliot had been expressing—sometimes harshly, even intemperately—in his prose, it would be much less of a poem than it is. His own distinction still holds: that prose may legitimately concern itself with ideals, while poetry can only deal with actuality. Eliot's sense of "actuality" was subtler and more complex than his social polemics could suggest. What is most moving about the *Quartets* is the way the poem tries to talk sense about ideas and ideals, addressing us in the second voice (the poet "talking to other people"), entertaining a formulation, apologizing for it ("That was a way of putting it, not very satisfactory"), faltering and losing confidence in the usefulness of what it is trying to do. Then pausing perhaps and, gathering impetus, beginning again but in a different key; moving out somewhere beyond us, no longer occupied with our needs and interests since it has something more intimate and private in sight. For adequate demonstration of such movement, one needs to read aloud an extended passage; here I simply draw attention to the fifth section of "East Coker," which begins, wearily, with a confession to us that twenty years have been largely wasted ("the years of *L'entre deux guerres*") and that the struggle to use words brings inevitable failure; that each "raid on the inarticulate" is also a deterioration; that the burden of the past is immense and overwhelming; that "conditions" (wartime England in 1940) seem "unpropitious" for any attempt at recovery. But (grimly) "For us, there is only the trying. The rest is not our business."

Then, after a space, the voice resumes, still addressing us evidently but with rather more "poetic" inclinations, speaking intensely about a "lifetime burning in every moment," or of "old stones that cannot be deciphered," and of the respective "times"—under starlight, under lamplight—in which we spend our evenings. After mention of the second evening comes a parenthetical phrase, "(The evening with the photograph album)," signaling to my ears the moment when the second voice turns into something else (you cannot speak a parenthesis to an audience) and the lines no longer are organized by an order of punctuation:

> Old men ought to be explorers
> Here and there does not matter
> We must be still and still moving
> Into another intensity

Then a glimpsed "union" changing into "communion," as through the cry of wave and wind, through "the vast waters / Of the petrel and the porpoise," the poetry explores, in associative monologue, its subject—the subject of the four poems taken together—continuously winding and unwinding itself. F. R. Leavis once named that subject, with special reference to the beginning of "Burnt Norton," as "a radical inquiry into the nature and methods of his exploration." Let us say rather, "of exploration," by way of noting the poem's reach beyond the merely personal. And what it explores is not merely the conditions of spiritual and religious possibilities, but other matters of intimate and ultimate concern that presented themselves to a man and poet very much in the "middle way" (Eliot was fifty-five when he published "Little Gidding"). It was an attempt to ascertain what things mattered and how much they mattered: questions of present, past, and future time; the writing of poetry; the love of worldly and unworldly things; stillness and speech; one's origins, one's ancestors, one's childhood; the meaning of history, of servitude, of freedom; the circumstances of a nation at war. What it has to "say" about these matters is not to be extracted from its poetry, which turns out to matter very much. When a saying is extracted and contemplated in its "translated" form, the result is unmemorable; but within the poem, from time to time, memorable things happen. In the language of the "dead master" in "Little Gidding" who comes to admonish the "I" about the gifts of old age:

> So I find words I never thought to speak
> In streets I never thought I should revisit
> When I left my body on a distant shore.

In the spring of 1933, during a nine-month stay in the United States (he had determined to separate permanently from his wife), Eliot visited the University of Virginia to deliver some lectures later published as *After Strange Gods.* In their reflections on orthodoxy (the subtitle was "A Primer of Modern Heresy") they figure as Eliot's most controversial prose utterance. But early in the first lecture there is an extraordinary passage in which he describes his impressions of the new world on arriving from England the previous fall:

> My local feelings were stirred very sadly by my first view of New England, on arriving from Montreal, and journeying all one day through the beautiful desolate country of Vermont. Those hills had once, I suppose, been covered with primaeval forest; the forest was razed to make sheep pastures for the English settlers; now the sheep are gone, and most of the descendants of the settlers; and a new forest appeared blazing with the melancholy glory of October maple and beech and birch scattered among the evergreens; and after the processions of scarlet and gold and purple wilderness you descend to the sordor of the half-dead mill towns of southern New Hampshire and Massachusetts.

He goes on to say that the "happiest" lands are those in which the long struggle between man and the environment had brought about a successful accommodation between landscape and "numerous generations of one race," and he concludes that "those New England mountains seemed to me to give evidence of a human success so meagre and transitory as to be more desperate than the desert." He would go on to speak to his Virginia audience about the importance of tradition, and in the preface to the published volume would characterize their university as "one of the older, smaller and most gracious of American educational institutions, one of those in which some vestiges of a traditional education seem to survive."

We need not dwell upon what certainly appears to be a bit of wishful thinking, if not just outright flattery, on Eliot's part; nor will we further consider the context of the previously referred to remark about how free-thinking Jews are undesirable in a traditional society. When called to the bar of judgment Eliot will probably be willing to negotiate with and revise his terms; at any rate he never reprinted the lectures. But non-negotiable, as I hear it, is the description of his stirred local feelings as he ventured through New England, observing and being saddened by the transitoriness of human success. It is the most authentic of Eliotic notes, and—for all the differences between early and late work—is there from the beginning of "Preludes," with its withered leaves and lonely cab-horses, right down to the end of "Little Gidding" with its children in the apple tree, "Quick, now, here, now, always—". Three decades ago, in "Fifty Years of American Poetry," Randall Jarrell surveyed our poets from the first half of this century. When he came to Eliot, Jarrell decided it was appropriate to speak, not from his own voice in the present, but from the point of view he imagined the future would take about this writer:

> Won't the future say to us in helpless astonishment: "But did you actually believe that all these things about objective correlatives, classicism, the tradition, applied to *his* poetry? Surely you must have seen that he was one of the most subjective and daemonic poets who ever lived, the victim and helpless beneficiary of his own inexorable compulsions, obsessions?...But for you, of course, after the first few years, his poetry existed undersea, thousands of feet below that deluge of exegesis, explication, source listing, scholarship, and criticism that overwhelmed it. And yet how bravely and personally it survived, its eyes neither coral nor mother-of-pearl but plainly human, full of human anguish!"

The voice of that future has not yet been heard; we should keep listening for it.

—*Columbia History of American Poetry,* ed. Jay Parini (New York: Columbia University Press, 1993).

Epistolary Eliot

In this beautifully appointed and superbly edited first volume of T. S. Eliot's correspondence (there will be four volumes in all), his widow, Valerie Eliot, uses as epigraph to the whole enterprise a passage from a lecture her husband delivered in 1933.[1] The lecture has not survived, but Eliot's brother Henry recorded two sentences which addressed, with TSE's usual originality, the matter of how one should feel about writing letters, or about having one's letters read by others, or about reading letters not written to us:

> The desire to write a letter, to put down what you don't want anybody else to see but the person you are writing to, but which you do not want to be destroyed, but perhaps hope may be preserved for complete strangers to read, is ineradicable. We want to confess ourselves in writing to a few friends, and we do not always want to feel that no one but those friends will ever read what we have written.

So although he might not have been thrilled at the prospect of a complete stranger like myself eavesdropping on a 1915 confession to Pound—"Besides, I am constipated and have a cold on the chest"—Eliot has tactfully allowed us to feel tactful about reading his outgoing mail.

In fact, and although he once wrote his friend Conrad Aiken that "Letters should be indiscretions—otherwise they are simply official bulletins," most of these letters, which extend through 1922 (the year *The Waste Land* was published and Eliot began his editorship of the *Criterion*), are neither

1. THE LETTERS OF T. S. ELIOT: Volume I 1898-1922, ed. by *Valerie Eliot.* Harcourt Brace Jovanovich.

indiscreet nor simply "official." The either-or choice laid down to Aiken fails to take into account the number of different ways in which Eliot's prose can be interesting. At least one reviewer of these letters has already found, however, that Eliot's ability to assume different voices depending on whom he is addressing ("He do the police in different voices," as the canceled allusion to Dickens from *The Waste Land* had it) is a measure of his inauthenticity or fragmentedness as a human being. This seems to me nonsense: why should one write one's mother, one's Harvard professor in Indian philosophy, and Ezra Pound all in the same voice? If one demands that a consistent voice permeate a writer's correspondence, one should go to D. H. Lawrence, who tended to harangue everyone he wrote to in the same terms and tone. Eliot is more discreet—even in his indiscretions—and the commendable manners of his epistolary style show in his taking the recipient into account.

For example, a 1914 letter to J. H. Woods, his Harvard philosophy professor, written from Merton College, Oxford, where Eliot is reading Aristotle, is partly an "official bulletin"—since Eliot had promised to keep Woods "au courant" on his studies there—but also something more. He tells Woods he is following three courses of lectures: Harold Joachim's on the *Ethics,* R. G. Collingwood's on the *De Anima,* and J. A. Smith's Logic. He is finding the *Posterior Analytics* "very difficult" and accompanies his study of it "with the commentary of Zabarella, which is remarkably good, and very minute, so that this reading takes most of my time." There follow descriptions of Joachim's good lectures and Collingwood's method with the *de Anima.* Although, from Peter Ackroyd's biography, we knew that Eliot studied Aristotle with Joachim at Oxford, the extent of his immersion in the *maestre de color che sanno* is now more clear. And Eliot's "bulletin" to Woods helps explain the passionate force with which Aristotle is invoked in "The Perfect Critic" (the opening essay in *The Sacred Wood*), where the "living force" of the philosopher is celebrated as well as the "universal intelligence" he applied to everything. Aristotle, says Eliot, wasn't a poet who looked to write critical prose in order to satisfy "impure"—creative—desires:

> In whatever sphere of interest, he looked solely and steadfastly at the object; in his short and broken treatise [the *Poetics*] he provides an eternal example—not of laws, or even of method, for there is no method except to be very intelligent, but of intel-

> ligence itself swiftly operating the analysis of sensation to the point of principle and definition.

This famous definition of "method," in other words, came out of some hard antecedent study.

A month after Eliot wrote Woods on how his Aristotelian studies were progressing, he struck a quite different pose to Conrad Aiken in wondering whether to return to America and take up a career of philosophy at Harvard. He is currently suffering, so he informs Aiken, from "indigestion, constipation, and colds constantly"; the university atmosphere is oppressive; the war is suffocating; and how can one like a country that is "satisfied with such disgusting food?" England is surely uncivilized, but then, on the other hand, there is Cambridge, Massachusetts, and the college bell, and the "people…whom one fights against and who absorb one all the same." The young man continues to put himself on stage for Aiken:

> The great need is to know one's own mind, and I don't know that: whether I want to get married, and have a family, and live in America all my life, and compromise and conceal my opinions and forfeit my independence for the sake of my children's future; or save my money and retire at fifty to a table on the boulevard, regarding the world placidly through the fumes of an apéritif at 5 P.M.—How thin either life seems! And perhaps it is merely dyspepsia speaking.

Dyspepsia perhaps, or perhaps the accents of "Portrait of a Lady," that very artful portrait of a young man who doesn't know his own mind.

In fact, this is one of the last glimpses we are given of the Laforguian or dyspeptic aesthete, conjuring up the world through apéritif fumes. By June of the same year, 1915, Eliot has married Vivienne Haigh-Wood, and a month later is writing his father in quite un-Laforguian terms: "I am *convinced* that she has been the one person for me. She has everything to give that I want, and she gives it. I owe her everything." It is extraordinary to think that this twenty-six-year-old, whose to-be-famous poem, "The Love Song of J. Alfred Prufrock," had just the past month been published in Harriet Monroe's *Poetry,* should without consulting or informing his parents suddenly decide to throw in his lot with Vivien (as she liked to spell it) and England. Eliot appears to have counted on his friends to convince his parents that the life he had chosen was a viable one. Two days after the marriage, Pound—under Eliot's request—sent a long letter to Henry Ware Eliot that was meant to serve as "some sort of apologia for the literary life in general, and for London literary life in particular." It is a fascinating letter, at least as much for what Pound says about himself as about Eliot; although one cannot feel confident that Eliot père was disarmed of his fears and reassured by such claims as "Again if a man is doing the fine thing and the rare thing, London is the only possible place for him to exist." (London was at any rate, as Pound put it in a letter to his own mother, some centuries nearer the "Paradiso Terrestre" than was St. Louis.) A few months after Pound's letter to Henry Ware Eliot, Bertrand Russell wrote Charlotte Eliot in an effort to convince her that, financially and intellectually, it made sense for her son to remain in England: that he could both teach school at High Wycombe *and* pursue the doctoral degree; and that not only was Vivien "thoroughly nice," but her good offices could already be observed insofar as TSE "is no longer attracted by the people who call themselves 'vorticists,' and in that I think her influence is wholly to be applauded." (Eliot's father had remarked, apropos of Pound and Lewis's Vorticist showpiece, BLAST, that he hadn't known there were enough "lunatics" in the world to support such a magazine.)

Five years after the marriage, with *The Sacred Wood* about to appear, Eliot wrote his mother a letter filled, among other things, with interesting literary gossip, an item of which concerned the arrival in London of the American "vagrant poet and man of letters" Maxwell Bodenheim. Bodenheim hoped to make a living in London by his pen, and Eliot noted sardonically that, as he had informed the new arrival, "getting recognized in English letters is like breaking open a safe—for an American, and that only about three had ever done it." Of course by this time he had broken open the safe, Pound having already instructed him that while he (Pound) threw rocks through the front windows of English Letters, Eliot was to climb in the back way and "make off with the swag." A year after marrying Vivien, Eliot was up to his ears in reviewing: "Philosophy for the *Monist* and the *International Journal of Ethics,* reviews for the *New Statesman,* the *Manchester Guardian* and the *Westminster Gazette...*" From the beginning of 1917 to the end of 1919 he produced roughly seventy-five reviews and essays—most significantly in the *Egoist* and *Athenaeum*—among which are to be found some of his most memorable and lasting prose work: essays on *vers libre,* Henry James, Turgenev, Kipling, Henry Adams, Stendhal, Marlowe,

Swinburne, *Hamlet,* Ben Jonson, "Tradition and the Individual Talent." (That the bulk of these reviews and essays still remains uncollected is one of the continuing frustrations of contemporary letters: Faber and Mrs. Eliot, please take note!)

At the same time—as is well known, but not till now so grindingly documented—the writer was not only working full-time at Lloyds Bank, but offering courses of lectures to fill out his income. Eliot comes through at his most appealing when he describes to his cousin Eleanor Hinkley (who always provokes him into lively letters) one of these courses, taught in early 1917:

> My greatest pleasure however is my workingmen's class in English Literature on Monday evenings. I have steered them through Browning (who arouses great enthusiasm), Carlyle, Meredith, Arnold, and am now conducting them through Ruskin. There are not many working *men* at present, except one very intelligent grocer who reads Ruskin behind the counter; most of them are (female) elementary schoolteachers, who work very hard with large classes of refractory children all day but come with unabated eagerness to get culture in the evening (stimulated, I hope, by my personal magnetism).

A year later he is in the midst of another series of lectures, "cramming George Eliot for the last two weeks in preparation," and he tells us that for the occasion he has read *Mill on the Floss, Scenes of Clerical Life,* and *Adam Bede* (after work hours at Lloyds and after the latest review had been sent off). By this time—the spring of 1918—one feels that the young man of twenty-nine has come into his full powers as a critic. The sweep and confidence of his literary judgments, as conveyed in the following sentences, again to Eleanor Hinkley, are all the more impressive for also being true:

> I am very glad you like James.... He is a wonderful conscientious artist, one of the very few, and more European than most English or Americans. I think he has about the keenest sense of Situation of any novelist, and his always alert intelligence is a perpetual delight. As a critic of America he is certainly unique. I am reading *R[oderick] Hudson* now in preparation for an article for the James number of the *Little Review.* I am writing on the

> Hawthorne influence on James, which comes out at the end in an astonishing unfinished book *The Sense of the Past* (read the scenario at the end). *Hudson* I find dull and stilted and old fashioned; but it is a very early one. I think you might like Turgenev. I admire him as much as any novelist, but especially in the *Sportsman's Sketches*. His method looks simple and slight, but he is a consummate master with it....I come more and more to demand that novels should be well written, and perceive more clearly the virtue and defects of the Victorians.

He then proceeds to have at Thackeray, Meredith, Samuel Butler and George Eliot (somehow he missed out on the genius of *Middlemarch*) in invigorating ways. There is some muscle-flexing here, but nothing empty or unfelt in the judgments and comparisons (comparison and analysis, the tools of the critic—as he would put it in *The Sacred Wood*).

His career as a critic coincided, in its beginnings, with the worry that it might be all up with him as a poet; that—as he wrote his brother in September of 1916—"'J.A.P.' [J. Alfred Prufrock] was a swan song." He worried that Vivien would be "bitterly disappointed" if he never equaled it, and confided to Henry that "The present year has been, in some respects, the most awful nightmare of anxiety that the mind of man could conceive"—though, he added, "at least it is not dull." Vivien felt that "Journalism" was bad for her husband, although he loved it: "But I am sure and certain that it will be the *ruin* of his poetry—if it goes on," she wrote to Henry at about the same time. There are a good many of Vivien's letters in this collection, consisting in the main of variations on the theme of her "wretched health" and her overwhelming sense that "life is so feverish and yet so dreary at the same time, and one is always waiting, waiting for something" ("What shall I do now? What shall I do?...What shall we do tomorrow? / What shall we ever do?"). The only way, it seems, she could ameliorate her own lot was to worry about her husband's, especially in letters to his mother: "It seems he has not average strength—and added to that he lives as no average man does. The incessant, never ending grind, day and evening—and always too much to do, so that he is always behind hand, never up to date—therefore always tormented—and if forced to rest or stop a minute it only torments him the more to feel that inexorable pile of work piling up against him." Vivien knew how to put words together—just pushing through the sentences, written in June 1917, makes one feel exhausted. Eliot by then had begun work at the bank (hours 9:15 to 5:30, with a break for tea at 4). Surely it was not only the experience of living in wartime London that caused him to describe, in July of that year, his sense of himself as "living in one of Dostoyevsky's novels, you see, not in one of Jane Austen's." As for his health, things weren't so bad—"My teeth are falling to pieces, I have to wear spectacles to read, and from time to time I am contorted with rheumatism—otherwise I am pretty well." He would get worse.

The litany of complaints holds more than the occasional bit of something like comic relief. Note the following italicizations of *key words* in one of Vivien's many letters to Tom's mother on the subject of Tom's clothes:

> Tom did *not* get a new suit, *or* new flannels. I am ashamed to say it. His old underwear is still thick and in *fair* condition, but it needs *incessant darning.* Darning alone takes me hours out of the week. He needs a suit, and I think *must* have one. His pyjamas too are all very old and want constant mending.

This was in March, 1917. Eight months later, with winter coming on and Charlotte Eliot having sent money for her son's underclothing, Vivien renders up an account of how that money was spent, in the process of which occurs a sentence-confession it is a delight to misinterpret: "So far the weather has been, and *is,* so unusually warm that neither Tom nor I have made any change in our underclothing since the summer! It is a good thing in a way, but it is *very* damp and enervating at present." Yes, "it" certainly must have been, and for them both. On and on runs the letter, through woollens, vests, underdrawers, socks, and the ever unsatisfactory pyjama situation: "He is still worse provided with pyjamas than anything...He is very rough with his pyjamas, and shirts—tears them unmercifully!" ("I was neither at the hot gates / Nor fought in the warm rain / Nor knee deep in the salt marsh, heaving a cutlass, / Bitten by flies, fought.") But at least he now has a "chest protector," purchased on the advice of Vivien's mother: "The chest protector is quilted satin, and fits around the neck and has a double breasted chest part. It is particularly valuable for when he goes out in evening dress—which leaves the chest much less protected..." And later: "Tom takes cold *very* much more easily than I do. Most of *my* colds are caught from him. I think he would be better if he had one side of his nose cauterised..." Who was it that doubted we could learn much from Shakespeare's laundry lists? Something like the banality of evil, the everpresent malady of the quotidian, is testified to by these pathetic and oddly gripping outcries of Vivien's, and they provide as much a sense as one could ask for of what the Eliots' life together was like.[2]

The most entertaining and enlivening sections of the correspondence are those in which Eliot is writing to or about Pound, Wyndham Lewis, Richard Aldington, and other modernists. These letters—along with others concerning *The Waste Land* and the *Criterion*—I can merely allude to here, since I wish instead to indicate two moments in which Eliot is particularly expressive about his relationship to his parents. The first occurs in a letter to his brother, written in February of 1919, after their father had died. Eliot says that he wished "father could have had more satisfaction out of his children," but doesn't think that his father's life was a very unhappy one—"and after all none of his children was made for the kind of success that he could have appreciated" (Henry Ware Eliot was President of the Hydraulic-Press Brick Company in St. Louis). He goes on to speak more personally:

> I always tried to give as powerful an impression as I could of my position here but it was a prominence essentially too esoteric to be of much use in that way. Now, I find that I think more of his own youthful possibilities that never came to anything: and yet with a great deal of satisfaction; his old-fashioned scholarship! his flute-playing, his drawing. Two of the Cats that I have seem to me quite remarkable. I feel that both he and mother in spite of the strength of their affection were lonely people, and that he was the more lonely of the two, that he hardly knew himself what he was like. In my experience everyone except the fools seem to me warped and stunted.

I think that the loneliness Eliot sensed in his parents' lives was at least as much projected as discovered; but it is the tone here that compels—for those who find Eliot's melancholy compelling—and that final surprising

2. There is one teasing, unannotated reference, in a letter of Vivien's [3 October 1919] written to her friend Mary Hutchinson, to what sounds like Another Man, or at least the possibility of one. After saying how she wants to buy new clothes, but hasn't yet begun, she adds "I dont know what will please Jim most either! Directly that horrible Belgian goes to Bermuda you must begin laying foundation stones for me with Jim." Eliot scholars, get to work!

sentence which seems to come out of nowhere and makes the best, glum case for the consequences of not being a fool. (He was about to review *The Education of Henry Adams.*)

The other moment occurs in a letter written to his mother a few weeks later, in which—in the words just quoted about his father—Eliot attempts "to give as powerful an impression" as he could of his literary position. He is explaining why he has turned down an editorial position on the *Athenaeum* and why he will continue on at the bank and avoid the "intrigues of journalism":

> I only write what I want to—*now*—and everyone knows that anything I do write is good. I can influence London opinion and English literature in a better way. I am known to be disinterested. . . . There is a small and select public which regards me as the best living critic, as well as the best living poet, in England. . . . I really think I have far more *influence* on English letters than any other American has ever had, unless it be Henry James. I know a great many people, but there are many more who would like to know me, and I can remain isolated and detached.

Such remarks, he admits, are "conceited." Yet they are also nothing less than a true measurement of the distance he had come. To be able to write it out to one's mother, as if to offer (in Yeats's words from "Among School Children") "A compensation for the pang of his birth, / Or the uncertainty of his setting forth"—this is the success story told by these letters, played out against marital failure, and against physical and psychic distress. Out of that distress he came to formulate his sense of the admirable writer—"perfectly cool and detached, regarding other people's feelings or his own, like a God who has got beyond them; or a person who has dived very deep and come up holding some hitherto unseen submarine creature" (19 Sept. 1917). One recalls, at this point, the familiar sentence from the "Tradition" essay about how "only those who have personality and emotions know what it means to want to escape from those things." To that may now be added a correction he made, not without its quotient of slyness, to John Gould Fletcher, who had read "The Perfect Critic" and decided Eliot was insufficiently generous to the claims of "emotion." Responding to Fletcher, Eliot wrote that "Certainly I don't deny the importance of emotion. I often find it present to me when other people find only frigidity..." That was a way of putting it, rather more than satisfactory.

—*Hudson Review*, Spring 1989.

T.S. Eliot as Critic and Editor

IN HER INTRODUCTION to T. S. Eliot's letters published in 1988, his wife Valerie explained that originally she had hoped the volume would run to the end of 1926 (the first half of Eliot's life), but the scope of correspondence made that impossible. Further volumes of letters were promised, none appeared; now, twenty-two years later, a second volume has been published along with a thoroughly revised and expanded Volume One.[1] Presumably Faber brought in the co-editor, Hugh Haughton, in order to get things moving at last; at any rate, the explanatory footnotes are full, informative, indeed exemplary. More than 200 letters have been added to the first volume, including additional ones written to Eliot's mother by his first wife, Vivien. As for the new volume, letters written over the brief three-year period 1923-1925 add up to a whopping 878 pages, making it slightly longer than its revised predecessor.

The most memorable letters from Volume One were those written by both Eliot and Vivien (especially to Eliot's mother) cataloguing the thousand ills flesh and spirit were heir to in the years immediately following their marriage in 1915. Eliot is trying unsuccessfully to find time to write poems while he teaches extension courses in English literature, reviews books for the *Egoist* and *Athenaeum,* and in 1917 begins his full-time job at Lloyds Bank. On the basis of letters from these years he may be credited when he tells a correspondent that the world he is living in is a Dostoevsky novel, rather than one of Jane Austen's. Vivien Eliot described his life to Eliot's mother as "The incessant never-ending grind, day and evening,

1. *The Letters of T. S. Eliot,* ed. Valerie Eliot and Hugh Haughton, vol. 1: 1898-1922, rev. ed. (Faber and Faber, 1990); vol. 2: 1923-1925 (Faber and Faber, 2009). Both volumes contain useful biographical comments and calendars for the respective years, also a glossary of names describing the main correspondents.

and always too much to do so that he is always behind hand, never up to date—therefore always tormented." The upside to this grind appeared in 1919 when he wrote his mother, giving her "as powerful an expression" as he could of his literary position in London: "There is a small and select public which regards me as the best living critic, as well as the best living poet, in England.... I really think I have far more *influence* on English letters than any American has ever had, unless it be Henry James." Coming from one who never bragged about his merits and virtues, even to his mother, the estimate rings with truth that will be borne out by the subsequent events of his career. But first there would be the nervous collapse in 1921, leading to his three-month stay at the sanatorium in Lausanne, Switzerland; then the completion and publication of *The Waste Land,* this last concurrently with his taking on the editorship of a review, *The Criterion,* subsidized by Lady Rothermere.

A large, indeed preponderant number of the letters from Volume Two are, as in the earlier volume, about the daily struggles of an editor whose letterhead address is for a time *The Criterion* 9 Clarence Gate Gardens—a combination of the magazine with Eliot's home address. More than once he rises to eloquent complaint about the absurdity of his editorial situation. One example will do for many, this to his brother in America, Henry:

> *The Criterion* is run without an office, without any staff or business manager, by a sickly bank clerk and his wife. The latter has had to be on her back half of the time and the former has conducted all his work in the evening in his own sitting room, without even a *desk,* till Christmas! after a busy and tiring day [at Lloyds Bank] and subject to a thousand interruptions. Until the last few months I have paid my own secretary, a woman who came in three evenings a week. When I finally add that I have not only taken no salary but have actually been considerably out of pocket for payment of a secretary, and for the time that I might have spent on writing for other papers, it is enough to make any outsider believe that I ought to be certified a lunatic.

He writes to the editor of *The Dial,* Scofield Thayer, that he has done no writing whatever "For the last two years, except the scrappy contributions and editorials which you may have seen from time to time in *The Crite-*

rion," and that "the scraps themselves have been drops of blood out of an exhausted stone."

Yet although not so painful and sometimes amusing as the negative complaints, many of the letters testify amply to Eliot's imagination and efficiency as an editor concerned to put out a superior organ of critical inquiry. In the interests of making *The Criterion* representative of European culture in its range, he suggests to the poet F. S. Flint that Flint should write a series of short pieces dealing with foreign reviews. Specifically he proposes to Flint, "I should be highly pleased if you would consent to let me have sent to you any Spanish, German or Norwegian periodicals which we may receive." He admits the remuneration would be less than an inducement, but "if the idea interests you, it ought not to take very much of your time. It would merely mean looking over the reviews as they came in and sending me a few notes once a quarter. I propose that the reviews should be initialled by the writers." A minor but typical example of a letter that shows the vigilance, even in small matters, shown by Eliot's scrupulous directing hand.

As for the larger matter of what *The Criterion* stood for, or against, he was characteristically shifty. To Herbert Read, who could be called one of Eliot's "lieutenants," certainly a frequent and valuable contributor to the magazine, he wrote what Read would later call an "apologia" that consists largely of raising possible criteria for what, as editor, he was after, then backing away from them even as they were raised. "If I say generally that I wish to form a phalanx [Read had suggested the word] a hundred voices will forthwith declare that I wish to be a leader, and that my vanity will not allow me to serve, or even to exist on terms of equality with others." He would wish, he told Read, to get "as homogenous a group as possible" of contributors, but he knows homogeneity is "in the end indefinable" and that he doesn't expect everyone to "subscribe to all the articles of my own faith or to read Arnold, Newman, Bradley, or Maurras with my eyes." He is convinced that "at the present time we need more dogma," and that one should have "as precise and clear a creed as possible"; yet "a creed is always in one sense smaller than the man, and in another sense larger; one's formulations never fully explain one, although it is necessary to formulate." The best he can come up with is to find persons "who have an impersonal loyalty to some faith not antagonistic to my own."

He had previously written to an Oxford historian and philosopher,

F. W. Bain, a "Tory" with special interests in Bolingbroke and Disraeli, that while *The Criterion* was not an organ of "literary interest only" its political interest was not in daily doings at Westminster: "We want it to be clear that *The Criterion* is apart from current political controversy, that it is independent of party politics, and leagued with an ideal rather than with the actual Tory party." He was anxious that the magazine become not a "party organ," but one that would concern itself with "the discovery and maintenance of the philosophy and history of politics." Eliot liked to make play with the Tory label, as when he praised, to Ford Madox Ford, "hereditary and ineradicable toryism." On another occasion, responding to Ford's praise of Ford's own brand of toryism that saw no salvation in anything except fourteenth-century feudalism, Eliot assured him that he, Eliot, was "an old-fashioned Tory: I am all for empires, especially the Austro-Hungarian empire." The exact component of mischief in some of these reactionary remarks is uncertain, as when he writes Bain, whose piece on Disraeli *The Criterion* would publish, suggesting a further essay "vindicating either Charles the Second or George the Third." Would he indeed have been pleased to publish a friendly essay on the latter, whom Shelley in his poem "England in 1819" had called "An old, mad, blind, despised, and dying King"? Given Eliot's dislike of Shelley, and his remark to Ford that for him "English literature ends well before 1800 (at least that part of it which is written in verse)," it very well could be. Reviewing these letters, Michael Wood put it aptly when he called Eliot an "imaginary Tory" whose aim was "a way of arranging a disliked world in your head."

In his brief paragraph on Eliot in "Fifty Years of American Poetry," Randall Jarrell paid tribute to what was going on in that head by imagining what the "future" would say to us about the poet:

> But did you actually believe that all those things about objective correlatives, classicism, the tradition, applied to *his* poetry? Surely you must have seen that he was one of the most subjective and daemonic poets who ever lived, the victim and helpless beneficiary of his own inexorable compulsions, obsessions? From a psychoanalytic point of view he was far and away the most interesting poet of your century.

These observations occurred to me as I noted, in the above letter to F. W. Bain, Eliot's belief that, with the intellectual hold of "socialism" loosening its grip on "the young," there was "the chance of establishing an austere classicism" directed against "romantic" culture. Socialism, romanticism, "whiggery"—and what he called in "The Function of Criticism" the "inner voice"—were important elements in the world he disliked. But underlying it all was the "psychoanalytical" profile he had discovered in himself and which, in the opening letter to his brother in this volume, he accounted for as follows:

> I am very tired. My fatigue, which has been growing for years, is not solely due to overwork and anxieties; it is largely due to a kink in my brain which makes life at all an unremitting strain for me, and which is at the bottom of a good many of the things about me that you object to.

This is footnoted by the editors with sentences from a letter to Richard Aldington, Eliot's sometime assistant at *The Criterion,* in which he tells Aldington of suffering from "an *aboulie* and emotional derangement which has been a lifelong affliction." I doubt that any psychiatrist informed him of his "kink"; rather that it was a homemade discovery. But the seeming confidence and inevitability with which Eliot puts it forth here makes one draw a sharp breath. In *The Use of Poetry and the Use of Criticism,* he teased Matthew Arnold's notion that poetry was, in Arnold's words, "at bottom" a criticism of life, by adding "[That] bottom is a great way down." So was the "bottom" that he confessed to his brother was central to his being.

The letters are full of testimonies to what might be called "emotional derangement" in Eliot's private sector, and it always involved, to one degree or another, the derangement of Vivien Eliot. I quote a single example of what was no isolated instance of collapse on her part, as Eliot writes to Ottoline Morrell from a cottage they had rented near Chichester. His wife, fatigued and exhausted,

> had the worst crisis, after tea, that I have *ever* seen, the worst she has ever had. I am sure that she was on the point of death. She went completely numb, terrible palpitations, and gasping for every breath, I telephoned to *four* doctors, all out—finally one came. But before he came she suddenly had a terrific colitis explosion—poison that must have been accumulating for two or three weeks.... I *think* we are through it now, but she

> has wasted in this week to an absolute skeleton, and it will take weeks to build her up.

Eliot's mother, whom he had recently scared by writing her that everything was "crumbling," notes in a letter to her cousin Thomas Lamb Eliot that "it was not a eugenic marriage."

More cruelly Virginia Woolf, always the sharpest tongue in any company, after receiving a letter from Vivien inviting the Woolfs to dinner, confided to her diary as follows: "Mrs Eliot—this last making me almost vomit, so scented, so powdered, so egotistic, so morbid, so weakly." Near the close of the volume, in November of 1925, when she was about to leave a nursing home near Southampton, Vivien writes Eliot with various directions and requests, then breaks out abruptly near the letter's end: "I am sorry I tortured you and drove you mad. I had no notion until yesterday afternoon that I had done it. I have been simply raving mad. You need not worry about me. I am really being saved but its [*sic*] hard work." In the margins she wrote, "Please write to this doctor instantly and tell him the truth, that we have had sexual relations." Only a reckless and foolhardy reader would know what to say in response to this. In the next letter, written by Eliot to Geoffrey Faber, whose publishing house he was about to join, we find, surprisingly, that Eliot hopes Faber can dine the next day with him and his wife. Of course the reader grows accustomed, even hardened, to health complaints like this minor one to Wyndham Lewis: "Thanks for yours. I am ill, harassed, impoverished, and am going to have five teeth out. I have managed to avoid seeing anyone for a very long time. I have several enemies." Here the conscious overdramatizing of suffering, performed not to the most sympathetic of ears, is what we have come to expect, almost—unconscionably—to relish.

Eliot's most searching attempt to speak to his relationship with Vivien was made to John Middleton Murry in 1925. Two years previously, in "The Function of Criticism," Eliot devoted some pages to criticizing Murry's position as regards romanticism and the "inner voice" to which Murry gave prominence.[2] When, after Katherine Mansfield's death, Murry remarried,

2. Eliot wrote as follows about the inner voice: "My belief is that those who possess this inner voice are ready enough to hearken to it, and will hear no other. The inner voice, in fact, sounds remarkably like an old principle which has been formulated by an elder critic [Matthew Arnold] in the now familiar phrase of 'doing as one likes.' The possessors of the inner voice ride ten in a compartment to a football match at Swansea, listening to the inner

Eliot wrote him a brief note saying he couldn't attend the wedding (he couldn't get away from the bank) and that although he was sure Murry had done the best thing for himself in marrying again, Eliot concluded, "but you know that it has always been impossible for me to understand any of your actions." Shortly thereafter he wrote to Frederic Manning that "everything that Murry believes in is anathema to me," and that he had never found any writer "whose views were so antipathetic to me." Then, surely to Eliot's surprise, Murry suggested his name to deliver the Clark Lectures in Cambridge for 1926. Eliot responded with strong gratitude: "You must have *realised* that your proposal of my name...would come as a ray of hope just at the *blackest moment in my life.*" Two months later, after he had decided to leave the bank and join Faber, he wrote Murry a confessional letter that begins "In the last ten years—gradually, but deliberately—I have made myself into a *machine.* I have done it deliberately—in order to endure, in order not to feel—*but it has killed V.*" He goes on to speculate on what will happen were he to come alive again: "Does it happen that two persons' lives are absolutely hostile?" The editors presume, probably correctly, that the American woman he loved, Emily Hale, was on his mind as part of his coming alive again. Eliot writes all this, in its apocalyptic, end-of-the-line manner, to Murry because he is "spiritually...much wiser than I." It is astonishing that he should have let the confessional bars down to a man who, however "spiritually" wise, believed in everything that was "antipathetic" to him. Retrospectively it is surely a moment predictive of Eliot's conversion in 1927 and his abandonment of Vivien in 1933.

I have written elsewhere about Eliot's playful sardonic humor as it informs his reviews and miscellaneous prose. Such wit is amply to be found in the lamentations—sometimes laced with vivifying energy—about being an ill, put-upon editor imprisoned in an impossible marriage. It plays no small part in keeping us turning the pages through so much repetitive and, it must be admitted, frequently transient matters. Yet sometimes such matters are much to be enjoyed. When an autograph hunter requests one from Eliot, the hunter received, in addition to the autograph, some writerly advice: Eliot hopes "in return for this trifling favor you will make me happy by ceasing to *split infinitives.*" Doubtless Glen Walton Blodgett of Buffalo, New York, took this to heart. When returning his income tax

---

voice, which breathes the eternal message of vanity, fear, and lust." "The Function of Criticism," in *Selected Essays* (Harcourt, Brace, 1932).

return for the year 1924 to the Collector of Inland Revenue in Baltimore, Maryland, Eliot enclosed a check for $12.44, explaining that his delay in doing so was due to "very exceptional personal difficulties" (we can imagine them, yes) and that if he had made further "inclusions and allowances" the check would have been "something between four and five dollars." Someone had suggested that Prince Wilhelm of Sweden, who was of a literary bent, might be a possible contributor to *The Criterion.* After Eliot invited him to do so and the prince demurred, Eliot followed up:

> I have to thank Your Royal Highness for Your letter of the 12th February and to express the hope that Your Royal Highness will reconsider judgment. *The Criterion* and its contributors would be in every way honoured by Your Royal Highness's collaboration. Your Royal Highness's letter indicates complete command of the English language, but if this should be a difficulty I have to inform Your Royal Highness that we are quite prepared to translate from Swedish any manuscript that Your Royal Highness might be good enough to allow us to use.
>
> I remain Your Royal Highness's
> obliged and obedient servant.

Was this done with a perfectly straight face? Perhaps so, since Eliot was soon to declare himself (in *For Lancelot Andrewes,* 1928) as, among other things, "royalist in politics." It was at any rate to no avail since His Royal Highness never appeared in the magazine. Nor is the humorous note absent when Eliot considers his own prose. In a letter to Aldington, he says that his style was formed by two years of studying the philosophy of F. H. Bradley, and "an inherited disposition to rhetoric" gotten from his ancestors and their engagements with church, the law, and politics. But he admits that, in a wonderful phrase, these influences give his prose "a rather rheumatic pomposity—I am conscious of this stiffness, but I do not trust myself elsewhere."

His devotion to the work of Pound and of Wyndham Lewis was already well established, and in his letters to each, one marvels at the good-humored patience he shows in dealing with such monsters of ego. Pound harangues him about money payments and tells him what a boring magazine ("unreadable") he is putting out: "But for yr. connection with the review I couldn't go on appearing with this bunch of dead mushrooms." Lewis, whose work Eliot regards at least as highly as Pound's, is continually being placated and encouraged to send in the material he's promised to send. In a long and somewhat reproving letter Eliot regrets there is not more of Lewis's material to publish and pledges his "continuous and disinterested desire to push your work as far as in my power." Rather stiffly-on-purpose he signs it "Thomas Eliot." More unexpected, at least to me, was his reaching out to writers whose work I had presumed he was cool to at best. Engaged in the composition of his verse play *Sweeney Agonistes,* he wrote Arnold Bennett soliciting his advice about dialogue, to which Bennett responded positively. They dined together at the Savoy Grill. He wrote the now-forgotten writer May Sinclair how much he admired D. H. Lawrence's work, and published "The Woman Who Rode Away" while urging Lawrence to contribute more regularly to the magazine—"I mean that I should like to have something of yours in almost every number, shorter essays, notes or reviews." (Five stories of Lawrence would eventually appear in *The Criterion.*) And although we knew that Eliot admired *The Great Gatsby,* I was unprepared for the extent of that admiration in the next to last letter from the volume, when he tells Fitzgerald he has now read the book three times and that it has "interested and excited me more than any new novel I have seen, either English or American, for a number of years." It was, Eliot told him, the first step taken in American fiction since Henry James.

One of the bonuses in this and the previous volume is the frequent presence of Eliot's brother Henry as someone to whom Eliot could unburden himself. There are also letters from Henry to TSE, the most charming of which is one in which he tells Tom he's engaged to be married, and worried about the prospect:

> Perhaps she will make a Man out of me. I never had any very strong ambition toward that end. The field is already overcrowded. . . .
>
> Good God, how does anyone get married? I would not accept a job as a traffic manager or shipping clerk because I know nothing about it, and yet here is a job which every man accepts apparently on the blithe assumption that knowledge of the business is innate in him.

He proceeds amusingly, finally telling his brother that if he has any advice to give him, now's the time. From Eliot's silence (no return letter to Henry appears) we conclude that marital matters were a subject on which he found himself reluctant to advise and pronounce.

Are these letters of Eliot from 1923 through 1925, added to the earlier revised volume, "great" letters? Are they, as for example the letters of Keats or Byron or Robert Frost, ones that we would want to return to, reread with pleasure? The answer pretty clearly is no, yet I can't think of a better epistolary account of what it's like to run a magazine from issue to issue; of who should be gotten in touch with and what tone of address to take towards the recipient. As for the private man, his miseries are now broadcast for all who may want to listen in. But what gives the most pleasure, however grim or humorous the subject matter, is nothing more or less than how Eliot puts sentences together. In his important, early essay " 'Rhetoric' and Poetic Drama," mostly about Rostand's *Cyrano,* he speculates on acting and being conscious one is acting—the "dramatic sense" that, he says, is almost a sense of humor. In the letter quoted above he found his "inherited disposition for rhetoric" to issue in "rheumatic pomposity." But in most of these letters the prose is a good deal more flexible, less rheumatic than he suggests. When a fellow editor sent him an essay on Rimbaud for consideration, Eliot wrote back that the article was very interesting but that its style left much to be desired. He ends by begging pardon for speaking frankly and explains:

> Ordinarily, I do not take the trouble to do so; but the material which you have presented speaks so well for your brain power that I feel it would be a great pity if you did not take the trouble to learn more about the writing of English prose. Study Swift and Newman.

Putting two such prose masters together is done in such a way that we take the advice personally, at least to the extent of wondering whether our own prose might have benefitted by such a course of study. Did anyone ever couple Swift and Newman in this way before? Its imaginative surprise is typical of Eliot the letter-writer.

—*Hudson Review,* Summer, 2010.

Prufrock Centennial

ONE OF THE quieter celebrations of a literary centennial may be the one for *Prufrock and Other Observations*, T. S. Eliot's first book of poems published in 1917. Eliot was then twenty-nine years of age, had published a number of poems, essays on philosophic topics, and reviews. Married to Vivien Haigh-Wood in 1915, he and his wife experienced a rocky marriage to say the least, both of them frequently ill with minor complaints, even as her psychological state grew increasingly disturbed. Eliot taught at a couple of private schools and gave evening extension lectures to adults; but his financial situation was unsettled until in March of 1917 he went to work at Lloyds Bank in London, in the Colonial and Financial Department. In the fall of the previous year, he wrote to his brother Henry describing that year as "in some respect, the most awful nightmare of anxiety that the mind of man could conceive." At about the same time Vivien wrote to Eliot's mother describing, among other things, the state of her husband's underwear: "Still thick and in *fair* condition...but it needs *incessant darning,* Darning alone takes me hours out of the week." In the letter to his brother Eliot had expressed worry that his poem, "The Love Song of J. Alfred Prufrock," published two years previously, might be his "swan song." Working at the bank brought some alleviation to both financial and domestic troubles; he began to write poetry again and in August of 1917 *Prufrock and Other Observations* was published.

It was a slim yellow pamphlet brought out by the *The Egoist*, a small publisher of which Ezra Pound was the leading force, and consisted of twelve poems, beginning with "Prufrock" and ending with *"La Figlia che Piange."* Pound had been instrumental in getting Harriet Monroe, editor of the American magazine *Poetry,* to publish "Prufrock" in 1915, after some forcible coaxing—"the best poem I have yet had or seen from an American," Pound insisted. Eliot as well thought it by far his best poem. In the volume he followed it with "Portrait of a Lady," then two poems—"Preludes" and "Rhapsody on a Windy Night"—written earlier and under the influence of Jules Laforgue. There were a number of shorter poems, like "Morning at the Window," "Cousin Nancy," and "The Boston Evening Transcript," that could be thought of as illustrations of the Observations of the book's title. Distinct from the other poems in the volume, *"La Figlia che Piange"* was, and would continue to be, the purest expression of lyric Eliot. In his biography of the poet, Peter Ackroyd summed up the character of these poems: "Examples of dramatic virtuosity, conceived in terms of monologue and dialogue, 'scene' and character." Yet this does little to suggest the originality—at least the oddity—of the poems taken singly and together.

Evelyn Waugh's father, Arthur, was not taken by such originality, reviewing (as a bookman he reviewed everything) an anthology of 1914 in which "Prufrock" and other Eliot poems had appeared. What Eliot and these young poets in their eagerness to be clever had forgotten was that "the first essence of poetry is beauty," and that the "unmetrical, incoherent banalities" of such upstarts would eventually be corrected. Waugh concluded his review by alluding to a "classic custom in the family hall" in which a drunken slave was displayed by way of warning family members of the perils of unbridled self-expression. When Pound came to review *Prufrock and Other Observations* he mocked "a very old chap," Mr. Waugh, for comparing the younger poets to "drunken helots," Pound providing words that weren't in the review.

In fact the reviewers of the Prufrock volume were more indifferent to the poems than outraged by them as Arthur Waugh had been. The anonymous reviewer in the *Times Literary Supplement* found them to be "untouched by any generous rush of feeling," while the *Literary World* thought they were satiric teasings aimed at reviewers. "Prufrock" "was found to be neither witty nor amusing and "Mr Eliot" was advised that "he could do finer work on traditional lines." "A keen eye as well as a sharp pen," said *The New Statesman*, citing the appropriateness of Observations in the title to characterize the poems. The only significant reviews aside from Pound's were by the novelist May Sinclair and the American poet and Eliot's friend at Harvard, Conrad Aiken. Aiken praised the poems' "psychological realism" and called Eliot an "exceptionally acute technician" (details unspecified). May Sinclair countered the charge of obscurity by admitting that in these poems "His thoughts move very rapidly and by astounding cuts," a fine summing-up of their technique. And that was it for the early reviews of Eliot's first book.

One hundred years later what has survived from *Prufrock and Other Observations* as permanent literature? All the poems would be permanent in the Eliot canon; he was not—unlike say W. B. Yeats or W. H. Auden—to revise, much less to expunge particular poems: with very minor exceptions they stand in Eliot's *Collected Poems* as they stood at the beginning. (Remember that Eliot's volume adds up to just over 200 pages.) An uncontroversial estimate of the poems that most count in his first book would single out three: "The Love Song of J. Alfred Prufrock," "Portrait of a Lady," and "*La Figlia che Piange*."

My introduction to Eliot in college came by way of the subtle classroom presence of Reuben Brower, close reader extraordinaire. Brower began his classes on the poet not with "Prufrock" but with "Portrait of a Lady," an easier poem partly because it has a more stable narrative presence. A young man visits an older lady (in Boston, say), then goes away (Paris?) and comes back to a changed, unsatisfactory, guilt-tinged relationship. What made the poem memorable for me was Brower's voicing aloud lines such as the following:

> We have been, let us say, to hear the latest Pole
> Transmit the Preludes, through his hair and finger-tips.
> "So intimate, this Chopin, that I think his soul
> Should be resurrected only among friends
> Some two or three, who will not touch the bloom
> That is rubbed and questioned in the concert room."
> —And so the conversations slips
> Among velleities and carefully caught regrets...

Brower introduced me to the pleasure of reading the lines as they might be heard (Frost called it "ear-reading"), and it is those accents that remain with me even as the "content"—never all that much of account anyway—has disappeared. Of the three poems mentioned above "Portrait" may be categorized as a monologue with analogies to Browning or Laforgue. Its overall apologetic note, diffident and uncertain, would not be heard for the last time in Eliot's work.

Eliot placed "*La Figlia che Piange*" at the end of the volume for good reasons: it is a beautiful (the word may be permitted) instance of the lyric poet able, at least at the poem's beginning, to catch an elusive, personal mode of feeling:

> Stand on the highest pavement of the stair—
> Lean on a garden urn—
> Weave, weave, the sunlight in your hair—
> Clasp your flowers to you with a pained surprise—
> Fling them to the ground and turn
> With a fugitive resentment in your eyes:
> But weave, weave the sunlight in your hair.

The poem goes on to complicate itself by introducing an "I" who seems to be arranging a tableau for the woman of the first stanza and her putative lover. Not the least of complicating aspects are the irregular lines of the three "stanzas" (each slightly different from the others), and the unpredictable but quite wonderful rhyming. In her perceptive review of the Prufrock volume, May Sinclair called "*La Figlia*" no less than "a unique masterpiece," a plausible claim.

But of course the poem that counts the most is "Prufrock":

> Let us go then, you and I,
> When the evening is spread out against the sky
> Like a patient etherised upon a table;
> Let us go, through certain half-deserted streets,
> The muttering retreats
> Of restless nights in one-night cheap hotels
> And sawdust restaurants with oyster shells...

It proceeds through various shifting rhythmical and emotional patterns, which project an overall eloquence of inadequacy that more than once pauses to consider itself:

> It is impossible to say just what I mean!
> But as if a magic lantern threw the nerves in patterns on a screen...

"Prufrock" threw the nerves in patterns that had not been seen or heard before in English poetry. Impossible to say just what he or it means, because impossible to hold Prufrock as a character in a dependable frame that binds together the poem's constituent parts. One of those parts is Prufrock's disclaimer of Shakespearean gravity and weight: "No! I am not Prince Hamlet nor was meant to be." When Harriet Monroe objected to this section as out of keeping with other parts of the poem, Pound wrote her that he too disliked it, but that it was an "early and cherished bit" that Eliot wanted to include and that would do the poem no harm. So much for the necessity of having a consistently dramatized speaker.

As noted in his review of *Prufrock*, Conrad Aiken called Eliot an exceptionally able "technician" but failed to hazard any remarks about that technique. One sympathizes with Aiken's silence on the subject, since Eliot himself was to write, in prefacing the second edition of his first book of essays, "We cannot define even the technique of verse; we cannot say at what point 'technique' begins or where it ends." Thus Eliot had to content himself with defining poetry as "excellent words in excellent arrangement and excellent metre." A bit of a leg-pull here surely, but the amount of words spilled about "Prufrock" in this and the preceding century suggests a never-ending effort to find adequate—or the least inadequate—words to describe it. Perhaps for that reason the poem, more than any other of Eliot's, has showed its continuing life to curious readers of poetry, many of them younger ones. Along with Robert Frost's "The Road Not Taken," it is one of the only modern poem today's undergraduates have read, or at least heard about.

The final six lines of the poem are presumably about the mermaids Prufrock has heard singing, but their words and word-music are such as to take us beyond any reference. In Denis Donoghue's excellent formulation about the poems generally, "We are not allowed to escape from the words into another place":

> I have seen them riding seaward on the waves
> Combing the white hair of the waves blown back
> When the wind blows the water white and black.
>
> We have lingered in the chambers of the sea
> By sea-girls wreathed with seaweed red and brown
> Till human voices wake us, and we drown.

After a hundred years, "Prufrock" remains as fresh and unaccountable as it seemed to its first readers back then.

—*Weekly Standard*, May 21, 2017.

Poet in his Youth

T. S. Eliot: Inventions of The March Hare
Poems, 1909-1917
Edited by Christopher Ricks. Harcourt Brace. 428 pp.

BETWEEN THE YEARS 1909 and 1917, T. S. Eliot kept a leather-bound notebook in which he entered his poems as he wrote them; in 1922, having published *Prufrock and Other Observations* (1915) and *Poems* (1920), and with *The Waste Land* about to appear, he allowed his American patron, John Quinn, to purchase the manuscript, many of whose poems Eliot more than once deprecated as "unpublished and unpublishable." The Notebook, whose location was unknown to Eliot when he died in 1965, ended up in the Berg Collection of the New York Public Library; for years, Eliot scholars have been allowed to refer to, though not to quote from, individual poems. Now, with the blessings of Valerie Eliot, the poet's widow, the Notebook poems have been published, including a number of ribald and scatological exercises, such as "The Triumph of Bullshit" and the King Bolo verses, which Eliot excised (they wound up in the Ezra Pound archive). "Inventions of the March Hare"—Eliot's title, which he had crossed out at the front of the Notebook—has been edited by Christopher Ricks, professor of English literature at Boston University, and published along with a number of appendices. (The most interesting of these, "Influence and Influences," consists of a selection of Eliot's relevant statements on the subject.) There are, of course, many sorts of editing, but the imaginative dimensions of this example are altogether extraordinary.

Ricks's editorial brilliance has been on display before, most notably in his three-volume Tennyson, and his critical intelligence established through a number of books, including a fine one on Eliot. Still, nothing quite prepares one for the breadth of reading and power of retentive memory that inform his 200 pages of annotation to 80 pages' worth of hitherto unpublished poems. Nor does the modesty with which Ricks states his principles prepare us for the audacity of his practice. He will try, he says, to "abstain" from writing what Eliot called notes of "explanation"—notes that are not primarily the supplying of information. Since, in Ricks's words, "the important thing is evidence of where the poems came from, and of where they went to in Eliot's other work," the notes will be concerned with suggesting parallels, leaving it to the reader to decide "what to make of what the poet made of the matter."

But what "the poet made of the matter," inasmuch as the matter is words, may be considerable—especially when the poet is Eliot, who said of Shakespeare, "The evidence that Shakespeare read with the most prodigious memory for words that has ever existed is almost indisputable." When Ricks reads Eliot, things happen, fireworks go off. Consider the opening line of an early Notebook poem, "Second Caprice in North Cambridge": "This charm of vacant lots!" Ricks's note on the lines directs us to Tennyson, Milton, and the Oxford English Dictionary for relevant uses of the word "charm," then fastens on "vacant lots," noting that it closes Eliot's fourth "Prelude" ("Gathering fuel in vacant lots"), then tracing the phrase as it shows up in Eliot's translation of St. John Perse ("in this quarter of vacant lots and rubbish"). There follow references to an unadopted revised ending to Eliot's "Sweeney Agonistes"; to Virginia Woolf's report in her diary that Eliot told her his father was a brick merchant and that "they lived in the slums among vacant lots"; to a resemblance to French poet Jules Laforgue ("terrains vagues"), and finally to three sentences from Henry James's *The Bostonians* that make expressive use of "vacant lots" and related phrases from the poem.

Given Ricks's astonishing auditory memory, one expects him to pounce on Eliot's rhyming of "tranquillity" with "sea" (in "Mandarins 2"), and note that it's "a rhyme dear to Shelley" (examples from "Episychidion" and "Rosalind and Helen" are produced). But when a line from "Mandarins 1"—"the centre of formalities"—is compared not only with something in Tennyson's "In Memoriam" but also with some language from Chapter 80 of Dickens's *Barnaby Rudge*, which contains both "the centre of the system" and "round-faced mandarins," we gasp in disbelief, even as the similarity enforces itself. How on earth did Ricks latch onto that moment in Dickens's little-read novel? And how, in encountering "irritate the imagination / Or the nerves" (from "Easter Sensations of April"), did he think of a passage from Hawthorne's *The Blithedale Romance*, where the narrator looks at Zenobia and announces, "It irritated my nerves"? Further comparisons—to one of Eliot's letters, to James's *The American Scene*, to Arthur Symons and Gerard de Nerval—follow by way of broadening the network of "nerves."

The weight of annotation borne here by even the most insignificant-looking poem is formidable: For example, "Suppressed Complex," an eight-line trifle about a sleeping "she" briefly visited by a mysterious "I," elicits more than two pages of packed commentary. The title is glossed by a letter from Eliot to his brother, the OED, William James's *Psychology*, Freud's *Interpretation of Dreams*, Pound's literary essays, a prose poem of Baudelaire's, a book on Eliot by Robert Crawford in which Eliot's attendance at an Oxford lecture by R. G. Collingwood on Aristotle's "*De Anima*" is described, Frazer's *The Golden Bough*, and F. H. Bradley's *Appearance and Reality*. Lines from the poem are compared to *Hamlet*, Samuel Butler's "Hudibras," Keats's "Isabella," another poem by Eliot, one by Shelley, and one by Robert Stephen Hawker from the 1900 *Oxford Book of English Verse*. In another poem, the single word "Defecations" provokes mention of, among others, Jeremy Taylor, Coleridge, Matthew Arnold, and Dante.

Given what at least this reader feels to be the overall slightness, the ephemeral and fugitive quality of these Notebook poems ("unpublished and unpublishable"), Ricks's over-the-top annotation might be judged excessive—interventions of the March hare at some mad editorial tea party. Such a judgment would be not only ungracious but dully uninventive on the part of any reader serious about Eliot and, even more so, about poetry. In his preface to the second edition of *The Sacred Wood*, Eliot wrote that in considering the notion of technique in poetry, "We cannot say at what point 'technique' begins or where it ends," and went on to add, "So we cannot stop at any point." In proposing to examine where the Notebook poems came from and where they went to in Eliot's other work, Ricks has in fact refused to stop at that seemingly measurable point and instead has shown how the study of poetry is inexhaustible, neither to be measured nor completed. His edition of these poems is a seminar in the uses of literary language whose dimensions are vast and against which readers will feel their own limitations, failure even. Yet confronted with the critical genius at work in this edition, such feelings may seem appropriate, even salutary.

—*Boston Globe*, March 9, 1997.

Sincerely, Young Possum: *The Letters of T.S. Eliot, Vol 3*

The Letters of T.S. Eliot,
ed. Valerie Eliot and John Haffenden
Volume 3. Yale University Press

"I DON'T LIKE reading other people's correspondence in print, and I do not want other people to read mine," wrote T. S. Eliot to his mother in April 1927. Sounds definitive enough, yet six years later he would confess in a lecture that there was an "ineradicable" desire to hope one's correspondence might be preserved for complete strangers to read: "We want to confess ourselves in writing to a few friends, and we do not always want to feel that no one but those friends will ever read what we have written," put with a circumspection native to the man his friend Pound called Possum; still, I think Eliot might have been slightly astonished that, with the publication of Volume 3 of his letters, their total page count reaches 2700. Since that only brings us up to the end of 1927 (Eliot died in 1965), there's a long way to go.

The new volume covers just two years of the poet's life, which has not only to do with the fact that he wrote a lot of letters, but that they have been edited in the fullest, most scrupulous and imaginative way by the project's general editor, the remarkable John Haffenden. (Eliot's widow Valerie is co-editor, but I suspect did little of the heavy lifting.) Haffenden's procedure is, whenever possible, to annotate any letter Eliot has written by providing pertinent sections, at the bottom of the page, of the letter or other communication he was responding to. In other words, none of these letters ever comes from out of the blue.

It would however be disingenuous to pretend that the bulk of the letters can be of interest to anyone but a fairly devoted student of Eliot, and not so much a student of his poetry but someone interested in his "prose" capacity as editor of his periodical, the *Criterion*, an organ that, beginning with its inception in 1922, Eliot hoped to make a forceful commentator on the art, politics, and religion of England and Europe. As with the previous volumes of letters, many of them concern *Criterion* business, and although they are exemplary of the subtleties and complications of running a literary magazine, there is more than some sameness about them; also a good deal of business worries concerning the magazine's future as it moves from a quarterly, to (in 1927) a monthly, then back again to quarterly status. Eliot now has a position on the board of the publisher Faber & Guyer (later Faber & Faber), so has the added responsibilities of considering various books for possible publication and of informing their authors that (often) the book is not quite "right" for Faber, would not be a saleable item, but please consider us... etc. He is masterly at this.

Earlier volumes of his letters prominently displayed Eliot's wife Vivien, whose sufferings were the stuff of melodrama, if not tragedy. For most of the two years covered in the new volume she is a patient in a sanatorium on the outskirts of Paris, where her husband visits her periodically. We get a sad glimpse of her as she writes to John Middleton Murry, Eliot's friend and intellectual antagonist, "I am quite alone and have nothing at all inside." In a more sportive mood she confides to Eliot's brother Henry that "Of *all* the 'roles' a woman enjoys and delights in, that of the brow-beaten wife is the most delicious." Eliot's own laments, less frequent than in earlier volumes, occasionally burst out as he writes, also to Murry, "I am oppressed by a sense of doom, against which I struggle." But mainly he soldiers on, not without sometimes showing the effects. Aldous Huxley, if he can be trusted, notes that at a lunch "Tom looked terribly grey-green, drank no less than five gins with his meal, and announced that he was going to join Vivien in the nursing home, to break himself of his addictions to tobacco and alcohol." This did not come to pass. Writing to his brother Henry, Eliot discusses the difficulty of getting Vivien into an asylum, but says no doctor would commit anyone "unless they have either tried to commit suicide or committed a criminal assault. We must therefore wait until she either annoys people in the public street (which I am always expecting) or tries to take her own life." It took six more years for him eventually to remove himself from the marriage.

The most notable event in Eliot's private life during these two years was his acceptance into the Church of England in the summer of 1927. This took place with some secrecy: he concealed it from his mother and later wrote his brother that he kept it from Vivien since it "might provide a fresh reason for domestic persecution." Later that summer he wrote an extraordinary letter to his mother, now ill and living in Cambridge, Massachusetts, who feared she would never see her son again. Eliot replied that he hoped to come to America soon, but that he had "a much more positive conviction than you have that I shall see you in a future life," even though that life would be not at all like anything imaginable. He assures her that whatever he has done that the world thought good, "It was something that you and I did together or even something that you had dreamt of and projected before I was born." He hopes to make "a deeper mark on English and European civilization," but at any rate salutes her as "the finest and greatest woman that I have ever known." His recent conversion may have strengthened assurance in an afterlife, but the testament is as movingly heartfelt as anything to be encountered in the letters.

Among his literary remarks and judgments, a few on American writers stand out. He calls Whitman "a great master of versification," and compares him in this regard to Tennyson. While disliking George Santayana, with whom he took courses at Harvard, he likes Santayana's fine essay "The Genteel Tradition in American Literature," and notes shrewdly that Santayana is best when he is "slightly mischievous" and when his essays fall "on the borderline of literary criticism." His admiration for Hawthorne grew ever more strong, not for his "preoccupation with American problems but in his preoccupation with general spiritual problems." Hawthorne's successor Henry James, shared in this concern but Hawthorne, Eliot says, is a much more "universal" writer, a "very much greater writer than James." At first glance this judgment seems a shocking one, especially when we remember Eliot's praise of James for his mastery over and escape from "ideas" ("He had a mind so fine that no idea could violate it"). But Eliot's main attraction was to the early Europeanizing James of *Daisy Miller* and *The Europeans*, and perhaps the later James interested him less; while as Eliot's own "spirituality" deepened, Hawthorne assumed more prominence.

The years 1926-27 for Eliot show little new poetry. His *Poems 1925* (a book he told Leonard Woolf he was unhappy about) concluded with the desperate fragmentation of *The Hollow Men*, and the parts he published in the *Criterion* from *Sweeney Agonistes*, his unfinished verse drama, failed to bring things together. The only finished poem was "Journey to the Magi," composed, he wrote Conrad Aiken, one Sunday morning in a forty-five minute interval between church and dinner "with the aid of half a bottle of Booth's Gin." Although he continued to review, and published an important essay, "Shakespeare and the Stoicism of Seneca," *The Waste Land* proved a difficult act to follow. The turn toward religion, which would culminate in *Ash-Wednesday* a few years later, was just beginning to make itself felt in his verse. As for stirring formulations about poetry, they are absent from the letters. He remarked to his spiritual counselor, William Force Stead, that he failed to see why so many people wanted to write about poetry: "God knows why; it seems to me the dullest subject going." No other great poet has made that statement.

But it is only one example among many of the original wit on display in all three volumes of letters, and that has kept this reader going as it lights up the correspondence with timely sparks. He writes F. Scott Fitzgerald (whose *Great Gatsby* he had admired) that Fitzgerald's letter had pleased him "in spite of the fact that you persist in misspelling my name." When during a discussion a religious topic is brought up, he declared "The only things I care for are dancing and brandy," and he offered to introduce Virginia Woolf (who better?) to new forms of dance steps like the Grizzly Bear and the Chicken Strut. "I have a frightful attack of rheumatism," he writes the day after a *Criterion* dinner party; "I'm afraid I sang too much." Many of the letters are written to Bonamy Dobrée, a member of the *Criterion* phalanx who had accepted a teaching position in Cairo. There is some rather heavy joking in the slightly obscene mode of Eliot's "King Bolo" poems, but also a couple of pertinent questions about life in Dobrée's new setting: "The only thing I want to know about the camel is whether, as American authorities assert, it is always necessary to walk a mile for one." Dobrée took that one more or less in stride, but it was followed by another query about the camel: "Do they fold their tents, and if so in how many folds, and if so is it always in the same folds like a napkin or a serviette (as called in seaside hotels)"? Dobrée couldn't answer that one.

—Originally published in the *Washington Examiner*,
December 31, 2012 as "Sincerely, Young Possum."

The Letters of T.S. Eliot, Vol. 6

THIS IS THE SIXTH volume of T. S. Eliot's letters, covering, as did Volume 5, only two years in his life, 1932-1933. At this rate, and since Eliot lived until 1965, one wonders how long the indefatigable editor of the correspondence, John Haffenden, can keep it up. As with previous volumes the individual letter, whenever possible, is fully situated in a context of to whom and to what Eliot was responding. Often the footnotes quoting liberally from the letter that provoked Eliot's are as interesting as that letter itself. Along with the currently appearing volumes of Robert Frost's letters, Eliot's provide a rich perspective on the modern poetry scene as observed by two masters. (Frost's letters are planned for five volumes and have just reached 1928, a generous-sized gathering but dwarfed by Eliot's.)

Previous volumes of Eliot's letters were significantly made up of business correspondence connected with the editorship of his magazine, *The Criterion,* and his position on the board of the publisher Faber and Faber. There are fewer of such letters in the new volume, which features instead two central events. The first is Eliot's seven-month visit to America, where he delivers some eighty lectures, the most important of which would be published as *The Use of Poetry and the Use of Criticism*, a survey of the central English critics from Sidney to Matthew Arnold. The other focal point concerns his decision to separate from his wife, Vivien, to whom he had been married, mostly unhappily, since 1915. The time in America helped firm up Eliot's resolution to leave Vivien permanently (as an Anglo-Catholic he would not divorce) despite the abrupt cruelty of such a move. He wrote to the widow of the poet Harold Monro that he had been contemplating such a step for years, and that a "sudden sharp break" would be best for both parties. His motive he described as that of "getting peace for work and throwing off the poison of uncongeniality and pretense" (552). This was an "excruciating decision," as the editor calls it; for such a "predominately charitable" man, the letters referring to his wife in their resentment and anger are "frank to the point of being shocking."

As for the months spent in America—his first visit there since 1915—he wrote his brother upon returning to England that it had been "the happiest year I can ever remember in my life." He lectured widely, taught a course at Harvard, got to California where he spent time with Emily Hale, the woman who meant so much to him. But his comments on the land were less than enthusiastic: "Most of the country I do not like; California is a nightmare" (545). Boston-Cambridge was the most agreeable spot, although in his first days living at Harvard's Eliot House he could hear "the wireless, the gramophone, the typewriter, and all the conversation of two undergraduates next door" (457). He wrote Geoffrey Faber about the grandeur of Eliot House although "The buildings don't seem real" and the house "gives in some inappropriateness an effect of burlesque" (459). He is displeased that "the dons...such as they dine at all, dine obscurely, at a small table in a corner, while the undergraduates dine at a dais." And then there are the presence of "waitresses," along with the family coat of arms on the backs of chairs causing a feeling of "distressing embarrassment, as if someone in the company had just made a joke in bad taste" (459). He meets Harvard's President Lowell, "an affable, mediocre, uninterested Boston business man too small for the job." All in all "The human life seems very insignificant" (459), although he hopes to become reconciled and see it all "in a more humorous light." He managed that humorous light when he later confessed that to live in Cambridge was "to be among a society which consists largely of one's own relatives... people who were fond of me before the malady of poetry declared itself" (xvii).

Eliot was addicted to formulations, comic or morose, that judged the world to be "an unpleasant place" (as he wrote to Stephen Spender), "a compound of knave and blockhead, chiefly moved by vanity and fear, and kept quiet by laziness" (291). Yet whatever gloomy sentiments he professed about mankind, his dealings with individuals were invariably thoughtful, generous, and enlivened by idiomatic energy, as when he hopes, in visiting friends in New York City, to encounter "a copious supply of BEER (not the synthetic article made by the Harvard Chemists...together with a Limburger cheese and quiet corner with no women in it" (504). After he returned to England and visited Virginia Woolf, she found him "settling in with some severity to being a great man"(xxxv). That would transpire presently.

—Originally published in the *Boston Globe*, August 31, 2016, as "A more personal volume of T. S. Eliot's letters."

The Prose Eliot

OVER THE PAST two months, I have been undergoing one of the more significant reading experiences of my life, the perusal of T. S. Eliot's complete prose from the first twenty-one years of his writing career. Eliot died in 1965, so these pages constitute a major recognition, after fifty years, of his contribution. The general editor is Ronald Schuchard, and anyone familiar with his edition of Eliot's Clark lectures of 1926 (*The Varieties of Metaphysical Poetry*, 1993) will be unsurprised at the extraordinary fullness with which these two large volumes are annotated.[1] The general editorial introduction to the volumes tells us that the notes are intended to "enhance and clarify" Eliot's "highly referential prose." The magnitude of this editorial task was enormous, since at the beginning of the present century more than 700 pieces of the prose were uncollected, nor were there

1. *The Complete Prose of T.S. Eliot: The Critical Edition*. Vol. l, *Apprentice Years 1905-1918*, ed. Jewel Spears Brooker and Ronald Schuchard. The Johns Hopkins University Press, 896 pp. Vol. 2, *The Perfect Critic 1919-1926*, ed. by Anthony Cuda and Ronald Schuchard. The Johns Hopkins University Press, 992 pp.

This is a good year for readers of Eliot. His English publisher, Faber & Faber, has commissioned a six-volume edition of the complete prose. It will not be textually annotated, but Archie Burnett will exercise his usual editorial scrupulousness. Also, to appear later this year in two volumes from Faber, *The Poems of T. S. Eliot*, edited by Christopher Ricks and Jim McCue. A very full biography of Eliot, taking him up to *The Waste Land*, has recently appeared (*Young Eliot*, by Robert Crawford, Farrar, Straus & Giroux).

Meanwhile, a fifth volume of Eliot's letters, covering the years 1930-31, has just been brought out by Yale University Press. As it has in previous volumes, John Haffenden's editorial genius is again on view. But Volume 5 contains an added bonus, a twenty-page account of Valerie Eliot's heroic labor over the decades in searching out the vast trove of correspondence. By quoting from her own letters about the project, Haffenden brings her alive in remarkable ways.

any critical editions of works published in his lifetime, the Clark lectures being the exception. In response to anyone who might question the need for such a comprehensive project, the editors quote Eliot himself on the importance of reading everything a major author has written: "To understand Baudelaire you must read the whole of Baudelaire." On the safe assumption that one hundred years after "Prufrock" appeared, Eliot qualifies as a major author, we may profitably address ourselves to these early volumes of prose.

Volume I is divided into three sections: Juvenilia and Undergraduate Writings; Graduate Essays and Ph.D. Thesis; Early Journalism: Reviews and Essays. Volume II, an especially rich trove, consists of essays and reviews from Eliot's great period of journalism (1919-1926). His first collection of them, *The Sacred Wood* (1920), has been disassembled, the individual items put in the order they appeared. Each volume has thirty pages or so of introduction that provides a capsule version of Eliot's life and writings during the period. Without question, the most forbidding section for the common reader to navigate is the one containing Eliot's graduate essays at Harvard and Oxford, and his Ph.D. dissertation in philosophy. As a once hopeful student of philosophy, I was unable to call up enough resources to find them of much interest, and I think that even an academic philosopher would need to have very specialized inclinations to follow the pages devoted to the arguments and concerns of late nineteenth- and early twentieth-century thinkers such as Bergson, Josiah Royce, Bernard Bosanquet, Bertrand Russell, and above all F. H. Bradley, Eliot's favorite philosopher-writer and the subject of his Ph.D. thesis. How alive for the contemporary student of philosophy are the concerns they deal with—post-Hegelian idealism, questions of immediate experience, the nature of relations, objects, and truth—I can't say, but would imagine not very alive except historically. In an address Eliot gave to the Harvard Philosophical Club in 1914, "The Relations Between Politics and Metaphysics," he affects some humorous detachment from such issues, as he observes "Mr. Bertrand Russell directing with passionate enthusiasm his unearthly ballet of bloodless alphabets," or "Professor Bosanquet...the prophet who has put off his shoes and talks with the Absolute in a burning bush," or "Professor Royce [to whom] we owe the resuscitation of Christianity by the method of last aid to the dead."

The first and most useful attempt to connect Eliot the philosopher with his behavior as critic and poet was made decades ago by Hugh Kenner in the chapter "Bradley" in *The Invisible Poet*.[2] Some letters of Eliot's, written after his four-year immersion in philosophy and not available to Kenner, suggest that he had had enough of it. In one he explains "I took a piece of fairly technical philosophy for my thesis and my relativism made me see so many sides to questions that I became hopelessly involved, and wrote a thesis perfectly unintelligible to anyone but myself." In another he declares that all philosophizing is a perversion of reality, and that any philosopher as his private system develops and approaches completeness will become "equally preposterous—to anyone but its author." Looking back on his Ph.D. thesis forty-six years later, he found himself "unable to think in the terminology of this essay, indeed, I do not pretend to understand it." The Possum may be on display here, but I also think the poet-critic of later years was speaking accurately about his early preoccupation. He admired Bradley's masterwork, *Appearance and Reality*, because it had "no positive results," and what the editors calls "the sauce of skepticism" seems to have been the truest thing he took away from his engagement with philosophy.

Having found modern philosophy to be a "logomachy," as he called it some years later in a letter to his mother, he decided to reject the fellowship Harvard offered him; instead he put English roots down by marrying Vivien Haigh-Wood in June of 1915. He did some teaching at London's Highgate School where, among the usual academic subjects, he also "taught" baseball. (One would like to have observed this.) In the next couple of years he gave a series of extension courses of lectures to adults in English and French literature, while with the assistance of Bertrand Russell, who very much took Eliot under his wing, he made reviewing connections with philosophical, social, and religious journals, along with the less specialized *New Statesman*. Of the eighty items he published between 1915 and 1918 the majority appeared in the *Egoist*, a small avant-garde press that also brought out his first book of poems, *Prufrock and Other Obsevations*, in 1917. After that he published most prominently in Middleton Murry's *Athenaeum*, then in 1919 began to write for the *Times Literary Supplement*.

In, *Seeing Through Everything* (1977), I sought to describe Eliot's prevailing style as a critic in these early pieces, by appropriating some words from

2. Still the best book on Eliot. Among its many valuable aspects is a chapter on Eliot's criticism that, among other things, introduced one to the many then-uncollected early reviews and brought out their often comic and satiric nature.

Kenner about the famous passage in "Gerontion" that begins, "After such knowledge, what forgiveness?" Kenner remarked of it, "No other Eliot poem exploits the ambiguity of dissolving key-words to this degree. There is no up nor down, no ground on which declaration may stand." As a lively prose example of such "dissolvent" activity, I quoted from a review of 1919, "The Education of Taste," in which Eliot set forth the following sentences about the critic's attempt to find the right language to describe a literary work:

> To communicate impressions is difficult; to communicate a coordinate system of impressions is more difficult; to theorize demands vast ingenuity, and to avoid theorizing requires vast honesty. Also, there is the generality, which is usually a substitute for both impressions and theory.

This is only one of many examples from Eliot's prose, the effect of which is to dissolve key-words to the point where "There is no up nor down, no ground on which declaration may stand." As with Bradley's philosophic writings, which issued in no "positive" results, something similar may be claimed for his own practice as a critic, especially in this early phase where his style was, in the editors' words, "elegant, ironic, authoritative." Who but this poet-critic, it might be supposed, would have something definitive to say about verse technique and the proper way for a critic to proceed in relation to it? Yet when Eliot wrote a brief preface to a second edition of *The Sacred Wood,* he was characteristically skeptical, some might well say evasive. He first took the afflatus out of poetry by calling it a "superior amusement," then quickly adding that although it wasn't a "true definition," "if you call it anything else you are likely to call it something still more false." He next disposed of Matthew Arnold's definition of poetry as a "criticism of life" as too frigid a definition for someone who has had a new experience of poetry. After dissociating it from morals, politics, religion, psychology, and history, he came to what looks to be a conclusion:

> Hence, in criticizing poetry, we are right if we begin, with what sensibility and what knowledge of other poetry we possess, with poetry as excellent words in excellent arrangement and excellent metre. That is what is called the technique of verse.

Are we finally approaching the nub of things? Not at all, since "we observe that we cannot define even the technique of verse; we cannot say at what point 'technique' begins or where it ends; and it we add to it a 'technique of feeling,' that glib phrase will carry us but little farther. We can only say that a poem, in some sense, has its own life... that the feeling, or emotion, or vision resulting from the poem is something different from the feeling or emotion or vision in the mind of the poet."

The doctrine of "Tradition and the Individual Talent" here reasserts itself, but not in such a way as to clear anything up. If the end of things is to declare, "a poem, in some sense, has its own life," then the activity of reading, listening, "realizing" the life of an individual poem is ongoing, never-resting. After all, the next time we read it, its "life" may have declared itself in a different manner. So, the preface ends, "We cannot stop at any point."

In an autobiographical note in 1925 for the Harvard class of 1910, *Quindecennial Report,* Eliot listed his publications as follows: *Prufrock*, 1917; *The Sacred Wood*, 1920; *Ara Vos Prec,* 1920; *The Waste Land*, 1922; *John Dryden*, 1925; *Literature and Export Trade*, 1925. His assiduous bibliographer, Donald Gallup, must have queried him about the final item, since Eliot replied, in one of the useful notes provided by the editors, "I cannot recall how *Literature and Export Trade* got into the Class List. It must have been either a small leg-pull of my own, or a confusion on the part of somebody else," and he assures Gallup that no such work by his hand is in existence. Leg-pull or not, Eliot's critical writings are full of such mischief (later on he was fond of playing practical jokes on his colleagues at Faber and Faber) and is central to the life of his prose.[3] In his review of these volumes (*The New Criterion*, Dec. 1914), Denis Donoghue singled out some sentences with a particular "aphoristic flourish." Here follow some different ones from those chosen by Mr. Donoghue. In reviewing an anthology, *The New Poetry*, Eliot notes at the end of a paragraph, "Rupert Brooke is not absent." Soon

3. My favorite leg-pull comes in a 1920 *Athenaeum* letter concerning William R. Polack, who had objected to some statements in Eliot's essay on the dramatist, Philip Massinger. It begins, "Mr William H. Polack's perplexity is a spectacle before which it is impossible for me to remain passive," and concludes with the following paragraph: Mr Polack "feels that T.S.E. deplores the fact that Dickens was not an artist. I feel that Mr Polack's feelings have run away with him. (So look'd he once when in an angry parle he smote...) But if Mr Polack is again mistaken, what then?" Eliot famously called *Hamlet* an artistic failure, but it provided him here with a first-rate bit of allusive teasing.

afterward he concocted a number of fatuous letters presumably written by readers troubled by something Eliot had written; for example, Helen B. Trundlett, from Batton, Kent, who while finding "occasional coarseness" in Brooke's early poem, calls it "dross" that "was purged away (if I may be permitted that word) in the fire of the Great Ordeal which is proving the well-spring of a Renaissance of English poetry." Of an obscure practitioner of *vers libre*, Eliot writes "One is annoyed with him for not having rewritten the small book before printing it." (Evidently it's always a good idea to rewrite your book.) In a 1917 review of the anthology *Wheels*, he calls Sacheverell Sitwell the most important poet in the volume; then, with an allusion to Matthew Arnold's characterization of Shelley as "a beautiful, *an ineffectual* angel, beating in the void his luminous wings in vain," Eliot calls Sitwell "a beautiful but ineffectual aeroplane, beating its propeller vainly in a tree." About Evelyn Waugh's brother Alec, Eliot opines "Mr Waugh is said to be very young, and to have written a novel. That is a bad beginning, but something might be made of him." The poet Lancelot Hogben possesses "a simple sincerity...which would stand the author in good stead if he would read the right things and work hard." Sometime the insolence gets out of hand: "Because we have never learned to criticize Keats, Shelley, and Wordsworth (poets of assured though modest merit), Keats, Shelley, and Wordsworth punish us from their graves with the annual scourge of the Georgian Anthology." A good hit at the now-forgotten Georgians perhaps, but that intolerably sniffy parenthesis ("poets of assured though modest merit") has to be condemned. There is an even sillier hit about how Marlowe's Mephistopheles renders Milton's Satan superfluous.[4]

All the above zingers but one are from the *Egoist*, 1917, and speak to a small, knowing audience; when Eliot began to write for the *Athenaeum* and then the *TLS*, he became not less clever but more searching in his formulations. In the *Athenaeum* between July and September, 1919, appeared "'Rhetoric' and Poetic Drama," "Marlowe," "Tradition and the Individual Talent," "Swinburne as Critic," and "Hamlet." In November of the same year appeared the first of his "leaders" for the *TLS*, the great essay on Ben Jonson. In 1921, along with a nervous breakdown, he published three of his most valuable essays, on Dryden, the Metaphysical Poets, and Marvell. At the same time he wrote a series of outspoken and entertaining letters

4. This occurs in "The Possibility of a Poetic Drama," an essay Eliot excluded from his *Selected Essays* (1932). Was he a trifle embarrassed at trashing Milton?

for the *Dial*, in New York, and he began, with the inception of his magazine *The Criterion*, in 1922 to produce, from time to time, a commentary on whatever currently engaged his attention. He had a penchant for striking off agreeable portraits of important figures, as in this London Letter of 1921 apropos of Bernard Shaw's *Back to Methuselah*, Shaw's lengthy five-part sequence of plays. Eliot calls him an insular Diderot, and *Methuselah* "a delightful farrago of...conversation about economics, politics, biology, dramatic and art criticism":

> Mr Shaw has never cajoled the public; it is no fault of his that he has been taken for a joker, a cleverer Oscar Wilde, when his intention was always austerely serious. It is his seriousness which has made him unpopular, which made Oscar Wilde appear, in comparison, dull enough to be a safe and respectable playwright. But Shaw has perhaps suffered in a more vital way from the public denseness; a more appreciative audience might have prevented him from being satisfied with an epigram instead of a demonstration. On the other hand Mr Shaw himself has hardly understood his own seriousness, or known where it might lead him: he is somehow amazingly innocent. The explanation is that Mr Shaw never was really interested in life. Had he been more curious about the actual and abiding human being, he might have been less clever and less surprising. He was interested in the comparatively transient things, in anything that can or should be changed, but he was not interested in, was rather impatient of, the things which have always been the same.

The almost friendly passage needs to be reread in order to detect just how much is going on under its bland façade. To this reader, discovering it for the first time and fresh from having taught a couple of Shaw's plays, it is satisfying to see Eliot dealing with a "modern" temperament as opposed to his own would-be classical one, and to find that the result is an original thought.

By way of suggesting the quality of Eliot's reviewing, without adducing yet once more the most famous essays, consider the following piece on a writer you may not have been reading recently, the early seventeenth-century playwright and pamphleteer, Thomas Dekker. (In his great Oxford survey of the period, Douglas Bush calls him the best of its journalists.)

Eliot had been given, for a *TLS* review of about 1200 words, Dekker's *The Plague Pamphlets*, a selection edited by the scholar F. P. Wilson. In an opening paragraph Eliot compares Dekker's contribution to the literature of plague with Defoe's more well-known *Journal of the Plague Year* and with Poe's "Masque of the Red Death." He notes that Dekker's pamphlets seem to have been written hurriedly and are not equal in interest to two other of Dekker's satirical tracts, and as a prose writer, Eliot places him considerably below Thomas Nashe (whom we also haven't been reading recently). All this in the opening paragraph. He then proceeds to distinguish Dekker's method from those of Defoe and Poe, both of whose narratives "gain their effect by structure and by their rates of speed." By contrast, Dekker has no movement whatever, the pamphlets being merely a collection of vague anecdotes and passages "of the purple meditation in which his age indulged itself." There is further commentary on Defoe's achievement; then the third paragraph places Dekker in distant relationship to Boccaccio and the fabliaux writers. Eliot picks out Dekker's most interesting pamphlet, *The Meeting of Gallants at an Ordinarie*, mentions the dramatist Middleton as a comparable comic writer, and tells us the names of the gallants, "as we might expect, Signors Shuttlecocke, Ginglespurre, Stramazon and Kickshow." Even Dekker's more "pathetical" tales are lighter than Defoe's: "They belong to a more reckless and a tougher world." Eliot then produces a fine paragraph from Dekker's *The Wonderfull Yeare*, about a bride taken ill of the plague at the altar, and quotes some of Dekker's sentences: "Nor was his divination true, she was a wife, yet continued a mayd; he was a husband and a widower; yet never knew his wife: she was his owne, yet he had her not: she had him, yet never enjoyed him." The tale concludes with the moral "that he lost her, before she had time to be an ill wife, and she left him, ere he was able to be a bad husband." For Eliot, this marks the difference between Dekker and Defoe, and he suggests that the sentiment of the whole passage "might fill a tragedy by Fletcher and Ford." He finds another tale "like a more scurrilous *Merry Wives*:" and the whole tone of the pamphlets impresses us with "a world before puritanism." A marvelous concluding paragraph of Dekker's (too long to quote here) reminds Eliot of the Elizabethan dramatists, and of Donne "in his more rhetorical and less theological mode."

All this within 1200 words, the allusions summoned up thick and fast even as Eliot hurries to get the copy to Bruce Richmond, obliging editor of the *TLS*. An editorial note has, "I hope to get the Dekker done in a week or so, but I want to re-read Defoe first." This seems to me a vivid and impressive example of how the briefest of reviews can, in Eliot's hands, strike off something valuable and something few reviewers, then and now, are capable of.

In June of 1927, Eliot was baptized and received into the Church of England. This collection of his prose stops at the end of 1926, but its strongest essay of that year is a September one on "The Right Reverend Father of God," Bishop Lancelot Andrewes, whose writings had come to prevail for Eliot over the sermons of Donne. There is a long paragraph in the essay that, by way of admiring Andrewes's preaching, compares his ideas about the Incarnation to the operations of a classical scholar, in particular (though without naming him) to Harold Joachim, with whom Eliot read Aristotle at Oxford in 1914:

> Reading Andrewes on such a theme is like listening to a great Hellenist expounding a text of the Posterior Analytics: altering the punctuation, inserting or removing a comma or a semicolon, comparing its use in its nearer and in its most remote contexts, purifying a disturbed or cryptic lecture-note into lucid profundity. To persons whose minds are habituated to feed on the vague jargon of our time, when we have a vocabulary for everything and exact ideas about nothing—when a word half-understood, torn from its place in some alien or half-formed science, as of psychology, conceals from both writer and reader the meaninglessness of a statement, when all dogma is in doubt except the dogmas of sciences of which we have read in the newspaper, when the language of theology itself, under the influence of an undisciplined mysticism of popular philosophy tends to become a language of tergiversation—Andrewes may seem pedantic and verbal.

But no, and Eliot concludes the long paragraph:

> It is only when we have saturated ourselves in his prose, followed the movement of his thought, that we find his examination of words terminating in the ecstasy of assent. Andrewes takes a word and derives the world from it; squeezing and squeezing the word until it yields a full juice of meaning which we should

> never have supposed any word to possess. In this process, the qualities which we have mentioned, of ordonnance and precision, are exercised.

It is a great peroration that, coming near the end of these 2,000 pages of prose, seems an appropriate way to end, even as it looks forward to a new beginning.

—*Hudson Review*, Spring 2015.

More Prose and Letters

The Letters of T. S. Eliot,
Volume 7, edited by John Haffenden and Valerie Eliot

The Complete Prose of T. S. Eliot,
Volume 5, edited by Iman Javadi, Ronald Schuchard and Jayme Stayer

"I AM NOT a good correspondent," flatly declared T. S. Eliot to his Harvard English professor friend Theodore Spencer. Really? asks the surprised reader as he embarks on the seventh volume of Eliot's correspondence, covering but two years (1934–1935), adding up to nearly 1,000 pages, edited yet again by John Haffenden. As with previous volumes, this bad correspondent manages to correspond in a quite inimitable way. The previous volume (1932–1933) contains letters from the seven months Eliot spent in America, where he delivered the Norton Lectures at Harvard and the Page-Barbour ones at the University of Virginia. Two books resulted from these lectures: *The Use of Poetry and the Use of Criticism*, a brief history of literary critics in England from Sir Philip Sidney to I. A. Richards, and *After Strange Gods*, which Eliot never reprinted, in part because of the infamous reference to "free-thinking Jews" as inimical to a traditional society.

The letters from America in the previous volume derived much of their energy from observations made about life as observed from the perspectives of Harvard College and relatives in Cambridge, Massachusetts. There is no comparable point of focus in the new volume. Eliot plugs away at his Faber desk pretty much nine to five with a few weekends visiting friends in the country. He has now ensconced himself in a "clergy house" in South Kensington, with two rooms, use of shared bathroom, "excellent servants and meals served in my room"—the house presided over by the vicar of St.

Stephen's, Gloucester Road. To Paul Elmer More, who had become a warm correspondent, he apologizes for the inadequacy of *After Strange Gods* and wishes he had a more "profound" knowledge of theology, since "Pure literary criticism has ceased to interest me." This is not exactly news: in the 1928 preface to *The Sacred Wood*, his first and most original book of criticism, he stated that poetry had "something to do with morals, and with religion, and even with politics, perhaps." Increasing interest in these questions caused him "to be leaving the domain of criticism of poetry."

The new volume of prose, covering the years 1935-1939, takes us up to the closing of his magazine *The Criterion* on the eve of World War II. That year, 1939, also saw the publication of *The Idea of a Christian Society*, three lectures that attempt to rationalize religious matters of intimate and ultimate concern. Eliot believed that prose could legitimately be concerned with ideas, while poetry must deal with the way things are. I haven't counted, but suspect that the pages devoted to poetry are outnumbered by ones devoted to religious matters. Some examples of the latter: "The Catholic in the Modern World"; "The Church Assembly and Social Credit"; "Save the Children Fund"; "The Church in an Ecumenical Society," just for starters. There is a parochial feel to these essays that does not tempt the reader (this reader) to explore further. Yet just as we become wearied of the ecclesiastical mode, we encounter two hitherto unpublished lectures given at Edinburgh titled "The Development of Shakespeare's Verse," full of complicated considerations of poetry, drama, the theater, and the Elizabethan literary scene. There are enlightening comparisons between Shakespeare and Marlowe, incidental treatment of John Webster's verse, and discussion of Shakespeare's most popular plays and what "popular" means. If, as Eliot claimed, pure literary criticism no longer interested him, he nevertheless practiced it admirably in these lectures.

Nor did Eliot as literary critic abstain from longer essays comparable to the ones published in the 1920s on Ben Jonson, Dryden, Shakespeare, and the Metaphysical poets. He accorded substantial treatment to Milton, Byron, and Tennyson, along with shorter considerations of George Herbert, two odes by Cowley, and Marianne Moore's poetry, plus short tributes to Kipling and G. K. Chesterton and a second look at Wyndham Lewis's book on Shakespeare, *The Lion and the Fox.* Rereading the essays on individual writers (they would be published after the war in *On Poetry and Poets*) I found the one on Byron particularly impressive, especially as it took on the early, now unread poem that brought him fame. You would not know from these probing, agile essays that the author had become increasingly preoccupied with larger matters, since the essays are wholly literary in their critical slant.

As this stupendous edition of the complete prose now heads into the years of World War II, one's gratitude is tempered by its on-line status only—hardcover print is promised at the completion of the series, three volumes hence. I don't know how many others like myself would have shied away from reading all this on-line without the assistance of someone willing to print them out. The letters, thankfully, are available in print, and unlike the prose collection the latest volume is thickly seasoned with humor, natural to the epistolary mode rather than the more formal address. Although not the most interesting, many are devoted to preparations for Eliot's church pageant *The Rock*, and after that the Canterbury production of *Murder in the Cathedral.* More arresting, though in a pathetic and painful way, Vivien Eliot is well represented in her efforts to get "Tom" to come back home and live with her. The door is always open, she promises. Notoriously, she shows up at one of his lectures, clutching her dog, Polly, who escapes and jumps up on TSE, who keeps repeating "I can't talk to you now." Desperate to find out an address for him besides the Faber one, she writes a birthday note enclosing a check for one pound and wishing him "every good thing in this life and for all eternity." A postcript urges him to "*Buy yourself some socks at Marshall & Snellgrove.*"

Since what most appealed to me in these letters is Eliot the humorist, the solemn pretender, the joker, I propose to list in no particular (though roughly chronological) order moments that especially pleased me. He advises Stephen Spender, whom Faber is publishing, to avoid "bookmaking if possible": "I know quite well the horrid slavery of reviewing but that has the spiritual advantage over some kinds of book-writing of being wholly ephemeral and irresponsible; whereas one can never escape from the consequences of a book one has published." Reporting on a visit from W. B. Yeats, he finds "Uncle Willie looney as ever. He will spell Balzac with an S... Never mind he goes on in his oldtime way about the phases of the moon etc." He advises the poet Gavin Ewart not to publish a translation from the French until he has "a more complete knowledge of the French language," and adds, "You will observe that I have corrected the French word for sausages." About a performance of Shakespeare's *Antony and Cleopatra* he finds Cleopatra "not only indecent, but worse, ridiculous. Her sea-fight costume made her look like a comic Brittania, and really, if a lady is to appear with bare legs, it should not be in a scene in which she has to kneel several times in supplication, so that she goes about with dirty knees and the effect is rather diminished."

Invited to write an essay on Henri Bergson, he demurs: "I might possibly consent to write an essay on Bergson, if you could induce Bergson to write an essay about me." Advising Marianne Moore, whose selected poems Faber is about to publish, Eliot says that she should not assume "*Everyone knows your work*" since "Some people, especially in cathedral towns, and the like, are very backward in this country." One yearns to know what is so special about those uninformed cathedral parishioners! He confesses in a letter to his Harvard classmates, "I cannot afford yachting, but I should like to breed bull terriers. I am afraid of high places and cows." To the editor of the *Times* in support of Sir John Squire's "spirited defence of Stilton Cheese" he recommends the formation of a Society for the Preservation of Ancient Cheeses, and advises that "Troops of members should visit all the hotels and inns in Gloucestershire, demanding Double Gloster." In respect to a Reader's report on a book about Aldous Huxley, he advises, "The way to deal with Huxley is exactly to sneer at him, and for this purpose there is, I think, a chance for a good pamphlet by some real ruffian—not a gentleman, and preferably not even an Etonian, but, let us say, one who has plumbed life to the very dregs of Carlton House Terrace... In short, I can think of no one except Wyndham Lewis or myself."

The most surprising item in these letters is one from his older brother, Henry Ware. What we've seen of previous exchanges between the brothers reveal Henry to be both a sympathetic and sharply critical observer of TSE's career. But I was unprepared for the missive he sent Eliot in late 1935, a sixteen-page critique and exploration of his Catholic propensities and philosophic situation as revealed especially in *After Strange Gods* and the two religious plays, *The Rock* and *Murder in the Cathedral.* Henry's wonderful phrase to characterize a frequent tone of his brother's is "elfin mischievousness," and he tells Tom that "Sometimes you remind me of a gentleman in full evening dress and white gloves attempting to put something right with the kitchen plumbing without soiling his attire." He adds, sympathetically, that his brother's literary position is now such that "whatever you may want to say, your public expects it to be a worthy permanent addition to the world's literature." Then he speaks directly to Eliot's religion, to the fact that "you—holding your beliefs—have done nothing at all to rescue the members of your own family, for whom I know that you have the greatest affection, from their peril, which, if I understand plain English, is regarded by the Catholic Church as infinitely more serious than moral peril." He adds that this is a "literal" way of putting it, and observes that due to the "unfortunate effects of mixing a Puritan conscience with Catholic doctrine [you] act in a more literal manner than do most sophisticated Catholics." There is a bit of teasing here, but with an underlying seriousness and concern about TSE's situation. Eliot did not reply to his brother, at least not in a letter.

It is fortuitous but surely fitting that the final letter in the collection, dated December 31, 1935, is to Eliot's American publisher, Donald Brace, informing him of the contents of his collected poems shortly to be dispatched, except for "one poem that is unfinished, and which I will forward if I can finish it within the next fortnight." The poem was "Burnt Norton," first of the *Quartets,* and it was delivered to the publisher in good time.

—*Hopkins Review*, Summer 2018.

Eliot's Mischievous Prose

IN A HANDWRITTEN note to his copy of Ezra Pound's *Selected Poems* edited by T. S. Eliot, I. A. Richards took up a side of Eliot that greatly dissatisfied him:

> Must "come out" about Eliot's prose. His unfortunate inability to comprehend what he is implying; what he must be taken as intending to assume; the vast liabilities he so often (thoughtlessly? no not without thought but without the right kind of thought) incurs.
>
> The pontification, the impossible claims, the ridiculously too conscious humilities, the gauche misrepresentations of other people's fairly obvious remarks—these things I am persuaded are not in Mr Eliot's mind so much as in his prose style: an instrument he can never keep on the right terms with for long.

At the end of his catalogue of how Eliot's prose failed to produce disciplined thought, Richards, who much admired Eliot's poems, called his prose "an amusing trail of logically incompetent manipulations of bogus information." We may assume from this assault that Richards thought of himself as, on the contrary, a writer of logically competent, disciplined, fair-minded prose whose disinterested procedures were not unlike those of the scientist. If we look at what is probably Richards's most lasting book, *Practical Criticism* (1929), we find such procedures exhibited in its later chapters, which bear titles such as "The Four Kinds of Meaning," "Irrelevant Associations and Stock Responses," and add up to 150 pages of reflective generalizations from the "experiment" Richards had conducted with his Cambridge students. As is well known, that experiment consisted in eliciting commentary from the students on thirteen poems, untitled and undated, names of the poets withheld. Writing up the results, Richards quotes from what he called the students' "protocols," making it clear which ones he admires and which he does not. This commentary, which makes up the first half of *Practical Criticism,* is what we remember and reread from the book, and its memorability has much to do with Richards's willingness to cultivate a humorously ironic tone in his remarks about the students' contributions. Such a tone is almost completely absent from the sober, "scientific" manner of the book's second half.

Without attempting to refute his enumerations of why Eliot's prose is faulty, we can at least entertain the idea that Richards's own prose is most rewarding when he allows himself some of the unscientific play he found so annoying in Eliot. Since I am convinced that Eliot's greatness as a critic is inseparable from the style in which his prose operates, I want to take up some examples of that style from reviews, essays, and other commentary that have never been collected between hard covers. Even sympathetic readers of the poet may know relatively little about the 700 or so items that remain uncollected or unpublished, and my endeavor is spurred by a recent announcement that Eliot's publisher, Faber, in collaboration with the Johns Hopkins University Press in this country, are projecting a seven-volume edition of his complete prose, supervised by Ronald Schuchard, a first-rate scholar and critic.

Most of the following collections of prose have been available since before Eliot's death: *The Sacred Wood* (1920) and *Selected Essays* (1932) were and are still the major ones through which he made his enormous impact. *The Use of Poetry and the Use of Criticism* (1933), a collection of his Norton lectures at Harvard, was followed by another series of lectures given at the University of Virginia and published as *After Strange Gods* (1934). Eliot never reprinted the latter, probably because of its infamous remark about "free-thinking Jews" being dangerous to a traditional society. *On Poetry and Poets* (1957) gathered up some fine essays on individual writers—Samuel Johnson and Byron, Milton and Yeats—plus a number of salient reflections on poetry, in particular "Poetry and Drama" and "The Three Voices of Poetry." A posthumous collection, *To Criticize the Critic,* appeared in 1965. Eliot's social and political thought are to be found in *The Idea of a Christian Society* and *Notes Towards the Definition of Culture,* books that have remained in print while exerting little influence. In 1994 Ronald Schuchard introduced and edited with generous commentary Eliot's 1925 Clark Lectures at Cambridge and his Turnbull lectures at Johns Hopkins.

This volume, *The Varieties of Metaphysical Poetry,* set a standard for editorial scrupulousness that the promised *Complete Prose* will strive to emulate.

I shall describe briefly some high spots in the uncollected prose, aware of having doubtless missed out on other interesting material, pieces which, in Faber's announcement, "remain scattered in numerous libraries and institutional collections around the world." Of the uncollected material I'm aware of, most appealing are the pieces that appeared in two English periodicals, *The Egoist* (1917-1918) and *The Athenaeum* (1919). Only a very small portion of these found its way into Eliot's published collections. In 1919 he began reviewing anonymously for the *Times Literary Supplement,* there producing his most famous essays—those on Ben Jonson, Dryden, Marvell, Blake, Swinburne—which appeared in *The Sacred Wood* and *Selected Essays.* Entirely uncollected are the London Letters he wrote for the American magazine *The Dial* (1922) and, in a similar vein of cultural commentary, his many items signed and unsigned about the state of things in London and elsewhere as they appeared in his magazine *The Criterion,* beginning in 1922.

In his excellent chapter on Eliot's criticism in *The Invisible Poet,* Hugh Kenner laid great stress on the anonymity provided by reviewing for the *TLS* as central to Eliot's daring brilliance as a critic. Kenner believes that after about 1925, when Eliot had become a recognized big name, his criticism became less vital. While it is true that Eliot would never surpass the essays mentioned above, those written anonymously for the *TLS,* Kenner's explanation may be too simple. It doesn't give sufficient credit to the signed, earlier pieces in the *Egoist* and *Athenaeum,* and it doesn't explain why the anonymous pieces he continued to write for the *TLS* are less weighty than the great ones of 1920-21. It is a fact that after *The Waste Land* appeared in 1922 and he became a literary power, Eliot was solicited by a wide variety of periodicals both English and American, among others *The Dial, Books and Bookmen, Nation,* and *Athenaeum, Vanity Fair, Time and Tide, The Listener,* and above all *The Criterion*—thus the *TLS* became just another place where he appeared. But it's certainly the case that as, in Kenner's phrase, the invisible poet and critic turned into a highly visible and extremely influential one, Eliot became more wary and circumspect in his pronouncements. There is, notwithstanding, valuable work (mainly uncollected) appearing in the later 1920s and early 1930s. Foremost are twelve brief talks he delivered over the BBC and published in *The Listener* in 1929-30. Partly the fruits of his Clark Lectures, they take up various aspects of

English writing in the late sixteenth and early seventeenth century. In 1931 he gave three further BBC talks, again published in *The Listener* and collected in a small volume published by an obscure American press (Terence and Elsa Holliday). This volume, *John Dryden: The Poet, The Dramatist, The Critic,* has been unavailable for decades except in good libraries.

At least since Randall Jarrell's tribute to Eliot in his 1962 lecture at the National Gallery in Washington, "Fifty Years of American Poetry," we knew that Eliot as poet was a very different figure from the devotee of various causes he championed: Classicism, Orthodoxy, Marvellian Wit (tough reasonableness beneath slight lyric grace). Instead of a poet who had effected a total severance between the man that suffered and the artistic creation, Jarrell, in the form of an enormous, disbelieving question, proposed a quite different Eliot:

> Won't the future say to us in helpless astonishment: "But did you actually believe that all these things about objective correlatives, classicism, the tradition, applied to *his* poetry? Surely you must have seen that he was one of the most subjective and daemonic poets who ever lived, the victim and helpless beneficiary of his own inexorable compulsions, obsessions?"

Although it would be mistaken to claim that such a wide divergence between truth and myth is to be found in Eliot the critic as well, there is more wildness, more anarchy, more sheer mischief in his prose writings than has been charted by those who see him as the steely-eyed scourge of Romanticism, the spokesman for all that is sane and orderly in the English tradition. As Graham Hough pointed out some time ago in his searching essay "The Poet as Critic," Eliot admitted in "The Three Voices of Poetry" that his poetry had always been, in Hough's words, "radically dependent on unconscious and uncontrollable processes." To some extent this was also true of his criticism, which in its early manifestations depended much upon serendipitous opportunities to review books for *The Egoist, The Athenaeum,* and *TLS.* The results, when some were gathered together in hard covers, made the whole operation look more systematic and planned than in fact it was. Hough also admired what he called, particularly with respect to the early reviews, a pervading quality of "intellectual charm." "Intellectual" may not be quite the adequate word for a manner that is by turns sly and feline, then suddenly revelatory in the occasional sentence that seems to have popped out from nowhere. A headshaking at human—especially English—literary folly alternates with the equivalent of practical jokes, of which in his later employment at Faber he was a great practitioner. In *The Invisible Poet* Kenner drew our attention to the letters Eliot wrote to *The Egoist,* full of preposterous sentiment that supposedly issued from British worthies with names and addresses like Charles Augustus Conybear, The Carlton Club, Liverpool; or J. A. D. Spence, Thridlingston Grammar School; or Muriel O. Schwarz, 60 Alexandra Gardens, Hampstead NW. The poetic sensibility that was indulging itself in the obscene "King Bolo" poems he shared with Pound and Wyndham Lewis, or the later humorist of *Old Possum's Book of Practical Cats* who composed a poem beginning "How unpleasant to meet Mr. Eliot," must have enjoyed writing prose in which he could say extravagant things and get paid for saying them. I don't mean to imply that Eliot as critic was frivolous or given to the trivial; rather that, as his rival Robert Frost liked to claim about himself, "I am never more serious than when joking."

"Joking" sounds much too loud and merry for the kind of humor in Eliot's reviews from these years. In one of them he has at hand an anthology of sixteen contemporary poets and he places it in a context of three older generations of what he calls "verse-producing units":

> The first, the aged, represented by the great name of Hardy, but including several figures in process of oblivesence; the middle-aged, including Mr Yeats and a small number of honored names; the ageing, including the Georgian poets and the curious shapes of Mr Eliot and Mr Pound: all these ages have already lined their nests or dug their graves. We could, at will, pronounce a fitting obituary over any one of these writers except the first mentioned.

In *Lives of the Modern Poets* I wrote about this paragraph,

> One is struck by the civilized humor tending toward mordancy, expressing itself sharply in particulars of diction and idiom; as in choosing an automaton-like phrase "Verse-producing units," to neutralize the creative pretensions of all these poets: or "oblivescence," imparting a suavely gentle air of decline to the "aged"; or "ageing" as a mock-weary epithet for himself and Pound (both

> in their early thirties) and with a nod to the Georgian poets whom Eliot mocks elsewhere and of whom everyone (such is the air) is by now tired. Finally there is the one-two punch of yoking these "units" together, all of them having "lined their nests or dug their graves," and the concluding boast about how the reviewer could write an obituary for any of them, except of course—in a graceful bow—Hardy, the first mentioned. The surface of the prose is so engaging and resourceful, the reader feels so flattered to be addressed in such a knowingly urbane way, that he is unlikely to have much interest in disputing Eliot's distinctions, even when they are more disputable than the ones brought forth here.

Eliot's criticism in the years 1917-19 is mainly a dissolvent of various terms and assumptions that other writers have too credulously invested in. His skeptical and astringent humor is directed at any sort of literary writing—creative or critical—that has emanated from minds more illusioned and less knowing than his own. In one of his earliest *Egoist* pieces in October 1917, the second of three "Reflections on Contemporary Poetry," he introduced a distinction he would elaborate two years later in "Tradition and the Individual Talent." He is comparing the poems of his London contemporary, Harold Monro, with those of a French poet, Jean de Bosschère. Monro's poems, Eliot writes, seek to present human emotions by decorating them in thoughts and images. De Bosschère, by contrast, "is an intellectual by his obstinate refusal to adulterate his poetic emotions with human emotions." De Bosschère aims not to tell us how we feel about a situation, "but how it is." His "austerity is terrifying"; his direct aim at "emotions of art," rather than human emotions, sometimes issues in "an intense frigidity which I find altogether admirable." We recall that when Eliot wrote this and similar pronouncements in praise of austerity, frigidity, poetic rather than human emotions, he was undergoing marital chaos, miserable health, and exhausting work that made him feel, as he put it in a letter, that he was living in a novel by Dostoyevsky rather than one by Jane Austen. The aims of art as against the claims of life, he would formulate in memorable sentences from the "Tradition" essay:

> Poetry is not a turning loose of emotion, but an escape from emotion; it is not the expression of personality, but an escape

> from personality. But, of course, only those who have personality and emotions know what it means to want to escape from those things.

When the American poet John Gould Fletcher read the opening chapter of *The Sacred Wood* ("The Perfect Critic"), he found it insufficiently generous to the claims of emotion. Eliot wrote Fletcher back that he wouldn't deny the importance of emotion, but that he often found it "present to me when other people find only 'frigidity'."

The sentence is typically Eliot in that it is both serious and humorous—a trace of mischief is surely visible. At about the same time Frost declared in a letter that humor was the "most engaging cowardice," a "form of guardedness" that kept "some of my enemy in play far out of gunshot." The "play" in Eliot sentences is not without its aggressive component, as when in a review of an anthology of recent poetry he ends a paragraph by stating, innocently, "Rupert Brooke is not absent." He then composed a letter to *The Egoist* by a presumably surprised woman who had taken offense at this abrupt dismissal of Brooke:

> Brooke's early poems exhibit a youthful exuberance of passions, and an occasional coarseness of utterance, which offended finer tastes; but those were but dross which, as his last sonnets show, was purged away (if I may be permitted the word) in the fire of the recent Ordeal which is proving the well-spring of a Renaissance of English poetry.

It was signed Helen B. Trundlett, Batton, Kent, and its mock daring parenthetical apology ("if I may be permitted the word") marks it as an Eliotic spoof.

Sometimes a sentence of his has to be read twice in order to catch the dismissive thing being said, as when in the beginning of a review of a certain Guy Rawlence, author of *Covent Garden, and Others,* Eliot observes that "One is annoyed with him for not having rewritten the small book," as if it were merely annoying of poor Rawlence to overlook such a crucial matter. From Alec Waugh's poems Eliot quotes some undistinguished lines and announces that "Mr. Waugh is said to be very young, and to have written a novel. That is a bad beginning, but something might be made of him." The list of such *mots* could be extended, and if the habit of facetiousness seems no more than something to be deplored as the arrogance of a young reviewer feeling his oats, it can also indicate something deeper, what Wyndham Lewis in *Tarr* called "the curse of humor," something its owner couldn't get rid of if he had tried.

Eliot's ironic humor is dry enough to exclude readers who if asked would insist that of course they had a good sense of humor. A related exclusiveness shows up in odd ways at unexpected moments in the early criticism, perhaps the most surprising of which occurs in a review of a book by George Saintsbury on the nineteenth-century French novel. Titled "Beyle and Balzac," it is dedicated partly to making the highest claims for Stendhal and Flaubert as opposed to Balzac. We may speak, Eliot writes, about how Balzac unites imagination with observation, carrying us—though not profoundly—through the pages of *Cousine Bette.* On the other hand, and with reference to *Le Rouge et le Noir:*

> It is impossible to say that certain scenes between Julien and Mathilde de la Mole are a union of imagination, etc; they go too deep for that. Stendhal's scenes, some of them, and some of his phrases, read like cutting one's own throat; they are a terrible humiliation to read, in the understanding of human feelings and human illusions of feeling that they force upon the reader.

This is extraordinary for the way it suggests a disturbing depth of feeling in the critic, which we (at least this reader) can't begin to lay claim to. What *are* those scenes in Stendhal that demand to be read in the extreme way Eliot reads them? And how do they produce the "terrible humiliation" he says they produce? If as he claims "Beyle and Flaubert strip the world; and they were men of far more than the common intensity of feeling, of passion," then can readers like the rest of us rise only to a common intensity—something a good deal less than stripping the world as Eliot says Stendhal does?

In a less extreme way, reviewing the letters of W. B. Yeats as edited by Pound, Eliot concludes by quoting some sentences that could, he suggests, be said of the man who wrote them:

> The solitary has charm whereas the companionable compels his followers. When the companionable says I am your friend and will help you, or to a girl that he loves her, his voice does

> not penetrate so deeply and so touchingly as when the solitary speaks.

So much for the penetration of the merely companionable person like you or me (or Balzac?). Something of a similar exclusivity is revealed in one of his most surprising turns of pronouncement, in a review of a volume of Kipling's. After various fertile and unobvious comparisons of the writer with Swinburne, with Tennyson, with Joseph Conrad, Eliot concludes with this consideration of Kipling's audience:

> It is wrong, of course, for Mr Kipling to address a large audience; but it is a better thing than to address a small one. The only better thing is to address the one hypothetical Intelligent Man who does not exist and who is the audience of the Artist.

Eliot never said this again; it was something that overtook him at the end of a review. If for a second at the opening of it we pride ourselves on being on the side of "minority" art, we immediately stand corrected when told that addressing a large audience, wrong as it is, is better than addressing a small one. Who would be bold enough to translate this pronouncement into more easily available terms? How enlivening but difficult it is to summon up this Intelligent Man who doesn't exist. Graham Hough's phrase "intellectual charm" as a way of taking Eliot's temperature in these early pieces is as good as any, as long as we don't try to say exactly what the phrase means.

After the First World War, in 1921, the year in which appeared his seminal essays on Marvell, Dryden, and the Metaphysical Poets, Eliot introduced himself to an American audience in *The Dial,* where *The Waste Land* would appear the following year. He did this through a series of London Letters in which he reported on the state of things, cultural and otherwise, in England. The manner in which he conducted himself in these relaxed expatiations was in some ways a continuation of the deadpan humor of the *Egoist* and *Athenaeum* pieces, but, less tethered to a particular book or writer, the prose's effect was more purely an independent creation. Here is part of the first paragraph of the letter of July, 1921:

> The vacant term of wit set in early this year with a fine hot rainless spring; the crop of murders and divorces has been poor com-

> pared with that of last autumn...Einstein the Great has visited England; and delivered lectures to uncomprehending audiences, and been photographed for the newspapers smiling at Lord Haldane. We wonder how much that smile implies; but Einstein has not confided its meaning to the press. He has met Mr Bernard Shaw, but made no public comment on that subject. Einstein has taken his place in the newspapers with the comet, the sun-spots, the poisonous jellyfish and octopus at Margate, and other natural phenomena. Mr Robert Lynd has announced that only two living men have given their names to a school of poetry: King George V and Mr J. C. Squire. A new form of influenza has been discovered which leaves extreme dryness and a bitter taste in the mouth.

The innocent juxtapositions, or rather the sequence of sentences that are and are not sequential—from Einstein to Bernard Shaw to the poisonous jellyfish and the discovery of a new form of influenza—must have caused some readers new to the writer to wonder exactly what was going on in these communicated "facts" about London 1921. Never did Eliot put himself forth as more unillusioned, weary (or mock-weary) of the spectacle of human follies and wishes, than in these bulletins. "The man who is tired of London is tired of life," Samuel Johnson's dictum, is all too resolute for the tone Eliot captured in a paragraph such as the above.

You would not guess from the enervated, thoroughly-small-and-dry atmosphere of the London Letters that their author was being an extremely productive figure on a number of fronts. In January 1922 he returned from his three month's visit to the clinic in Lausanne, had accepted Pound's excisions and revisions of *The Waste Land* manuscript, and was preparing to launch *The Criterion,* where *The Waste Land* would be published in England. In April 1922 he began a London Letter by saying that, after his time away, he found London unchanged, "the same things one liked, the same things one detested, and the same things to which one was indifferent." He decided to contemplate the particular "torpor" that struck him on becoming again a citizen of London, and ascribed it to English provinciality, the complacent belief that English literature was already so good that adventure and experiment were too risky. Such "torpid indifference" distinguished London negatively from other cities, which as they decayed "extend a rich odour of putrefaction; London merely shrivels, like a little bookkeeper grown old."

Dispiritedly, or such is the pose, he considers an anthology of contemporary American poets edited by Louis Untermeyer. In this he fails to find "one or two of the writers who interest me most" (they are unnamed) and finds in those present the same "commonplace and conventionality" as is present in current English poets. One by one he ticks them off—Sandburg, Vachel Lindsay, Masters, Amy Lowell, eventually arriving at Frost, at which point the letter doubles back on itself by alluding to the condition with which it began:

> Mr. Frost seems the nearest equivalent to an English poet, specializing in New England torpor; his verse, it is regretfully said, is uninteresting, and what is uninteresting is unreadable, and what is unreadable is not read. There, that is done.

Although he makes a serious mistake about Frost, the really irritating thing here is the tone: the passive voice excusing itself as it performs an unpleasant task; the pained sigh of relief at the end. It represents, I should say, some extreme of cultivated, yawning insolence, and would provide food for despisers of Eliot did they but know of the item tucked away in a never republished London Letter. The only claim that might be made for it is that as insolence it is absolutely distinctive: no one but Eliot would have been capable of it.

The urbane spectator of human foibles, a persona developed in the London Letters, made many appearances in the Commentaries (signed and unsigned) that Eliot wrote for *The Criterion* during his editorship at that magazine. Usually his observations were directed at things going on in England, particularly in London, and special note was taken of the fate of various churches condemned to disuse and dereliction. The most vividly amusing of these is a commentary of January 1928, the year after Eliot had entered the Anglican church. In it he addresses himself to the "problem" of Westminster Abbey, "particularly the fear that available space for interring great men will soon be exhausted (if, that is, we go on producing great men at the present alarming rate)." He is skeptical of plans for extending the space and also points out that the Abbey was designed originally as a church, not a Pantheon. He then cocks a wary eye at the fact that, increasingly, the great men memorialized were not only not Church of England but had dissociated themselves from any communion, and he asks "why should great men be buried in a church of which they are not members?" The concluding paragraph proposes a brilliant solution to the whole difficulty:

> Fortunately, there is a way out, which has just occurred to us, and which is both more practical and more sensational than anything the newspapers have thought of yet. The French have a poor little Pantheon at the end of the Rue Soufflot in Paris. Let us have one six times the size, and prove that we have six times as many great men. Some piece of waste ground could be provided, near London (Wembley would be a good spot, if it is not engrossed by greyhound courses; and the greyhounds would be an attraction). Our Pantheon should be built of course of reinforced concrete, with statuary by Frampton. But let this monument for the World's Finest Pantheon be set on foot at once, so that the edifice may be ready for Mr. Bernard Shaw, and Mr. H. G. Wells, and the Dean of St. Paul's.

I have no doubt Eliot was troubled by the fact that Westminster Abbey was both a church and a tourist attraction (patronized by visiting Americans), but his "solution" turns the whole matter into farce by building a creative fantasy that becomes increasingly bizarre as it develops. After the "piece of waste ground," currently put to no good use, has been activated in Wembley, the possible difficulties caused by the dog races quickly becomes an asset to tourists—"the greyhounds would be an attraction." Tilting at what pass for great men in the modern world—Shaw, Wells, and Dean Inge are always favorite targets for Eliot's condescension—he puts a crown on the whole edifice of reinforced concrete. Satire is deliberately unfair, said Eliot's friend Wyndham Lewis; Eliot is quite deliberate and ingenious about his unfairness, and we may think of Jonathan Swift.

In selecting for inspection sentences and paragraphs from "early" Eliot prose, I may be laying disproportionate emphasis on his performances as an ironist, a satirist, while paying insufficient attention to his ideas and principles, his "positive" contributions as a literary and cultural critic. Yet since matters of "content" in Eliot have received more attention than the manner of style, I attempt to redress the balance. The fact that Eliot never reprinted the bulk of his early writing (he did include "Reflections on *vers libre,*" one of his most humorous ventures, in *To Criticize the Critic,* but that was the exception) probably meant that he thought them slighter efforts than the pieces collected in *The Sacred Wood* and *Selected Essays*. It may also have been that after his conversion in 1927, he looked somewhat more severely on youthful mischief. At any rate the writings he produced at the end of the 1920s and early '30s are contemporaneous with "Ash-Wednesday," with its parenthetical question ("Why should the agèd eagle stretch its wings?"). The prose equivalent of this resigned posture seeks to inform and direct a reader, rather than shake him up, and is accordingly mainly devoid of fireworks and mock-heroics.

But there is an easier, less speculative answer to this question about Eliot's changed manner, and it has to do with the medium he employed. Both the eleven talks he gave in 1929-30 on Renaissance and early seventeenth-century writers, and the three talks on Dryden in 1931, were delivered over the BBC and published in its organ, *The Listener.* The aim of each talk was to address something like the general listener, no specialist in Renaissance writers or in Dryden, but ready to be informed. The sort of teasing that Eliot liked to do in the early pieces and the London Letters was to be avoided in favor of something altogether more straightforward. He succeeded admirably in adapting his style to the possibilities of a still relatively untried medium of communication. These expository talks, very much pitched at an introductory though not simplified level, were undeniably enhanced by Eliot's drawing upon his experience of giving extension lectures in London and elsewhere fifteen or so years previously. Unlike these earlier lectures, Eliot knows nothing of the individuals in his radio audience, so must address something like, to modify an earlier formulation, the Intelligent Man who does not exist but is the audience for the lecturer. For example, in "The Genesis of Philosophic Prose: Bacon and Hooker," Eliot begins by apologizing for the forbidding sound of his title, then surveys in an opening paragraph some of the chief prose writers who flourished at the end of Elizabeth's reign and the beginning of the seventeenth century. Some of these he has discussed in earlier lectures: the lively prose of the Tudor translators; the popular journalism of Greene, Dekker, and Nashe; the prose of the great dramatist Ben Jonson ("the most intelligent man of his time") and of Shakespeare, whose unique prose is unsurpassable ("There is no finer prose than Shakespeare's"). He then introduces the contributions of Richard Hooker and Francis Bacon by suggesting what, if these two writers were ignored, would be left:

> I think that you would find in all of it either a certain boyishness, as in the people we looked at last week, or a certain pedantry and quaint stiffness, as in Donne and Andrewes, or a kind of luxuriance of style, as in Donne and Andrewes and later in Jeremy Taylor, and especially Browne and Burton, all of which are qualities to be enjoyed, but which seem to us antique. Of all the writers we examine, Bacon and Hooker seem to me among the most modern. That they are the fathers of modern philosophy and theology respectively is not the point with which I have to deal: my point here is that they are the fathers of the modern abstract style. We do not all study philosophy, but we must all make use of a kind of writing which these two men made possible; make use of it, I mean, either when we write or read. Any kind of argument, legal, political, or general; any kind of scientific exposition or explanation, from the theory of relativity to how to clean a typewriter or oil a motor car, owes something to Bacon and Hooker.

"I think...," "seem to me," "my point here is," "I mean,"—this is the cautious, uneventful style of the patient expositor making a thoughtful presentation of material in the time allotted him. Even if the listener or reader has heard or read the previous lectures, quite a lot is demanded of him: the assumption that he will nod his head, in reference to the preachers Donne and Lancelot Andrewes, at their "quaint stiffness"; or that Sir Thomas Browne and Robert Burton and Jeremy Taylor had "luxuriance" of style that was also (compared to the prose of Hooker or Bacon) "antique." The "modern" aspect of the two central subjects of this talk is brought out by invoking their utility as makers of an argument—from explaining the theory of relativity to instructing one how to clean a typewriter or oil a motor car. It is the opposite of tendentiousness: nothing is declared from on high, as in so many of Eliot's early pronouncements. The effect rather is quietly persuasive—one wants to agree with such low-keyed, modest judgments.

Even as Eliot invites us to look, in these old poets and prose writers of the early seventeenth century, for evidences of "life," the life of his own prose is patent. Except for one or two specialists, no one reads the late Elizabethan pamphleteer, novelist, and poet Thomas Nashe, but Eliot makes a case for why this writer might just possibly be rewarding by quoting a paragraph from Nashe's *Piers Penniless His Supplication to the Devil:* "With the enemies of poetry I care not if I have a bout, and those are they that term our best writers but babbling ballad makers, holding them fantastical fools, that have wit, but cannot tell how to use it etc." He then focuses:

> But when one becomes a little used to the long breathing sentences, the torrential phrases, and the perpetual surprises of conceit, one finds something more than archaic quaintness: one finds life in this style, a life from which our language can still be renewed.

And he proceeds to make a case for the qualities we look to find in such "old prose."

His 1921 essay "John Dryden"—occasioned by Mark van Doren's book on the poet—contained a memorable formulation: "To enjoy Dryden means to pass beyond the limitations of the nineteenth century into a new freedom." Ten years later he returned to the subject more fully in the radio talks on Dryden as poet, as dramatist, and as critic. It is a model of just, perspicuous observation, dedicated to no more and no less than what its final sentence sums up: "But it is worthwhile to know what Dryden did for the English language in verse and in prose, because we shall understand better what that language is, and of what it is still capable." The essays are mainly written in a manner similar to the talks on Renaissance writers noted above. But there is one extraordinary moment in which Eliot's critical genius shines forth. He is comparing Dryden's *All for Love* with Shakespeare's *Antony and Cleopatra* and is occupied by what it means to use the words "poetic" and "dramatic" in speaking about these plays. To elucidate the tricky matter he focuses on the moment at the end of the play when, Cleopatra having poisoned herself and died, her maid Charmian (Charmion in Dryden) herself utters last words. In Shakespeare she says,

> It is well done, and fitting for a princess
> Descended of so many royal kings.
> Ah, soldier!

Dryden has it thus:

> Yes, 'tis well done, and like a Queen, the last
> Of her great race. I follow her.

Eliot says that if you take the passages by themselves you cannot say that Dryden's lines are any less dramatic, or poetic, than Shakespeare's, and that a great actress could make much of either of them. Then he asks us to consider "Shakespeare's remarkable addition to the original text of North, the two plain words *ah, soldier*":

> You cannot say that there is anything peculiarly *poetic* about these two words, and if you isolate the dramatic from the poetic, you cannot say that there is anything peculiarly dramatic either, because there is nothing in them for the actress to convey in action; she can at best enunciate them clearly. I could not myself put into words the difference I feel between the passage if these two words *ah, soldier* were omitted and with them. But I know there is a difference, and that only Shakespeare could have made it.

Christopher Ricks, who first drew my attention to the passage, writes that if he had to adduce a single paragraph to prove Eliot was a great critic, this would be the one. To his excellent account of the passage in *T. S. Eliot and Prejudice,* I would add that what generates the special power and surprise of Eliot's writing here occurs at the end of the paragraph: first, his confession that he can't put into words (what? Eliot at a loss for words?) the difference made by the addition "Ah, soldier!"; second, that he insists there is such a difference and only Shakespeare could have made it. A lesser critic couldn't have gotten away with this, much less done it triumphantly by making the very inability to put something into words—surely the critic's task—an indication of how powerful is the dramatic and poetic effect, the kind of effect only Shakespeare could have brought off.

These are some examples of uncollected Eliot that will be welcomed back into print as of permanent value. One should add to them the brief but trenchant essay of 1930 titled "Johnson's *London* and *The Vanity of Human Wishes,*" later titled "Poetry in the Eighteenth Century." (He would expand some of its insights in his much longer essay "Johnson as Poet and Critic" published in *On Poetry and Poets.*) It is most notable for some remarks about how the virtues of later eighteenth-century poetry such as Goldsmith's and Samuel Johnson's are in part the virtues of good prose. He lays down the following caveat:

> Those who condemn or ignore en bloc the poetry of the eighteenth century on the ground that it is "prosaic" are stumbling over an uncertainty of meaning of the word "prosaic" to arrive at exactly the wrong conclusion. One does not need to examine a great deal of the inferior verse of the eighteenth century to realize that the trouble with it is that it is not prosaic enough. We are inclined to use "prosaic" as meaning not only "like prose" but as "lacking poetic beauty"...Only, we ought to distinguish between poetry which is like *good* prose, and poetry which is like *bad* prose.

"To have the virtues of good prose," he concludes, "is the first and minimum requirement of good poetry." This is surely a response to Matthew Arnold's downgrading of the eighteenth century as an age of prose and reason that, for all its virtues, lacked the higher virtues to be found in the Elizabethans, Milton, and the Romantics. Both Eliot and Pound had been insisting that poetry should be, in Pound's phrase, at least as well-written as prose; to my knowledge Eliot was the first to make a case in these terms for some eighteenth-century poetry.

In the later 1930s and '40s, when his attention became more and more focused on religion and its current relation to culture and society, his memorable literary efforts became fewer and farther between, the main ones to be found in *On Poetry and Poets.* In 1937 he gave a lecture in Edinburgh titled "The Development of Shakespeare's Verse," never published, but from which significant parts were used in "Poetry and Drama." Near the end of his life he produced a pamphlet for the British Council on George Herbert, who by that time had become just about his favorite English poet. Despite that fact, the pamphlet is undistinguished as criticism. More rewarding, partly because more pointedly sardonic, are his reflections in 1962 on the new English Bible. After producing various examples of its "monotonous inferiority of phrasing" ("sweated all day in the blazing sun" having replaced "borne the burden and heat of the day"), he ends with the following paragraph:

> It is good that those who aspire to write good English prose or verse should be prepared by the study of Greek and Latin. It would also be good if those who have authority to translate a

> dead language could show understanding and appreciation of their own.

Finally, in a compendium of Eliot's formulations, many of which take their bite from a somewhat acidulous humor, we can note how, in his way with questionnaires, he maintained an admirably skeptical temper. One of his most provocative definitions of poetry, that it was "not a career but a mug's game," has been preserved in *The Use of Poetry and the Use of Criticism.* Not as well known are three responses to well-meaning and pointless questions from a variety of publications. In 1922, responding to the *Chapbook's* query about the particular function of poetry as distinguished from other kinds of literature, his answer was that it "Takes up less space," an appropriately space-saving response. When in 1938 *transition* wondered whether he had ever felt the need of a new language to express the experiences of his "night mind" (*Finnegans Wake* was on the horizon) he said definitely not, adding that he was not "particularly interested in my 'night mind'," but qualified this by disclaiming any suggestion about "other people's interest in their night-minds." "It is only that I find my own quite uninteresting," he concluded with a most notable use of "only." Finally, in 1949, after *The Cocktail Party* had been performed at the Edinburgh Festival, he was provided with a list of fourteen questions, the final one of which invited him to give "a definition of Comedy which seems to you precise for our time and place." His answer may give the right note on which to end:

> Instead of answering the question, I should like to suggest to you a useful exercise. Imagine that you have just seen the first performance of *Hamlet,* and try to set down fourteen questions for Shakespeare to answer, parallel to these fourteen. Then consider whether it is not all for the best that Shakespeare never answered these questions, or if he did, that the answers have not been preserved.

—*Hopkins Review*, Summer 2008.

The Gifts Reserved for Age: *The Collected and Uncollected Poems of T. S. Eliot*

T. S. Eliot's *Collected* Poems, 1909-1962 was published in 1963, two years before he died. More than one review remarked at the time how austere was Eliot's decision to let these two hundred and some pages stand for the poems by which he wished to be remembered. By comparison, the collected poems of contemporaries such as W. B. Yeats, Wallace Stevens, or Robert Frost ranged from two to three times longer. This disparity is due in part to the fact that after *Four Quartets* was published in 1943, Eliot wrote very few poems (he was in part preoccupied with writing poetic dramas), while Yeats, Stevens, and Frost continued with undiminished energy to turn out lyrics until overtaken by death. It is thus with something like shock that we note that fifty years after Eliot died appears this outsized—to say the least—edition of his poem in two volumes, adding up to a total of almost two thousand pages. None of Eliot's contemporaries, three of them mentioned above, has received such an editorial tribute—in fact have been only slightly annotated if at all.

The contents of the two volumes are arranged as follow: Volume I contains 219 pages of collected poems, followed by uncollected ones, then an "Editorial Composite" of *The Waste Land,* and about a thousand pages of commentary, plus introductory material, bibliography and index. Volume II contains *Old Possum's Book of Practical Cats,* Eliot's translation of St. John Perse's *Anabasis,* followed by other verses, then "Improper Rhymes," featuring Eliot's "Columbo" and "King Bolo" poems, scatological and humorous (or so the poet hoped) in character. Concluding the two volumes are 350 pages of textual history for all the poems. The two volumes weigh ten pounds and are hard on one's wrists and knees.

Christopher Ricks, head of the Editorial Institute at Boston University, is the most authoritative scholar and critic of Eliot in the world; his co-editor, Jim McCue, has published, while these volumes were in preparation, essays on the challenges and difficulties of editing Eliot. In the introduction to their commentary, they address the question any interested reader is likely to ask: Is all this necessary and does it not smother rather than illuminate Eliot's work? In Ricks's introduction half a century ago to his splendid edition of Tennyson's poems, he spoke directly to what a fully annotated edition consists of, and justified the frequency with which sources were brought into play in annotating Tennyson's (or Eliot's) lines. It is a commitment to "illustrate the range of possible likenesses... from conscious allusion to another poet, then unconscious reminiscence, then phrasing which is simply an analogue and not a source." The notes should refrain from interpretative explanation but proceed from a "point of information" rather, which leaves the reader free to make up his own mind about how useful is the proffered parallel.

The seeking out of parallels is the most controversial aspect of an annotated edition such as this one, and sometimes the recipient of comparable scholarly attention has not been appreciative of the honor. When, in his *Illustrations of Tennyson*, John Churton Collins, a late nineteenth-century critic, put his encyclopedic mind to work in detecting echoes of all sorts in Tennyson's poems, the bard responded as follows:

> There is, I fear, a prosaic set growing up among us, editors of booklets, book-worms, index hunters, or men of great memories and no imagination, who *impute themselves* to the poet, and so believe that *he*, too, has no imagination but is forever poking his nose between the pages of some old volume to see what he can appropriate. They will not allow one to say "Ring the bell" without finding that we have taken it from Sir P. Sidney, or even to use such a simple expression as the ocean "roars," without finding out the precise verse in Homer or Horace from which we have plagiarised it.

Whether the echo was a source, an allusion, or an analogue mattered not a bit to the annoyed Tennyson, who allegedly called Churton Collins "a louse on the locks of literature." (Subsequent research has determined that Tennyson's name for him was "Jackass.")

As for Eliot, he was of two minds about the propriety of annotating his poems at all. He declared emphatically, in a letter written near the end of his life to the master of a Cambridge college, "I will not allow any academic critic (and there are plenty of them in America only too willing) to provide notes of explanation to be published with...my poems." In Ricks's edition of Eliot's early uncollected poems, *Inventions of the March Hare* (1997), he quoted the letter but balanced it somewhat by pointing out that Eliot had sometimes "applauded" an annotated edition, and that he himself provided notes for the most allusive of his poems, *The Waste Land*. The editors' statement in *The Complete Poems*, that the notes "proceed from a point of information," leaves open possible disagreement about whether a particular note does or does not constitute "information" and whether it may constitute interpretive explanation. We shall never know whether Eliot would have admired this massive work, been appalled by it, or subtly expressed mixed feelings about it.

That said, we can remark more particularly on features of the two volumes. First, if we may momentarily detach him from his co-editor, Jim McCue, a word about Christopher Ricks. In *Inventions of the March Hare*, Ricks quotes Eliot saying about Shakespeare that he "read with the most prodigious memory for words that has ever existed." I think it fair to say that on the evidence of a lifetime work of criticism, scholarship, and editorial practice, Ricks has exhibited a comparably prodigious memory for words. We know that Harold Bloom possesses a prodigious memory (he can recite the whole of *Paradise Lost* or the lyrics of Hart Crane), since he has told us about it more than once. But Bloom consistently shirks the task of describing the verbal interanimation of poems he has brought up for commentary. Ricks's own style in his essays, in which his words are so interanimated with puns, anti-puns, double-entendres, playful twistings of language in every direction, has bothered critics who prefer a plainer style. But there is no denying his unbelievable ability to call up analogies and parallels from earlier writings to the particular line under consideration. To take but one example, and to refer perhaps unjustly to Ricks rather than in team with his co-editor: Eliot's "What the Thunder Said" (*The Waste Land* Part V) has a memorable evocation of aridity in the lines "But sound of water over a rock / Where the hermit-thrush sings in the pine trees / Drip drop drip drop drop drop drop." The drip drop line we are told was anticipated by Coleridge, Poe, and W. E. Henley, and the Coleridge citation is brief: "Drip! drip! drip! drip!—in such a place as this / It has nothing else to do but drip drip drip." The citation is to *Osorio* opening Act IV. Only a Coleridge specialist will have even heard of *Osorio*, which turns out to be a failed play from early in Coleridge's career, eventually retitled and produced in 1812 with the help of Lord Byron. Such a calling-up from this obscure source is beyond the reach even of Google; but no one is going to say "Aha! This is what I've been waiting for—now I understand Eliot's line."

But in many instances we are helped by a note to fill in something we only imperfectly understood, if at all. In the lines from "East Coker"—"Had they deceived us / Or deceived themselves, the quiet-voiced elders"—it may or may not have occurred to us to think about the Biblical anecdote of Susannah and the Elders, but it occurred to the editors, and they provide possibly relevant sentences from the four-page story of Susannah in the Apocrypha to the Book of Daniel. The editors gloss "deceived themelves" by adducing similar phrasing about "elders" in Eliot's essay "Thoughts After Lambeth," and they conclude with a parallel which, like the drip drop Osorio one, will occur to nobody, but is pleasant to have anyway, citing Henry Adams, who referred to Garibaldi as "A quiet-featured, quiet-voiced man in a red flannel shirt."

At a higher level of annotative usefulness and interest, here is part of the commentary on lines opening the second part of "Little Gidding": "Ash on an old man's sleeve, / Is all the ash the burnt roses leave. / Dust in the air suspended / Marks the place where the story ended." We may remember that during World War II Eliot was an air raid warden, and sometimes "watched" at Faber, his place of business, as well as near his home in Kensington. But the particular salience of these lines is enriched by sentences from a letter of Eliot's to William Levy about such firewatching: "During the Blitz the accumulated debris was suspended in the London air for hours after a bombing. Then it would slowly descend and cover one's sleeves and coat with a fine white ash. I often experienced this effect during the long night hours on the roof." Or there may be an unexpected enrichment of a particular moment in a poem—even a moment not to every reader's taste. In perhaps the prosiest section of *Four Quartets*, the follow-up to the beautiful lyric about the fishermen in part II of "The Dry Salvages," we are instructed about what's involved in happiness as a "sudden illumination" rather than what's involved in lesser sorts of happiness: "Not the sense of well-being / Fruition, fulfilment, security or affection, / Or even a very good dinner." A friend of mine used to writhe over that business about the good dinner as an unattractive example of Eliot at his most man-of-the-world yet churchwardenly self. The editors quote a letter to Eliot's boss, the publisher Geoffrey Faber, about moments of illumination, quoting St. John of the Cross about how the soul must be divested of its cravings for worldly things: After this happens, says Eliot, "One returns (I do anyway) to the Canard Aux Oranges or the Moules Marinières or whatever it is with a keener pleasure....If we are rightly directed, a good dinner can lead us toward God, and God can help us to enjoy a good dinner." My friend wouldn't have been won over, but I shall now read these lines in a slightly enhanced way.

It would be disingenuous for a reviewer to pretend he has followed most of the Commentary: I singled out the 163 pages devoted to *Four Quartets* as a good spot for concentration, especially the fifty-five pages given to "Little Gidding," which Eliot once called the best thing he had written. Before the notes on individual lines and passages, there are introductory pages dealing with the history of the poem, its composition, the "Dante" section, and matters of its post-publication. The twenty-four pages of notes about the seventy-line encounter with the ghost ("some dead master") in the aftermath of an air raid are unforgettable, as the ghost speaks its message:

> Let me disclose the gifts reserved for age
> To set a crown upon your lifetime's effort.
> First, the cold friction of expiring sense
> Without enchantment, offering no promise
> But bitter tastelessness of shadow fruit
> As soul and body begin to fall asunder.

The unrhymed tercets both remind us of and are distinct from Dante's terza rima and were described by Eliot in a letter: "(What is quite interesting is that the austere Dantesque style is more difficult, and offers more pitfalls than any other.)" The commentary on this passage, filled with illuminating statements about it by Eliot, is perhaps the most revealing one in the volume.

In fact the fineness and human resonance of what this edition has surrounded the poems with is not found mainly in its notes on particular lines but in the more general commentary, drawn from Eliot's letters and other communications, which show the depths of ennui, despair, and self-recrimination that marked the man. Often the sardonic bite, a darkly humorous one, is apparent, as when, asked by W. H. Auden why he liked to play patience, Eliot responded that it was the nearest thing to being dead. Or a quite unhumorous confession, perhaps the most bleak self-assessment I'm aware of in any writer, comes in a summing-up he made to his close friend, John Hayward, in 1936:

> I have no family, no career, and nothing particular to look forward to in this world. I doubt the permanent value of everything I have written. I never lay with a woman I liked, loved or even felt any strong physical attraction to. I no longer even regret this lack of experience. I no longer even feel acutely the desire for progeny which was very acute once.

This assessment stops the curious reader in his tracks. What rescued Eliot from the despair he located in *The Hollow Men*—"the lowest point I have reached in my sordid, domestic affairs"—was his Anglican commitment begun in 1927, but more dramatically his marriage to Valerie Fletcher eight years before he died. In an undated communication he wrote, with reference to the grim ending to *The Waste Land*, "If I had known that I was, late in life, to have the felicity to have this radiant angel, Valerie, my Valerie, as my wife...I should have been myself radiant with joyful hope."

New to me, and I suspect to most readers, is the existence of an "exercise book" made for his wife and titled "Valerie's Own Book." It consists, in no special order, of many poems Eliot had previously written and then copied into the book for his wife. The contents range from famous poems like "Prufrock" to a few of the infamous obscene verses, gathered in our edition under the title "Improper Rhymes." On a wedding announcement card he sent to his old friend Conrad Aiken in 1957, he declares himself "intensely happy, except for the fact that Valerie wants to learn about King Bolo and thus far I have resisted her attempts." But in fact he shared them with her, and what is more surprising wrote three poems about their marriage: "How the Tall Girl and I Play Together," "Sleeping Together," and "How the Tall Girl's Breasts Are." They contain such revelatory vouchsafings as this:

> I love a tall girl. When we lie in bed
> She on her back and I stretched upon her,
> And our middle parts are busy with each other,
> My toes play with her toes and my tongue with her tongue,
> And all the parts are happy. Because she is a tall girl.

What happened to Old Possum? Who would have thought that the author of *Four Quartets*, on the one hand, or "King Bolo and his Big Black Bastard Queen" on the other, would have been capable of such unprotected, intimate sincerity to a beloved, not meant for our eyes, yet preserved after both his and his wife's death? It is one of the more unsuspected of the Eliotic selves displayed in this magnificent, overwhelming edition.

—Originally published in *Commonweal*, April 20, 2016 as "The Gifts Reserved for Age."

Eliot's Last Prose

Five years ago I saluted the inauguration of what would eventually become eight volumes of T. S. Eliot's collected prose, edited by Ronald Schuchard and copiously annotated by his team of editors. Thus far it is available only on line, although a print edition is promised (printed out, the online edition runs to roughly 6,000 pages). As one who after a manner of speaking has "gone through" these pages I can't say that the final three volumes (1940-1965) weren't a falling off. It was easy to pay less than full attention to essays titled "Toward a Christian Britain," or "The Place and Function of the Clerisy." The great criticism Eliot wrote in the 1920s and 1930s (and the years leading up to 1920) is only minimally expanded by these final volumes, filled with often obligatory performances for this or that committee on one or another cultural or religious subject. He noted in 1947 that one of the more "exhausting" aspects of being the prime man of letters in the literary world was that "There was a general expectation on the part of many whom I met that I would deliver myself on almost any occasion of some profound and oracular piece of wisdom about life in general." As we near the end of these items, it is always a surprise to find, in a comparison between Walt Whitman and Tennyson, or a talk "The Last Twenty-Five Years of English Poetry," the old brilliance quite unaltered except for a somewhat more benign tone of address.

Marvin Mudrick sharply reviewed *On Poetry and Poets,* the main book of criticism Eliot produced during the war and postwar years. Eloquent in finding ways of dismissing much of it, Mudrick conjured up the sixty-year-old smiling public man (Eliot was sixty in 1948) and, referring to one of his last significant essays, "The Frontiers of Criticism" delivered in a football stadium before a University of Minnesota audience of 15,000, Mudrick found it typical of the essays in the book directed at poetry as subject. "The Social Function of Poetry" or "What is a Classic" were examples of "hollowly simplified classroom platitudes" in contrast to the essays about poets—Yeats, Milton, Byron. The public occasion of these essays, all or most of them lectures, facilitated the appearance, said Mudrick, of "Grandfather Eliot": the great critical pieces of the two previous decades disappeared as the Eliotic prose style "has thickened into a means of shutting out fresh perceptions." Mudrick worked hard to find appropriate phrases to convey his dislike for Eliot's prevailing tone: "Opaquely official; disingenuousness, special pleading, waspish authoritativeness, elaborate confessions of humility." In the earlier Eliot, he wrote, these rhetorical devices were a strategy for "maneuvering the reluctant reader into a closer look at the objects"; now they had "become themselves the chief visible objects."

I can imagine Eliot reading these charges of Mudrick's and wearily agreeing with him, as if they didn't cause him the least surprise or embarrassment. On occasion Eliot turns the charge against himself into an occasion for satisfying wit, as when, in "American Literature and the American Language," he justifies his scrupulous engagement with his own sentences as merely being consistent, "as I have a reputation for affecting pedantic precision, a reputation I should not like to lose." Such an explanatory turn goes a long way toward assuring us that we can relax, since the lecturer knows exactly what he's doing. But the essays on poetry from *On Poetry and Poets* are not as uniformly stiff and artificial as Mudrick claims. There are a number of places where the critic succeeds in saying something very much worthwhile about poetry in practice. One such contribution occurs in "The Music of Poetry," a worthy attempt to speak about a very complicated subject indeed. In Eliot's attempt to suggest how "verse rhythm" in a poetic drama may have an unconscious effect on the audience he devotes a couple of pages to the first scene in *Hamlet*. The opening exchanges between the sentries are "transparent" in that we attend to the meaning of the lines, not to their "poetry." He proceeds to note further transitions in the scene, from a staccato effect to one where the verse glides into a slower movement, concluding with Horatio's lines after the Ghost's disappearance at daybreak: "But look, the morn in russet mantle clad / Walks o'er the dew of yon high eastward hill." These lines contribute to "a kind of musical design" that has "checked and accelerated the pulse of our emotion without our knowing it," in which "we are lifted for a moment beyond character, but with no sense of unfitness of the words coming, and at this moment, from the lips of Horatio." It is as convincing a comment on the musical aspect of a brief dramatic sequence as I'm aware of. At the end of the essay he appends a "Note" in which he performs a similar piece of listening to the balcony scene in *Romeo and Juliet*, describing the musical pattern of their duet "as surprising in its kind as that in the early work of Beethoven." We may not want to press him too closely on just what in Beethoven's early work he had in mind or ear, but the impulse of this criticism assists in bringing out the music of poetry.

If I were to choose one moment or sequence from these late essays where the Eliotic genius appears, it would be his attempt, in "The Three Voices of Poetry," to find words for what he called the First Voice—that is, the poet speaking to himself or to nobody. He is in agreement with the critic Gottfried Benn about this "obscure impulse," calling it "meditative verse" rather than lyric. He formulates it this way:

> In a poem which is neither didactic nor narrative, and not animated by any other social purpose, the poet may be concerned solely with expressing in verse—using all the resources of words, with their history, their connotations, their music—this obscure impulse. He does not know what he has to say until he has said it, and in the effort to say it he is not concerned with making other people understand anything. He is not concerned, at this stage, with other people at all, only with finding the right words, or, anyhow, the least wrong words. He is obsessed by a burden or haunted by a demon which he must exorcise through the words he chooses.

I think it likely that Eliot would have agreed that the following lines in *Four Quartets* from the end of "East Coker" are a strong example of that "obscure impulse":

> Old men ought to be explorers.
> Here and there does not matter
> We must be still and still moving
> Into another intensity
> For a further union, a deeper communion
> Through the dark cold and the empty desolation,
> The wave cry, the wind cry, the vast waters
> Of the petrel and the porpoise. In my end is my beginning.

These lines seem to me a prime example of the music of poetry Eliot was concerned with: spare of punctuation and impossible to attach to a specific tone of voice, they are rather Voice itself.

In reviewing these essays I came across much I hadn't fully registered, often in a more relaxed mode than the taut formulations of his earlier criticism. The 1940 essay on Yeats, written soon after that poet's death, is marvelously open and revealing, as when Eliot quotes lines from Yeats's late poem "The Spur" ("You think it horrible that lust and rage / Should dance attendant upon old age") and notes that they are "not very pleasant" but that they are the confession of a man who was like other men, just possessed of more "clarity, honesty and vigour." He asks rhetorically, "To any honest man old enough, can these sentiments be entirely alien?" Not alien it seems to Eliot at age fifty-two, his wife dead and the possibility of further sexual experience unlikely (and unwanted). I noticed also how willing he was in writing about Yeats to let his guard down, call "The Folly of Being Comforted" a "very lovely poem" and the late poem "To Eve Gore Booth and Con Markiewicz, "beautiful," which indeed it is. One comparison he left out of the Yeats essay was made in "The Last Twenty-Five Years of English Poetry": by way of pointing out the change from Yeats's early style to a less mellifluous one, he adduced the early "Who Goes with Fergus," terming it "more exciting than any other English poetry of its period, but very obscure." By contrast, in the Robert Gregory elegy, two decades later, Yeats avoids the poetic in approximating to normal unaffected speech "resulting in increased intensity." A common observation about Yeats now, but not so much back then.

The writing of this review was interrupted by the arrival of *The Times Literary Supplement* containing an account of Eliot's complete prose by Lachlan Mackinnon. The account is confidently patronizing of a career that for Mackinnon was unpleasantly narrow, even prissy in some of its outlines. Mackinnon finds in an early TLS "leader" by Eliot an "almost snobbish" tone. He eagerly pounces on Eliot for what seemed to me some amusing sentences about Gertrude Stein: "Her work is not improving; it is not amusing, it is not interesting, it is not good for one's mind." Eliot found that her prose had a kinship with the saxophone, and Mackinnon thinks the comparison might be "racist," since Stein was Jewish. (But what about the saxophone?) He finds also that Eliot's increasingly sought-after status as a lecturer is a mark of his "extraordinary willingness to supply what people asked for," as if such willingness were to be slightly frowned on. The infamous much-criticized scientific analogy in "Tradition and the Individual Talent" about what happens when a "filament of platinum" becomes the mind of the poet, is found by Mackinnon to be as "preposterously lofty" as he found it at age fifteen. He attributes Eliot's "parsimonious" output of poems to his adherence to the "depersonalization" theory of poetry set forth in that same essay. He notes that Eliot, as opposed to other "major critics like Johnson, Coleridge and Auden" had little to say about Shakespeare ("a book composed of his Shakespearean thoughts would be a very short one"). He is unhappy with Eliot's talk about the "objective correlative" (in the "Hamlet" essay) and finds that his "theory" in "The Metaphysical Poets" is no more solidly grounded than Ted Hughes's imaginative history of Shakespeare (Why bring in Hughes?). As for Eliot's admiration of what he called "the mind of Europe," Mackinnon finds his range "significantly less than European." *After Strange Gods,* the book which Eliot himself declined to reprint, having had second thoughts about some of its content, consists of nothing more or less than "perfervid, half-demented lectures." While not accusing Eliot directly of anti-Semitism, Mackinnon finds his use of the word "deplore" (in relation to Pound's anti-Semitism—"I am sure that not one of us does not deplore Pound's way of referring to Jews"—very "thin stuff," and recommends Christopher Ricks's demonstration of "the unease of many of Eliot's self-exculpations..." while giving no credit to Ricks's admirably even-handed treatment of the issue. "Eliot wrote of Polish and German suffering but said precisely nothing about the Shoah," which, presumably, shows in its "astonishing silence an appalling moral failure." In sum, Eliot's "reversion to a narrow Anglicanism" was a "shabby, diminished thing" compared to the early prose that now seems "odd and lonely" compared to later examples.

Instead of attempting to refute all or any of Mackinnon's charges, I recommend a letter of Dwight MacDonald's in which he speaks of Eliot as combining "qualities not so often found together: intelligence, humor, and what I can only call a kind of reckless generous nobility." In his review Mackinnon shows himself impervious to anything like humor, even "fun" in Eliot's prose. When we remind ourselves that a hundred years have passed since the "odd and lonely" fact of Eliot's critical genius began to be apparent, the temptation to argue with one or another of his verdicts or his omissions, early or late, is muted; it would be almost tantamount to taking issue with Matthew Arnold or Coleridge about a critical pronouncement;

or setting out to show Samuel Johnson why Milton's "Lycidas" is a great poem instead of the one Johnson read. As the immediacy of Eliot's many formulations becomes less immediate, we read him not to be instructed or corrected, but—in a more disinterested approach to him—as "literature." This is a readerly attitude not much different from the way we read his poetry, our judgments suspended rather than provoked to argument.

But he was a great provoker throughout his career, and as a single example we may consider the number of potshots he took at Bernard Shaw, a literary contemporary who rivaled Eliot in public status, even as they disagreed about everything. I have no idea of what Shaw thought of Eliot as a poet, but Eliot's appreciation of Shaw as a dramatist, certainly as a critic, was minimal or absent entirely. So the feline Eliot comes into play where the now aged rival is concerned: "One is compelled to admire a man of such verbal ability as not only to conceal from his readers and audiences the shallowness of his own thought, but to persuade them that in admiring his work they were giving evidence of their own intelligence as well." I yield to no one in my admiration for many of Shaw's plays and for his criticism, especially his music criticism; yet—or is it therefore?—I find Eliot's jab invigorating. In a letter he extended his attack, admitting that Shaw was "like a red flag to a bull to me." He dismisses one of Shaw's very best plays—"*Pygmalion* I have never approved of"—but then concedes a bit, by liking it "very much better as a musical comedy. In fact I sometimes think that Shaw is best at musical comedy, for *The Chocolate Soldier* [that would be *Arms and the Man*] and *My Fair Lady* are the only two of his works I should like to see again and again." One thinks of him, rapt, listening to Julie Andrews sing "I Could Have Danced All Night"! So the dismissal of Shaw is turned into something more agreeable, and as always the turning is accomplished through a style hard to resist.

Even more irresistible is the following formulation from a late essay titled "Becoming a Poet" where he ponders the relation between parent and child as it pertains to the matter of writing poetry:

> I don't think any parents have brought up their child with a view of his becoming a poet; some parents have brought up their children to be criminals; but for good and loving parents a poet is about the last thing they could want their child to be, unless they thought it was the only way to save him from becoming a criminal.

That should be read twice for full satisfaction, and I recommend it to Lachlan Mackinnon in case he missed it.

> *The Complete Prose of T. S. Eliot*, ed. Ronald Schuchard. *Volume 6, The War Years, 1940-1956*, ed. David E. Chinitz & Ronald Schuchard. *Volume 7, A European Society, 1947-1953*, ed. Iman Javadi & Ronald Schuchard. *Volume 8, Still and Still Moving, 1954-1965*, ed. Jewel Spears Brooker & Ronald Schuchard. Johns Hopkins University Press. A smaller edition is in the works, edited by Archie Burnett (Faber).

—*Hudson Review*, Spring 2020.

More Letters from T.S.E: *The Letters of T. S. Eliot, Vol. 9*

THE NINTH VOLUME of T. S. Eliot's letters covers the years 1939-1941 in slightly over a thousand pages. Eliot died in 1965, and even though this installment like previous ones has appeared at a reasonable pace, there is a long road ahead. As with previous volumes (except for the first two), Valerie Eliot is listed as editor along with John Haffenden; but since she died in 2012 Mr. Haffenden has been the moving force. Although the acknowledgments contain a number of names, none is singled out as anything like chief assistant. That task, however it was managed, is a mighty one, since it involves setting each letter in the fullest of contexts—quoting, sometimes at length, from the document or letter that provoked Eliot to respond. In other words, most of the pages carry substantial footnotes of elucidation. Sometimes even a conscientious reviewer such as yours truly gave them a less than thorough reading.

Eliot wrote modestly but trenchantly about how he regarded his correspondence: "We want to confess ourselves in writing to a few friends, and we do not always want to feel that no one but those friends will ever read what we have written." He once declared to his friend from Harvard days, the poet Conrad Aiken, that "letters should be indiscretions, otherwise they're simply bulletins." Yet anyone who picks up this volume in search of Eliotic indiscretions will be disappointed. The most notable person encountered in previous volumes was his first wife, Vivien. Now confined to a sanatorium, she is present only very occasionally with reference to her financial situation, her jewels, her piano—never in the living voice that her husband had finally managed to escape. He informs his partner, Geoffrey Faber, in 1941 that he thinks he is "somewhat mellowed in a more personal way, the years 1933-39 having been a period of relative serenity in my life such as I had never known before." (He left Vivien for good in 1933.)

The relative serenity takes on point when he describes to John Hayward the extremity of his personal drought:

> I have no family, no career, and nothing in particular to look forward to in this world. I doubt the permanent value of everything I have written; I never lay with a woman I liked, loved, or even felt any strong physical attraction to; I no longer even regret this lack of experience; I no longer even feel acutely the desire for progeny which was very acute once; and since I became a Christian I feel that the only difficulty I should have in a monastic life—which is easy to say because I am not free to enter a monastery—would be the deprivation of French tobacco.

He then recurs to the alleviation of the last six years, "the only happy years of my life—but that is a good many." Perhaps more than any moment in the letters thus far, reading this one makes us stop to let it sink in.

Looking up Hayward in the index discloses that he is by far the leading correspondent of Eliot's in these three epistolary years. He and Eliot had lived together for a time, when Hayward, a fine critic and editor, severely handicapped with muscular dystrophy, took up residence in Cambridge during the Second World War. The years 1939-1941 were of course the ones of Eliot's near-completion of *Four Quartets,* for which Hayward supplied valuable editorial criticism. Along with the war the central event of Eliot's life in these years was the demise of *The Criterion* after seventeen years of his leadership. This meant a dramatic lessening in the social and literary matters over which he presided, and a corresponding thinning-out of literary correspondence. There are still letters to and from Herbert Read but fewer from Bonamy Dobrée, who always brought out Eliot at his liveliest (he shared the "obscene" King Bolo poems with Dobrée), and there is a general decline in connection with the writers Eliot published and criticized. In his letter announcing the end of the magazine he noted "A feeling of sadness has crept over me, and a suspicion that I ought to retire before I was aware that the feeling had communicated itself to the readers." A more than graceful way to bow out, but though as a director at Faber he still worked steadily the range of literary exchange is smaller. Hayward took up some of the slack, with his incisive commentary on *East Coker, The Dry Salvages* and *Little Gidding.* Eliot thanks Hayward for his suggestions about "Spittle-Skidding."

A relatively small percentage of the letters deal with the subject of Eliot's own poetry, and they reveal his impatience at being thought of as a difficult, nay obscure "highbrow" poet and dramatist. His second poetic drama, *The Family Reunion* (1939), stimulated him to think of his work as very much not obscure. He warned Ronald Duncan, whom Faber would publish, to avoid verse whose density would put off an audience: "I think that for the theatre, one has to write much simpler poetry than you realize. A good many of the verses are very interesting but are difficult to understand even in reading. Spoken to an audience which had not made itself very familiar with the text, I am afraid they would be quite unintelligible." Responding to a student at an adult education college who objected to what he called the "classicism" of his work, Eliot pointed out that classical allusions were not the same as classicism, which in itself is not obscure; thus "If my poems are obscure, it is therefore for some other reason. I would deny, however, that I have deprived the literary-minded working class of the right to enjoy my poems. It is not I, but the half-educated reviewers who have told people that my poems are unintelligible, who are guilty." He suggests that if people would read his poems "without wondering whether they understood them or not, I venture to think they might enjoy some of them." We're reminded of his important insistence that poetry can communicate before it is understood. His advice to an aspiring writer who had submitted his poems for consideration at Faber was to suggest he could learn to write better verse by trying to write good prose, and he recommended "the habit of looking up words in the dictionary and making quite sure of their meaning." The danger to avoid would be to use words "without making them mean anything at all" (172). The homespun nature of such advice was consonant with an earlier recommendation to another aspiring writer: "Read Swift and Newman." His campaign against obscurity especially as it revealed itself in the work of "younger men": "The only younger poet whose *obscurity* I can tolerate is Empson, and I suspect some twist in him similar to my own."

Making Empson the exceptional case is interesting especially since he goes on to expatiate to his colleague Geoffrey Faber and to air reservations about what he calls "the second phase of 'modernist poetry,'" by which he means the Auden group he himself was instrumental in publishing at Faber: The new or "second phase" of modernist poetry was really the first phase of a reaction to it:

> The revolution, if it deserves that name, which began *before* the last war, was abortive. The Leninists went out, and the Stalinists came in: Auden, Spender preserving external trapping of versification, allusiveness, obscurity, contemporary imagery, and adding the still more modern-seeming graces of homosexuality, leftwingery and an interim taste for Germans. Auden seems to drop with relief into the position of being a queer epigone of Kipling (no disrespect to the latter). The quickest way to becoming old-fashioned is to be Modern."

The accent of George Orwell is almost detectable. But this piece of literary-social criticism is the exception to the usual habit of these letters. For example, it would have been nice to have some comment on the "twist" Eliot suspected he shared with Empson, thus making Empsons' poetry tolerable. Instead we get the following PS to John Hayward: "Bill Empson lunched with me on Saturday.... He is dirtier and more distrait than ever. It was most refreshing to see him." This perhaps is livelier than something directed at his verse; and I was surprised and pleased that he found "Bill" (who?) dirtier than ever and (therefore?) found him refreshing.

Also refreshing in this trove of letters, so many of which are directed at matters of religion—he published *The Idea of a Christian Society* in 1939—are moments when the Christian Poet relaxes into an earthier idiom and addresses bodily matters in an amusing way. John Hayward is just about the only recipient of such confidences. On September 6, 1939, with war declared comes this revelation: "I woke suddenly at 6.30 this morning with an unmistakable attack of emerods [sic], very surprising, and was just dozing off again when I came to with a cramp in my leg. Fifteen minutes later came an air raid warning, which goes to show that it is emerods that cause air raid warnings and not vice versa." A canny reader like myself was able to take in this new word for an old complaint—though the "sic" further alerts us to its verbal novelty. He has wonderful advice for anyone who finds himself, like him, an air raid warden: "The first thing to do, when you hear the Syrens or the gun fire preliminary ...is to have a good Piss: after that you are ready for the Jerry." (I think he was right to capitalize Piss.) He is eloquent on the pains of morning ablution when the plumbing is out of order: "To get up and dress without washing or shaving not only ruins any appetite for the egg and marmalade but makes work impossible. Then there is the horror of having nowhere to rear" (followed by a complicated, heartfelt explanation). And even while staying with friends in the country, away from the blitz, the untoward may intrude upon privacy: "This morning, while preparing to give my body ease, I looked out of the bathroom window and saw one of the sheep from the field apparently trying to deliver some message at the front door. That shows how rural we are." Eliot praised George Santayana's criticism for its "slightly mischievous" air; Eliot's mischievousness is more than slight.

The pervading air of minor illnesses and time spent in bed recovering from them is so much a feature of these letters that a reader grows accustomed to them, and their effect is minimized. (At one point Eliot is tempted to list for his correspondent various times and places where he did *not* catch cold.) At the close of this ninth volume of letters, Eliot is fifty-three, has completed the *Quartets,* his final triumph as a poet, and has written the essays for which he will be remembered. John Haffenden, most exhaustive of editors, may be contemplating the remaining twenty-four years of his subject's life with complicated feelings.

—Originally published in the *Hudson Review,*
Spring 2022 as "More Letters from T.S.E."

Acknowledgments:

PIECES IN THIS VOLUME have previously appeared in the following publications:

Commonweal

Dymock Poets and Friends

New England Review

The Atlantic

The Boston Globe

The Hopkins Review

The Hudson Review

The Wall Street Journal

The Washington Examiner

The Weekly Standard

The Yale Review

"The Designs of Robert Frost" originally appeared in *The New Pelican Guide to English Literature, volume 9: American Literature* edited by Boris Ford (London: Penguin, 1988).

"Frost's Biography and *A Witness Tree*" originally appeared in *The Cambridge Companion to Robert Frost* edited by Robert Faggen (Cambridge Companions to Literature. Cambridge: Cambridge University Press, 2001).

"Frost's Mischievous Grip" was originally delivered as a talk at the Jones Library in Amherst, Massachusetts as part of the ALA's Frost Literary Landmark Celebration, October 21, 2009.

"T. S. Eliot: A Revaluation" originally appeared in *Columbia History of American Poetry*, edited by Jay Parini (New York: Columbia University Press, 1999).

About the author

William H. Pritchard is the author of several essay collections and literary biographies including *Randall Jarrell: A Literary Life, Updike: America's Man of Letters*, and *Ear Training: Literary Essays* (Paul Dry Books, 2023). He is professor of English emeritus at Amherst College where he taught for sixty years. He lives in Western Massachusetts.

www.ingramcontent.com/pod-product-compliance
Lightning Source LLC
Jackson TN
JSHW080158280826
107249JS00001B/4